150 years of
Lincolnshire Co-operative

Written by Alan Middleton

Written by Alan Middleton

The moral right of the author has been asserted.

Copyright © Lincolnshire Co-operative Ltd 2011

Published and Printed by Ruddocks

ISBN No. 978-0-904327-11-3

Foreword

Opening the archive of imposing volumes of the Society's reports and accounts, you enter a world now long passed from living memory. The flimsy sheets of narrative and figures reveal a picture of co-operation in the county stretching back 150 years.

My enduring impression of our founders is of their passion, determination and ambition to improve the everyday lives of ordinary people; to feed, clothe, house, educate and inspire.

They had an absolute belief that the twin co-operative motives of collective self help and social responsibility could take people from the breadline and hopelessness to dignity, health and prosperity.

From humble beginnings, co-operators in Lincolnshire have taken this vision forward over successive generations. In 2011 we take on the baton and strive to stay true to our founding principles, as we work to improve the lives of our members today.

I hope that our founder Thomas Parker would be proud of the Society's achievements. We look forward to the opportunities and challenges of the 21st century with the same spirit of optimism and determination which has delivered so many benefits to our communities since 1861.

The Society's thanks go to Alan Middleton for undertaking the challenge of researching and writing this book. As a Director of Lincolnshire Co-operative for over 40 years, his knowledge of our history is immense and this book will be a valuable record and resource for future generations.

For those who'd like to delve further into the Society's history, we've put our entire archive online as part of our 150th birthday celebrations. Please visit our website www.lincolnshire.coop to find out more.

Ursula Lidbetter
Chief Executive Officer

Acknowledgements

I am indebted to many people who helped with this publication, in particular:-

Don McInnes, from Washington State in the USA, Great Grand Nephew of our illustrious former Secretary, Duncan McInnes

Ruth Tinsley, Methodist Historian

Gillian Lonergan, Co-operative College Archivist

George Kirkby, Retired Branch Manager

John Burgess, former Trading Club Collector

Ken Lidbetter

Bill Goodhand, Isobel Morley, Saxilby History Group and Lincolnshire Echo helped with photos

Many of the Society's own staff also helped, including:-

Marcus Stead, from the Retail Division

Bob Doe, Paul Halfpenny, Nigel Coates and Sarah Bradley from the Marketing Services Team

Debbie Jolliff, Rachel Sampher and Clare Wilkes from the Secretariat

...and the wonderful Ann Cumpstone, who typed the whole thing from hand-written notes or audio tapes and who worked in an unbelievably calm and patient manner throughout

Ursula Lidbetter was Editor-in-Chief and I am grateful for her advice, guidance and constant encouragement

Last, but not least, thanks to my ever-supportive and long-suffering wife Patricia, without whom none of this would have been possible.

Alan Middleton, July 2011

Board of Directors and Executive - 2011

Back row: Margaret Tranter, Amy Morley, Stuart Parker, Susan Neal, Julia Romney,
David Maltby, John Levine, Barbara Hutchinson, Malcolm Hoskins, Carol Bratton
Front row: Ursula Lidbetter, *Chief Executive Officer*; Stephen Hughes, *President 2011;*
Jane Powell, *Group Secretary.*

Senior Management Team - 2011

Back row: Ray Yeardley, *Head of Retail Operations;* Alastair Farquhar, *Head of Pharmacy;*
Andrew Turner, *Head of Group Services;* Jim Thomson, *Chief Retail Officer;*
David Dernley, *Head of Funeral Services*
Front row: Heather Lee, *Head of People & Performance;* Steve Galjaard, *Chief Financial Officer;*
Ursula Lidbetter, *Chief Executive Officer;* Jane Powell, *Group Secretary.*

CONTENTS

Horse Fair on Lincoln High Street
mid 1800s

SETTING THE SCENE

'...subtle changes are taking place which will prove to be a great significance for the future.'

4

Our story begins in the middle of the 19th Century. Queen Victoria is on the throne. On the political front, things are rather quiet, the Whigs and Tories seem satisfied with the constitutional equilibrium they have set up. There is no hint of the massive democratic change which is, as yet, still beyond the horizon. As Walter Bagehot, a prominent businessman, essayist and journalist of the time put it "the working classes contribute almost nothing to our corporate public opinion". But there were advocates for reform, emerging briefly with a campaign, then slipping back into the shadows, perhaps to review and plan their next activity. Although the working classes have not yet secured the vote they are, very gradually, starting to be a force which has to be reckoned with or at least acknowledged. The Trade Unions are gaining strength and the first Industrial and Provident Societies Act, passed in 1852 has led to a great upsurge in co-operative activity. The bankruptcy laws have also been amended to provide a much needed measure of protection in times of speculation.

The prophets of doom who forecast chaos with the ending of the Corn Laws 15 years earlier have been proved wrong but repeal has brought an important change; Britain has changed, almost overnight, from an agricultural nation, which raises all the food it needs for its six million people, into a mainly industrial nation,

fed on imported wheat. Agricultural wages are low but prices have also fallen. One pound of candles can be bought for 6d (2½p), a loaf of bread cost 7d, sugar is 4¾d, a pound of tea 4s (20p), a lb. of beef or pork is 7d, with bacon a little more at 9d. Agricultural labourers are earning 12s (60p) a week and waggoners slightly less. Income tax is 10d in the £.

Agricultural expansion has reached its peak and more than half the people of Britain are now living in towns, probably for the first time. The coming of steam power has revolutionised life and this is driving even more people from country to town in search of higher wages. It is an age of coal and iron. Horse traffic, both for travellers and goods, has been overtaken by the railways. The social system in the countryside remains largely unchanged and it will not see any significant change for many years, despite the efforts of Joseph Arch and his Agricultural Labourers Union.

So what sort of a place is Lincoln in the mid 1800's? It is of course the centre of one of England's richest agricultural regions and is dominated by the mighty towers of Lincoln Cathedral. At first glance it may present as a scene largely unchanged for centuries, but subtle changes are taking place which will prove to be of great significance in the future. The slow-moving barges still bring their cargoes up the River Witham to Brayford pool, but the sails, like those of the great

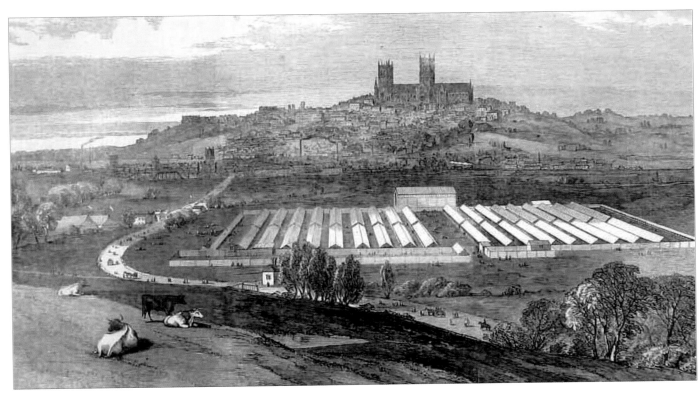

Meeting of the Royal Agricultural Society, Lincoln 1854

5

corn mills, are being challenged by the new power of steam. Before the middle of the century the Midland Railway Company's extension from Nottingham to Lincoln has been opened and in 1848 the London to York line through Lincoln has linked the city to the capital. A year earlier the Sheffield to Lincoln line had been completed and by 1850 Lincoln's virtual isolation of centuries, except by waterway, has been ended. The population of the city is around 23,000 but it is growing steadily. In little more than ten years it has risen by 10,000 and many more are to come, attracted by the prospects of higher earnings as the great engineering works develop. Messrs Clayton and Shuttleworth, barely heard of ten years earlier, are soon to become household names as are those of Joseph Ruston, Burton and Procter, Robey & Co. and William Foster, as their factories employ thousands of Lincoln's men. Yet the city still retains its character as the commercial capital serving the surrounding countryside. Its industries are still mainly those ancillary to the countryside – brewing and malting, corn-milling and tanning. The Corn Exchange still provides a vital link between City and County attracting

farmers and millers from a wide area, who come in each week, by their gigs and dog-carts or even, latterly, by rail and market days see the rural population flock in with their produce and livestock. Then the tradesmen and inn-keepers are busy, for market day is also a holiday for the folk from the fens and the wolds.

The carriages of the gentry are also to be seen andon big county occasions, like the annual "Stuff" ball,long queues of them wait to deposit their passengers outside the doors of the County Assembly Rooms where they are intent on an evening of merry-making. For humbler folks the pleasures are simpler. There are walks beside the Fossdyke Canal followed by a picnic at the Pyewype Inn, or for some the surreptitious pleasure of prizefighting on Pyewype Green for stakes of £2 a side, but are as likely as not to be interrupted by the police before the bout is over. The adventurous are able to take a railway excursion to the Great Brass Band Festival at the Crystal Palace or there are cheap day trips to Manchester. For those with an interest in sport there is plenty of choice. There is an annual cricket match between an England X1 and a Lincoln and District team played on the Lindum or in high summer there is the annual Regatta on the Brayford. For racing enthusiasts a visit to the Carholme may be attractive to see the "Lincoln Spring Handicap" started in 1853 and run over a distance of 1½ miles. In 1859 the name was changed to the "Lincolnshire Handicap", reclaiming a name which had been used previously for a two mile event run in August. Along with the name change in 1859 the distance was reduced to one mile. For those bored with cricket, rowing and racing an unusual spectacle was afforded by the Society of Lincolnshire Archers where prizes were actually awarded to women archers! The musically inclined are looking forward to a return visit to the Theatre Royal by Messrs Braham and Manley with their operatic company. The Lincolnshire Rifle Volunteers are also entertaining with a performance of the comedy "Still Waters Run Deep". There is a performance of Handel's "Dettingen Te Deum" but a local newspaper records "the audience was very slender as to numbers". But greater numbers attend a production of "Hamlet", by Mr and Mrs Charles Keen and even more gather to watch the intrepid "Blondin" perform on the high wire. One of the big events of the year is the Lincoln Exhibition of Arts, Science and Manufacturers held in Temple Gardens each July when the exhibits include many rare and valuable works of art lent for the occasion. There is not a great deal of civic development happening in this period but premises at the top of the Fish Market on Saltergate are being converted into a day police station. Not that lawlessness is on the increase in spite of the influx of newcomers, although the City is persistently troubled at this time by gangs of young men who play practical jokes, rob gardens and carry out other pranks under cover of darkness, so maybe some things never change. For the most part, however, the citizens are a law-abiding lot and the police courts record little more than petty crime.

Politically the city is quiet with very little activity to be observed. The representation of the City in Parliament by members of a local family, the Sibthorps, has continued for many years, but the line was broken in 1861 by the death, at the age of 45, of Major Gervaise Tottenham Waldo Sibthorp, of Canwick House who had succeeded his father in the representation in 1856. Seized with a "sudden and severe illness whilst on a fishing expedition in Derbyshire" the Major never recovered. He is described as "a Liberal Conservative". Mr George Fieschi Heneage is the City's other member.

There is also a strong temperance movement in the City led by the Lincoln Temperance Society. An American revivalist, the Rev. J Caughey is preaching to overflowing congregations, although a local newspaper finds it necessary to say, **"we cannot forebear to observe that on Sunday evening the revival prayer meeting after the service was anything but solemn......"**. And if too much high living should take its toll in spite of temperance advocates and revivalists, the county newspapers are full of advertisements for wonderful cures. There is a choice of "Old Doctor Richard Hewitt's Anti Wind Pills, priced at 1s. 1½d per box" or "Kaye's Worsdell's Vegetable Pills, which thoroughly purify the blood – sold throughout the empire, also at 1s. 1½d per box", and which have effected "extraordinary cures for rheumatism, eruptions and disorders of the stomach". For winter ills "Farrant's Balsamic Lozenges", are available to deal with coughs, colds, hoarseness, shortness of breath, or almost anything, in boxes costing 7½d.

KAYE'S WORSDELL'S PILLS,

THE BEST FAMILY MEDICINE.

A REMEDY FOR PAIN AND DISEASE so effectual as the *Vegetable Restorative Pills*, prepared solely by JOHN KAYE, Esq., of Dalton Hall, near Huddersfield, and St. John's Wood Park, London, has never been presented to the public. It is daily effecting the most astonishing cures of diseases differing materially in their symptoms and consequences. Thousands who had suffered greatly, some of whose cases had long been given up by eminent medical practitioners, and considered hopeless by themselves, have been speedily and thoroughly cured. The unprecedented popularity which these Pills have acquired may be readily accounted for. In the first place, they are purely vegetable, and are free from everything that can possibly injure the most delicate constitution. The infant, the mature, the aged, and even the most delicate female, may take them with perfect safety. Secondly, they are compounded upon philosophical principles, and go at once to the root of all disease. All diseases owe their origin to one primary cause—namely, the impurity of the blood ; and no medicine, in whatever quantities taken, can be effectual, unless it becomes assimilated with the blood, and assist that principle or vitality to pursue its course through the system, charged with the power of exterminating every unhealthy obstruction. This is precisely the office of these Pills ; they have power speedily to remove all obstructions, to purify the blood, and to promote the healthy circulation of all the fluids. Another remarkable excellence in these Pills is, that while they operate thus readily to remove what is injurious, while they are invaluable as *aperients*, they also prove admirable *tonics*. So far from weakening by their operation, as is common with ordinary active medicines, they materially strengthen the whole system. Those who have given them a fair trial bear grateful testimony to the fact, that by the use of these Pills, their appetites have been quickened, their digestion assisted, all their bodily powers braced and invigorated ; at the same time that a pleasing serenity has been imparted to their minds, so that they could engage in the various duties of life with cheerfulness and satisfaction.

And these testimonials have been borne, not by a few individuals, placed in very peculiar circumstances, or whose veracity is questionable, but by thousands of persons, of both sexes, moving in various ranks, whose integrity is unimpeachable, and the majority of whom have requested the publication of their cases, in order that the afflicted might indulge the confident hope of receiving the *relief*, the CURE, which is so earnestly desired.

ASTHMA, RHEUMATISM, GOUT, TIC DOLOREUX.

Mr. NICHOLAS TAYLOR, Lichdon-street, Barnstaple, was for many years afflicted with rheumatism, attended with excruciating pains in the nerves and muscles, and could scarcely even dress himself without assistance. After taking one box of Kaye's Worsdell's Pills he was freed from pain and by occasionally using them he has continued so ever since.

Kaye's Wordsell's Pills ..."compounded upon philosophical principles, and go at once to the root of all disease."

The Sheriff's *Parade*, another highlight of Victorian Lincoln, passes through the Stonebow

Conditions for working people in those days were harsh with none of the luxuries many of us take for granted today. For those in work they were long hard days and even then, everything they earned was spent on ordinary living expenses, nothing was left over. Wages were poor even for those in the new engineering factories in Lincoln. But there is some good news, Messrs Dawber & Co. have announced the availability of their new brew of Harvest Ales at 1s (5p) per gallon in 9 gallon casks, with good table beer costing as little as 3d per gallon. For those out of work, it was at the soup kitchens that they sought sustenance. A local newspaper reported that **"the Below Hill Soup Kitchen Committee are distributing soup twice a week to the deserving poor, while the Above Hill Soup Kitchen Committee are said to have obtained suitable premises near to Newport Arch for the purpose of making and distributing soup".** In the shops they paid prices for food and goods of often doubtful quality.

The controls and hygiene regulations which are in place today were non-existent then. Pure and unadulterated food was rarely available to working people and certainly not at affordable prices. Flour was often diluted with chalk, tea with sawdust and, if butter was obtainable, it was invariably rancid. Many people were at the mercy of unscrupulous private traders. Weights were frequently tampered with and as a result, people were served short measure.

Little wonder then that people wanted something better and it seems that improvement was just around the corner, a tentative solution was starting to emerge, a self-help solution, a co-operative solution. This is the story of Lincoln (now Lincolnshire) Co-operative which, together with other co-operatives across the UK and throughout the world, were to change the lives of working people, and the face of shop-keeping forever.

or in high summer there is the annual Regatta on the Brayford. For racing enthusiasts a visit to the Carholme may be attractive to see the "Lincoln Spring Handicap" started in 1853 and run over a distance of 1½ miles. In 1859 the name was changed to the "Lincolnshire Handicap", reclaiming a name which had been used previously for a two mile event run in August. Along with the name change in 1859 the distance was reduced to one mile. For those bored with cricket, rowing and racing an unusual spectacle was afforded by the Society of Lincolnshire Archers where prizes were actually awarded to women archers! The musically inclined are looking forward to a return visit to the Theatre Royal by Messrs Braham and Manley with their operatic company. The Lincolnshire Rifle Volunteers are also entertaining with a performance of the comedy "Still Waters Run Deep". There is a performance of Handel's "Dettingen Te Deum" but a local newspaper records "the audience was very slender as to numbers". But greater numbers attend a production of "Hamlet", by Mr and Mrs Charles Keen and even more gather to watch the intrepid "Blondin" perform on the high wire. One of the big events of the year is the Lincoln Exhibition of Arts, Science and Manufacturers held in Temple Gardens each July when the exhibits include many rare and valuable works of art lent for the occasion. There is not a great deal of civic development happening in this period but premises at the top of the Fish Market on Saltergate are being converted into a day police station. Not that lawlessness is on the increase in spite of the influx of newcomers, although the City is persistently troubled at this time by gangs of young men who play practical jokes, rob gardens and carry out other pranks under cover of darkness, so maybe some things never change. For the most part, however, the citizens are a law-abiding lot and the police courts record little more than petty crime.

Politically the city is quiet with very little activity to be observed. The representation of the City in Parliament by members of a local family, the Sibthorps, has continued for many years, but the line was broken in 1861 by the death, at the age of 45, of Major Gervaise Tottenham Waldo Sibthorp, of Canwick House who had succeeded his father in the representation in 1856. Seized with a "sudden and severe illness whilst on a fishing expedition in Derbyshire" the Major never recovered. He is described as "a Liberal Conservative". Mr George Fieschi Heneage is the City's other member.

There is also a strong temperance movement in the City led by the Lincoln Temperance Society. An American revivalist, the Rev. J Caughey is preaching to overflowing congregations, although a local newspaper finds it necessary to say, **"we cannot forebear to observe that on Sunday evening the revival prayer meeting after the service was anything but solemn......"**. And if too much high living should take its toll in spite of temperance advocates and revivalists, the county newspapers are full of advertisements for wonderful cures. There is a choice of "Old Doctor Richard Hewitt's Anti Wind Pills, priced at 1s. 1½d per box" or "Kaye's Worsdell's Vegetable Pills, which thoroughly purify the blood – sold throughout the empire, also at 1s. 1½d per box", and which have effected "extraordinary cures for rheumatism, eruptions and disorders of the stomach". For winter ills "Farrant's Balsamic Lozenges", are available to deal with coughs, colds, hoarseness, shortness of breath, or almost anything, in boxes costing 7½d.

KAYE'S WORSDELL'S PILLS,
THE BEST FAMILY MEDICINE.

A REMEDY FOR PAIN AND DISEASE so effectual as the *Vegetable Restorative Pills*, prepared solely by JOHN KAYE, Esq., of Dalton Hall, near Huddersfield, and St. John's Wood Park, London, has never been presented to the public. It is daily effecting the most astonishing cures of diseases differing materially in their symptoms and consequences. Thousands who had suffered greatly, some of whose cases had long been given up by eminent medical practitioners, and considered hopeless by themselves, have been speedily and thoroughly cured. The unprecedented popularity which these Pills have acquired may be readily accounted for. In the first place, they are purely vegetable, and are free from everything that can possibly injure the most delicate constitution. The infant, the mature, the aged, and even the most delicate female, may take them with perfect safety. Secondly, they are compounded upon philosophical principles, and go at once to the root of all disease. All diseases owe their origin to one primary cause—namely, the impurity of the blood; and no medicine, in whatever quantities taken, can be effectual, unless it becomes assimilated with the blood, and assist that principle or vitality to pursue its course through the system, charged with the power of exterminating every unhealthy obstruction. This is precisely the office of these Pills; they have power speedily to remove all obstructions, to purify the blood, and to promote the healthy circulation of all the fluids. Another remarkable excellence in these Pills is, that while they operate thus readily to remove what is injurious, while they are invaluable as *aperients*, they also prove admirable *tonics*. So far from weakening by their operation, as is common with ordinary active medicines, they materially strengthen the whole system. Those who have given them a fair trial bear grateful testimony to the fact, that by the use of these Pills, their appetites have been quickened, their digestion assisted, all their bodily powers braced and invigorated; at the same time that a pleasing serenity has been imparted to their minds, so that they could engage in the various duties of life with cheerfulness and satisfaction.

And these testimonials have been borne, not by a few individuals, placed in very peculiar circumstances, or whose veracity is questionable, but by thousands of persons, of both sexes, moving in various ranks, whose integrity is unimpeachable, and the majority of whom have requested the publication of their cases, in order that the afflicted might indulge the confident hope of receiving the *relief*, the CURE, which is so earnestly desired.

ASTHMA, RHEUMATISM, GOUT, TIC DOLOREUX.

Mr. NICHOLAS TAYLOR, Lichdon-street, Barnstaple, was for many years afflicted with rheumatism, attended with excruciating pains in the nerves and muscles, and could scarcely even dress himself without assistance. After taking one box of Kaye's Worsdell's Pills he was freed from pain and by occasionally using them he has continued so ever since.

Kaye's Wordsell's Pills ..."compounded upon philosophical principles, and go at once to the root of all disease."

The Sheriff's Parade, another highlight of Victorian Lincoln, passes through the Stonebow

Conditions for working people in those days were harsh with none of the luxuries many of us take for granted today. For those in work they were long hard days and even then, everything they earned was spent on ordinary living expenses, nothing was left over. Wages were poor even for those in the new engineering factories in Lincoln. But there is some good news, Messrs Dawber & Co. have announced the availability of their new brew of Harvest Ales at 1s (5p) per gallon in 9 gallon casks, with good table beer costing as little as 3d per gallon. For those out of work, it was at the soup kitchens that they sought sustenance. A local newspaper reported that **"the Below Hill Soup Kitchen Committee are distributing soup twice a week to the deserving poor, while the Above Hill Soup Kitchen Committee are said to have obtained suitable premises near to Newport Arch for the purpose of making and distributing soup"**. In the shops they paid top prices for food and goods of often doubtful quality.

The controls and hygiene regulations which are in place today were non-existent then. Pure and unadulterated food was rarely available to working people and certainly not at affordable prices. Flour was often diluted with chalk, tea with sawdust and, if butter was obtainable, it was invariably rancid. Many people were at the mercy of unscrupulous private traders. Weights were frequently tampered with and as a result, people were served short measure.

Little wonder then that people wanted something better and it seems that improvement was just around the corner, a tentative solution was starting to emerge, a self-help solution, a co-operative solution. This is the story of Lincoln (now Lincolnshire) Co-operative which, together with other co-operatives across the UK and throughout the world, were to change the lives of working people, and the face of shop-keeping forever.

Lincoln Flour Mill Co-operative building - now converted to flats

PRE LINCOLN CO-OPERATIVES

'...no amount of capital is proof against mismanagement, want of knowledge and skill, or of unity of purpose.'

It is often said that the worldwide co-operative movement started in Rochdale in 1844. That is not true – it is a complete myth.

There are many examples of co-operative activity much earlier than Rochdale. Most of these early co-operatives were single product enterprises, some dealt in coal, some in bread and many dealt in flour. This was nothing more than an attempt by hard pressed working people to obtain for themselves cheaper supplies of what was, at that time, a vital commodity.

Some very early attempts at co-operative trading were, amongst others, made by the dockyard workers in Chatham and Woolwich, whilst closer to home, the Hull Anti Mill Industrial Corn Mill Society was started in 1795.

Their views at the time were expressed powerfully in a petition to Hull Corporation for help.

"We, the poor inhabitants, (of Hull) have lately experienced much trouble and sorrow in ourselves and families on occasion of the exorbitant price of flour and we judge it needful to take every precaution to protect ourselves from the invasion of covetous and merciless men in the future."

At around the same time a watermill was built and worked for the benefit of the poor by the corporation at Louth and a co-operative mill was started at Stamford.

The first co-operative venture in Lincoln was again a corn milling enterprise. There is some dispute as to whether the business was registered under the Joint Stock Companies Act or the Friendly Societies Act (the Industrial and Provident Societies Act was not passed until 1852) but there is no clear evidence available to resolve this dispute.

However, whatever legal form it took the **Lincoln and Lincolnshire Flour Mill Society**, came into being in 1847. Based on the experience of other ventures elsewhere in the country, the pioneers of this flour mill co-operative believed that they could produce flour at at least 4d a stone cheaper than it was being sold by millers and bakers in the city at that time.

Regular weekly meetings were held and on 5 February 1847 the **Stamford Mercury,** which covered the whole of Lincolnshire at that time, (the Lincolnshire Echo did not start until 1893) reported: **"Already the organisation consists of 190 members, all of the working classes, who hitherto have gone on unaided by their wealthier neighbours. Each has taken a share of £1 which is paid by instalments. The intention is, if sufficient capital can be raised, to buy or build a mill for the company to buy their own corn and after grinding it, sell the flour to the shareholders at a small percentage above the prime cost which is sufficient to cover the expenses."**

The **Mercury** points out that a similar affair at Hull had been very successful. The co-operative mill at Hull was said to be a standing object lesson to the surrounding district to the power of association. Maybe the inspiration for the Lincoln Flour Mill Co-operative came from Hull, as was claimed by some historians at the time.

By March 1847 the number of shareholders had reached 1,127 but it was still only a paper exercise, no money had yet been called for. The Society started to receive subscriptions in April 1847 and the first instalment amounted to more than £50.

In July 1847 an architect was appointed and the search was on for a site on which to build a mill. Shortly afterwards the Society acquired a plot of land on the banks of the Upper Witham at the end of Salthouse Lane for £175. The conveyance was completed on 7 October 1847 and in total, 8 men were named on the deed as representatives of the Society. Little is known about these early pioneers, but it is clear that the "working classes", as the **Mercury** described them, had been joined by a number of tradesmen and businessmen who, perhaps because they had a little more substance than the working men, were more acceptable to the vendors of the land, as mortgages and bank loans were to be involved.

A building contract was let in September 1847 but one of the contractors later withdrew and from that point the project seems to have been beset with problems. From then on the committee often appear to have been more optimistic than realistic. Real cash subscriptions were, however, now being received but for a variety of reasons, poverty and unemployment amongst them, only

Illustration from the1840s shows a meeting at the City Assembly Rooms.

1,048 out of 1,600 shareholders had fully paid up. This led to something of a crisis in the Society's affairs and there was insufficient capital left to complete the building and equip the mill.

A meeting was held in the City Assembly Rooms at which it was agreed to appeal to the fully paid up shareholders to pay additional subscriptions of 10 shillings per share, which many did, and that the others should be called on to pay up.

Flour was eventually produced and made available to members in November 1848 and the Mercury reported that this was being sold at 3d a stone below shop prices.

So the mill was up and running, producing some flour, but it had many ups and downs, mainly downs, until February 1857 when a meeting of the Society was held in the Guild Hall chaired by Revd. E. R. Larkin. At that meeting a resolution was carried calling for the sale of the mill and the winding up of the affairs of the Society.

They had debts at the bank and insufficient funds to meet those debts and other liabilities.

On 26 March 1857, what was described as "an excellent Steam Corn Mill, four storeys high", was put up for sale by auction with:-

"A steam engine of 16 horse power, boiler and shafting, 4 pairs of french stones and one pair of grey stones,

Le Tall's mill - still standing and converted to flats

dressing machinery and other requisite machinery and apparatus, together with the yard and warehouse belonging thereto."

Interested parties were invited to obtain further information from Mr. Charles Pratt, wine merchant, or at the offices of Messrs. Mason and Dale, solicitors.

A postscript, or obituary notice to the whole affair, was provided by the **Mercury** for 24 July 1857, in these terms: **"Lincoln Proprietary Mill Society – This very useful society which was once the pride and glory of many of the working classes of this city has at last become defunct after a period of trials and losses. The whole of the £1,630 subscribed by the members has been expended and the mortgagees have been obliged to sell the property for nearly £300 less than the mortgage and two persons who made themselves personally liable to the bank are minus a sum of £20 or £30. This, like many other schemes would doubtless have paid a good percentage but no amount of capital is proof against mismanagement, want of knowledge and skill, or of unity of purpose. We wish the working classes success in every local attempt to benefit their condition and hope the failure of this society will act as a salutary admonition as well as to evidence that unless they place the right men in the right places their endeavours will be in vain, though every nerve be strained for the accomplishing of their object."**

So, after a ten year struggle the city's first co-operative venture had ultimately failed and people had lost their investment. Blame was attributed variously to – loose management, lack of ability and experience and dishonesty.

The mill still stands on the banks of the River Witham at the bottom of Salthouse Lane, which has now been re-named Princess Street; in the 19th and early 20th Century that part of the street closest to the High Street was called Salthouse Lane, only the part nearest the river was known as Princess Street. For a number of years the old co-operative mill building was used as a seed warehouse by Pennells. It has since been converted into flats.

Alongside this building is a former windmill, popularly known as "Le Tall's" mill. This was built some time between 1828 and 1841 and by 1849 wind power had been supplemented by steam.
The co-operative mill, sometimes described as the "proprietary mill" or "subscription mill", may have had some impact on the fortunes of "Le Tall's" mill.
In 1849 the then owner of "Le Tall's", a Mr Lister, was

13 of the
Rochdale
Pioneers
in 1865

declared bankrupt. It was reported at the time that, following the opening of the co-operative mill, he and other millers in the city had been forced to reduce their prices. This may have been the reason for Lister's bankruptcy, but presumably the lower prices brought some benefits to Lincoln's working people. "Le Tall's" mill continued as a mill well into the 20th Century but it too has now been converted to flats.

Lincoln was not alone: many or most of these early corn milling co-operatives failed for similar reasons to Lincoln. Dividends, when they were paid, were based on the amount of capital invested, but generally these early co-operative pioneers were content to sell their flour at a few pence lower than normal shop prices and paid no other benefits.

In the more conventional consumer co-operative sector, Rochdale (1844) is the best known but it was not the first. Rochdale was different in a number of ways; they established some principles, wrote them down and travelled the country telling people about them. These are some of the **Rochdale principles.**

One member one vote (whereas voting was normally weighted according to the amount of capital invested)

Sexual equality (how's that for ahead of its time in 1844)

New members have equal rights with existing

And probably the best known of all

An equitable distribution of dividend (this to be based on the member's purchases with the Society, rather than on capital invested)

But Rochdale was not even the first to adopt this *dividend on purchases principle* – Lockhurst Lane Society in Coventry, established in 1832, had already adopted this same principle. What Rochdale had that the others did not was, what we would probably call today, a good PR machine.

They also had the great good fortune to have as one of their supporters, George Jacob Holyoake (1817-1906), a prolific writer on co-operation, and described in at least one publication at the time as an eminent orator. Holyoake was to become one of the all time great co-operative pioneers. His great age and his contacts with the earliest figures in the co-operative movement made him a much revered figure in his latter years. On his death the movement levied 3d per member to acquire a site in Manchester and erect a building as the headquarters for the Co-operative Union (now Co-operatives UK) which was named Holyoake House in his memory and still carries that name to this day.

Such is the magic and the myth of Rochdale, despite the fact that Holyoake actually came from Birmingham, just a few miles from Lockhurst Lane.

Many early co-operatives may have failed but not all. Lockhurst Lane and Rochdale both continued well into the 20th Century.

Despite all the setbacks, the seeds of co-operation had been well and truly sown and the co-operative bandwagon was now unstoppable.

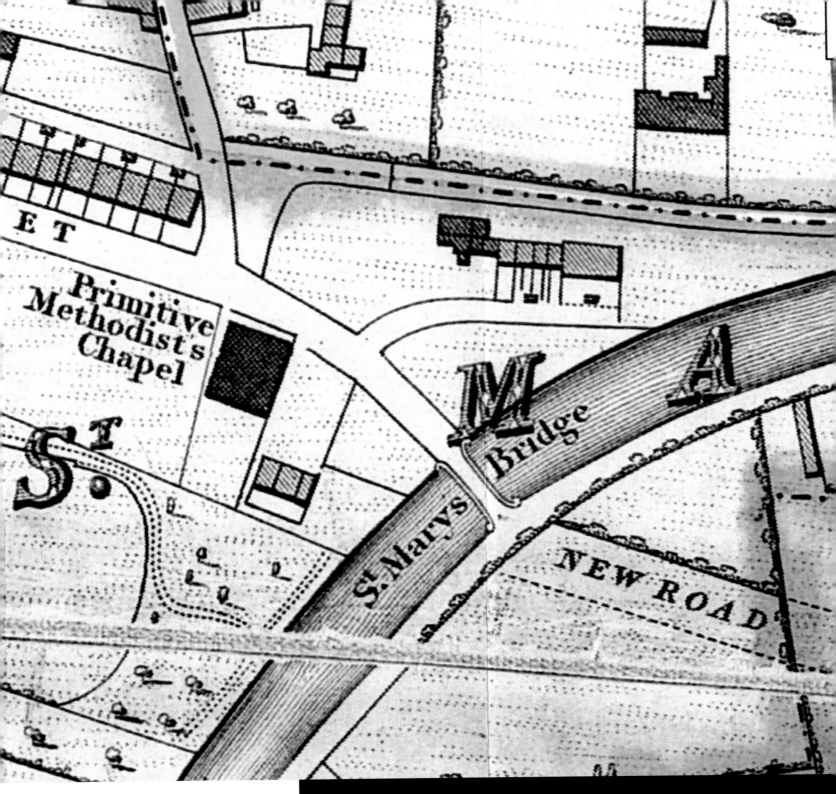

Primitive Methodist's Chapel
site of the first general meeting

A CO-OPERATIVE STAR IS BORN

3

'For a group of ordinary working men their achievement is little short of astonishing. Their record is very impressive, indeed inspirational'

In the years covered by the short life of the Lincoln Flour Mill Co-operative, the City of Lincoln changed a great deal. Large numbers of strangers had come to live and work in its rapidly growing industries, skilled craftsmen attracted by the new opportunities which were emerging and farm labourers in search of higher wages. Building trade workers had been drawn from many parts of the country and they found employment in the construction of the new factories which were springing up at Stamp End and elsewhere. Clarke's Crank & Forge Works was established in 1860 whilst a block of offices were under construction at Stamp End in the same year. With them the incomers brought new ideas and to some extent a new way of life. It also seems fairly certain that they were largely responsible for giving organised co-operative trading a second chance in the city.

Thomas Parker was undoubtedly the inspiration behind Lincoln Co-operative Society and it was he who was credited with the drive and initiative which brought the Society into being. Parker was a joiner by trade who was born in Market Rasen. He had come to Lincoln from Gainsborough and lived in Newton Street, off Melville Street. He was described as an ardent Methodist and was Secretary of the Lincoln Temperance Society which had been formed in 1847. In the Society's jubilee history book, "History of Co-operation in Lincoln", published in 1911, the author Duncan McInnes makes the following comments about Parker.

The course of social evolution since he passed away to an early grave (Parker died of consumption in June 1863 aged 34 and is buried in Canwick Road Cemetery) has proved the keenness of his insight and the soundness of his judgement.

To dream away his life in wishes and aspirations was no part of his disposition. To back up thought, by prompt and decisive action was the very essence of his nature.

He was an enthusiast but not one of the mercurial or inconstant type. He possessed creative as well as administrative capacity, and while his enthusiasm was electric and contagious, his honesty of purpose was transparent.

Some testimonial from a man who, although he did not know Parker personally, was writing in the lifetime of some of the society's founders, who undoubtedly did.

It is recorded that at meetings of the Lincoln Temperance Society, "discussions frequently took place as to whether something supplementary to the advocacy of temperance was not necessary, to provide an object of

Thomas Parker

interest and a centre of attraction outside of and apart from their daily round of toil, and permanently to ameliorate the condition of the working classes". In co-operation, Parker saw what he thought was the surest means of improving the lives of himself and his fellow workers and the less privileged members of society.

This is how it seems to have developed. Parker was a frequent visitor to the home of Joseph Watson in St Hugh Street. Watson, a few years earlier had been the manager, for a time, of the Co-operative Flour Mill. Based on all that we know, it is fairly clear that co-operation was a subject of discussion on these visits. Subsequently, at Parker's request, one of Mr Watson's sons, known only as F Watson, secured a copy of the Rochdale Pioneers' almanac and the society rules, as well as the rules of the Hull Anti-Mill Society and other successful co-operative ventures. From these, Watson senior drew up some simple notes to enable Parker to explain to a few working men who he had called together, "the principles of co-operation, how successful co-operatives worked and how a co-operative might operate in Lincoln". We do not know where or when this meeting took place, but we do know that it

No 1
Napoleon Place

was agreed, there and then, to work towards the opening of a co-operative store. It is highly likely that these "few working men", one report speaks of a dozen, were some of the building trade workers who had recently come to the City and some of whom later became committee members in the new society. The fact that they did not appear in editions of the Lincoln Directory before 1859 suggests that they were newcomers, and equally the fact that several of their names quickly disappeared from subsequent editions suggests that they were perhaps, migrant workers in search of employment.

Writing in **The Co-operator** of June 1862, Josiah Simpson, the first Secretary of the society, speaks of: **"A few earnest, undaunted and self-sacrificing men met together in a private room, to talk over the all-absorbing subject of co-operation. Our small contributions were weekly deposited in the savings bank until we opened our store with capital of £40."**

Such was the enthusiasm for the co-operative idea that, as a direct result of this meeting, a provisional committee was appointed and its first meeting was held on 17 April 1861. Records indicate that those present were Thomas Jackson, John Whitworth, Henry Taylor, William Godson, Josiah Simpson, John Harrison, Christopher Goy, Thomas Parker, Richard Harrison, Thomas McTurk and Thomas Mottershead.

At this meeting the decision was taken to form a co-operative society and to hold meetings every Saturday evening from 6pm to 7pm for the purpose of receiving contributions of the members, such meetings commencing 27 April. Another decision was that "we purchase from Mr Hayes for the use of the Society a glass ink stand, six pen holders, half a quire of blotting paper and a box of pens". Mr Jackson, Mr McTurk and Mr Taylor were appointed to a committee to seek out "a suitable place for carrying on the business of the Society". At another meeting it was agreed to adopt the whole of the Rochdale Pioneers' rules with the exception of number 42, which required the establishment of a fund for the intellectual improvement of the members and their families and for the maintenance of a library; such fund to be allocated 2½% from profits each year. It is interesting to note that the provisional committee did not feel that they needed to go down that road, at that time, or perhaps they objected to part of the profit being diverted in this way. (Lincoln Society did later open a library and also provided some funds for educational purposes.)

The provisional committee spent much time discussing whether the Society should be called equitable or industrial and since they could not agree, opted for both, hence the rather cumbersome title.

The Lincoln Equitable Industrial Co-operative Society Limited
This was changed in 1927 to
Lincoln Co-operative Society Limited
and in 2003 to
Lincolnshire Co-operative Limited

On 17 July 1861, just three months after the first meeting of the provisional committee, it was agreed that one room be taken in the house, No 1 Napoleon Place on a quarterly tenancy for use as a store. Amongst other early decisions was one to build up a modest capital by imposing an entrance fee of one shilling and by asking members to pay 3d a week each or more until enough had been subscribed to buy stock and start business.

The first general meeting of members was held on Saturday 10 August 1861, in the Primitive Methodist School, known as Portland Place, which was on the site of the present Lincoln Central Station in St Mary's Street, when the first officers of the new society were elected. They were: President, Thomas Jackson; Treasurer, John Harrison; Secretary, Josiah Simpson; Committee, H Taylor, T McTurk, H Richardson, W Godson and J Pacey; Auditors, H Millson and W Lamb; Trustees, J Whitworth, T Parker and H Beaumont.

Apart from its election of officers we have no record of what other business was carried out at this first humble general meeting of members or how many were present. Four days after this meeting the committee met again and appointed one of their number, Thomas McTurk, as the Society's first storekeeper. The former stonemason began his duties on 26 August, receiving as wages 21s per week and being allowed to live on the premises rent free, with the proviso that he should provide coal and gas and should keep the place clean. His place on the committee was taken by John Newsam. Also at this meeting it was decided to have a new counter made by a local joiner who was also given the job of placing a new door in the north window (probably a shutter). The Secretary was also asked to write to wholesale grocery firms for price lists. Shortly afterwards he was writing to the Secretary of the York Society for more general information.

No reports exist of the actual opening of the store. All we do know is that it happened on 8 September 1861. It was an event ignored by press and public alike, but this is when and where Lincoln Co-operative Society was born. It would appear from such flimsy records as do survive that the stock comprised butter and tea.

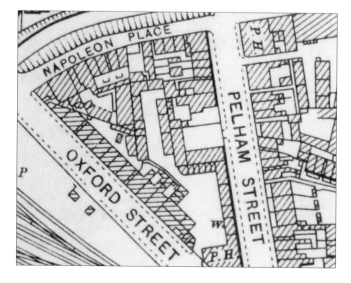

1905 map shows the location of Number 1 Napoleon Place at the junction with Pelham Street

The original pony delivery cart
was soon replaced by a horse drawn version similar
to the example shown here

We do not even know what the first day's sales were but we can be sure that it would have been a very nervous time for the committee. Within a day or two, the committee were deciding that 20s should be left in the hands of the storekeeper and that his accounts should be settled with the Secretary every Monday and Friday; that six small scoops be bought for use in the shop; and that Mr Parker obtain 20lbs of good butter on Friday, the implication being that there was plenty of bad butter around at that time. Another decision was to purchase four half-stones of tea to be retailed at 4s to 5s per pound.

But what sort of a place was this first shop in Napoleon Place? The old building stood until 1956 when, with other property in the Pelham Street area, it was demolished to make way for the new Pelham Bridge. The picture we have shows that it was part of a three storey, double fronted house, which presents a very unimpressive image. Its lower windows were provided with shutters and it stood a few feet away from a gas street lamp. Many of the rooms were let to lodgers.

One person who remembered the place well was quoted as describing it as "an uninteresting building, in poor surroundings, with an unsavoury history". It may be best not to delve too deeply into the nature of that history. The shop was open for business from 7 in the morning to 8 at night and "all goods were sold for ready money only". In the beginning the committee carried the goods from the store to the members' homes at night or on Saturday afternoons, if they were unable or unwilling to do this for themselves. Later a boy was engaged, wages 6s per week for delivery duties, then two, then a handcart was acquired, until trade increased to such a level that a pony and cart could be justified. The application of the "cash only" principle seems to have been called into question somewhat at a very early stage, as a practice developed whereby members left their orders at the store at the beginning of the week, they were delivered by the boy, either on a bicycle or by pony and cart and the member then called at the store later in the week to pay, or at least was expected to do so. Inevitably, some did

TO THE MEMBERS OF THE
LINCOLN EQUITABLE CO-OPERATIVE INDUSTRIAL SOCIETY.

BALANCE SHEET FOR FIRST QUARTER ENDING DECEMBER 17, 1861.

GENERAL STATEMENT.

Dr.	£	s.	d.	Cr.	£	s.	d.
To Contributions	128	11	1½	By paid for Goods	439	5	9
„ Sale of Groceries, &c.	365	3	5	„ Fixed Stock	44	4	1½
„ Entrance Fees	6	10	0	„ Salary	17	6	6
„ Cash received for Empties	0	14	2	„ Postage and Post Orders	1	4	3
„ „ from Treasurer	14	13	1	„ Printing and Stationery	3	16	6½
„ „ Discount	2	9	1½	„ Carriage on Goods	2	7	1
				„ Management Expenses	1	3	4
				„ Rent, Rates, and Gas	5	10	5
				„ Packages charged for	3	2	11
	£518	0	11		£518	0	11

STOCK.

Dr.	£	s.	d.	Cr.	£	s.	d.
To Members' Contributions	128	11	1½	By Stock-in-Trade	101	16	10
„ Interest on paid-up Shares	0	15	3	„ Fixed Stock	44	4	1½
„ Cash due to Treasurer	14	13	1	„ Empty Packages	2	8	9
„ Balance	13	9	4½	„ Entrance Fees	6	10	0
				„ Discount	2	9	1½
	£157	8	10		£157	8	10

PROFIT AND LOSS.

Dr.	£	s.	d.	Cr.	£	s.	
To Balance	13	9	4½	Depreciation of Fixed Stock	1	4	
				Nett Profit, allowing a Dividend of 9d. in the Pound upon £326, being the amount of Members' Purchases	12		

THOMAS PARKER,
JOHN WHITWORTH,   } Members of the Committee.
JOHN NEWSAM,

January 8th, 1862, Audited and found Correct,
(Signed)   WILLIAM LAMB,
HENRY MILLSON, } Aud
JOSIAH SIMPSON

THE STORES ARE OPEN FROM SEVEN IN THE MORNING TO EIGHT IN THE EVEN

N.B.—ALL GOODS SOLD FOR READY MONEY ONLY.

Balance sheet for the first quarter
ended December 17th 1861

not pay for one reason or another, and a form of credit, although it was never acknowledged as such at the time, had however been introduced. Bad debts were a problem for many co-operative societies for at least the next century and led to the demise of many.

As soon as the co-operative store was opened, existing traders, who had always charged top prices for poor quality goods, suddenly found that they had to cut their prices and began to get difficult with co-operative members over their existing debts. They also started vicious and completely false rumours about the alleged financial instability of the co-operative. But the committee were resolute and determined, tackling each problem as it arose and pressing on towards their

objective, coming through stronger each time. One cannot help but be struck by their integrity and honesty of purpose; they were indeed men of principle and ideals, co-operative principles. These were not businessmen or economists, but the quality of the work they did is a cause for considerable admiration.

The first quarter ended on 17 December 1861 and what was called the balance sheet records sales of £365.3s.5d, a sum of £439.5s.9d had been paid for goods and £17.6s.6d as salary to storekeeper McTurk. A remarkable entry in these accounts is one of £1.4s.10½d as "depreciation of fixed stock", an early indication of the financial prudency which has characterised the Lincoln Society throughout its life and which still exists to this day. Net profit amounted to £12.4s.6d, allowing a dividend of 9d in the £ on members' purchases. There were 74 members and capital of £128.11s.1½d had accrued.

For a first venture, by inexperienced people, with a stonemason as storekeeper and faced with competition and dishonourable tactics from established traders, scorn and criticism from others, this first quarter's result must have been very satisfying for those involved. For a group of ordinary working men their achievement is little short of astonishing. Their record is very impressive, indeed inspirational. They demonstrated perseverance, determination and a degree of probity which many 21st Century business and political leaders would do well to copy.

By the second quarter sales had risen to £436. In the fourth quarter sales were recorded as £550 and there is an entry in the accounts of £2.2s as "compensation to Mr McTurk, late storekeeper". There is no record as to why it was necessary to compensate McTurk. Possibly the committee felt that it was necessary to replace him with someone more experienced in the retail trade as the business grew, but felt some obligation to him as a former committee man. It was not necessarily a great move, at least not in the short term.

With the fifth quarter's report and balance sheet a new name appears, that of Edwin Teesdale who shortly afterwards became President. It was a hand-written sheet and a footnote to it indicated that the books had been made up by Mr Teesdale. The quarter had evidently been one of crisis for the young society: dividend had fallen to 1½d. This state of affairs, which might well have proved fatal to a society controlled by less determined men, was attributed to the dishonesty of a storekeeper who had come from Nottingham Society with first-class references to take the place of Mr McTurk. When results began to turn out unexpectedly poor, enquiries were made about the storekeeper's activities at Ruddington where he had previously been employed. It was found that during his last quarter's service there, no profit was made despite a turnover of £513 and there was a stock deficiency of £32. No doubt getting wind of the enquiries this ingenious young man intercepted letters sent to the society's Secretary from Ruddington. A trap letter was sent by Parker himself and when this failed to reach the Secretary, the storekeeper, or salesman as he was sometimes described, was dismissed and replaced by another from Leicester. No wonder that Josiah Simpson was impelled to write, "we had our trials to encounter and overcome and dishonest or incompetent shopmen seems to be amongst them". Thomas Parker wrote to his friend, William Godson, who had by now

left the area, "we have had a nice bit of bother with our salesman at the stores......".

The balance sheet re-appeared in printed form in the 7th quarter, ending 16 June 1863. It was introduced with a note of pride and pleasure on the part of the committee at being able to pay a dividend of 8d after paying 5% interest on paid up shares. **"We feel that nothing is required to make the Society a decided success but the thorough co-operation of each member. During the coming quarter let all purchase largely and induce others to join us."** The motto **"slow but sure"** and **"union is success"**, headed this and very many subsequent reports. It also proudly announced that the society now dealt in tea, coffee, sugar, ham, bacon, tobacco, dried fruits, cheese, flour, etc. and that non-members were allowed dividend at 6d in the £ on all purchases. **This report also included quotations from two members of parliament, W J Fox MP and Richard Cobden MP and ended with this note:**

"What is co-operation? Co-operation is a united movement of working men to realise better times for themselves and their families. How? Through co-operation or union in getting benefits and saving. Oh! the vast strength of unity. Remember the 'bundle of sticks', brother workmen, and band yourselves together. Be of one mind in support of the truth; have faith in the lovely principle of co-operation and cast your mountain of woe into the sea of oblivion. Enough has been accomplished in a few years to make the hopeful happy and encourage the most despondent. Free yourselves from the carking cares that chain millions to a merely animal existence. MEN OF LINCOLN – CO-OPERATE. Working men, buy your food and groceries at your own shop where you can depend on the genuine article and full weight. Nothing is tampered with to please the eye. There is no trust, therefore no risk. Shares may be paid up at once or by instalments of 3d per week."

Many more exhortations of a similar nature appeared in later reports. Reporting on the 9th quarter, ending 22 December 1863, the committee were able to declare, "not withstanding the great competition amongst the grocers in this city, your committee are thankful to state that this society of earnest, well-meaning men and women has not only been able to hold its own during the quarter, but has increased its members and capital".

Very soon a true picture began to emerge and that truth was that in the shop at Napoleon Place progress was bound to be limited. It was badly placed, in a poor neighbourhood and often very crowded as well as being remote from the homes of most of the members. Announcing that " the committee now have the offer of a much larger and very central place", the report for June 1864 declared: "if on examination we find it suitable we will at once take and enter upon it". The committee added "Lincoln with its hundreds of mechanics ought certainly to occupy a prominent position in co-operation and in order to attain this desirable end the committee hope that you will as an individual member purchase all you possibly can at the store so that the full benefit may be felt".

There was a note of regret in this report too, that during the quarter "many good members have been compelled to leave the town; others through sickness or distress have had to withdraw a good deal of their capital". This note was to be sounded many times in later reports; boom and bust were not inventions of the 20th Century. Lincoln with one foot in agriculture was subject to the effects of poor harvests and bad seasons. Equally with its other foot in engineering, which in turn was linked very largely to agriculture, it was liable to be affected by industrial depression. The society's balance sheets, through the years, particularly in the capital account, reflect the changing fortunes of the City's trade and commerce and also that of its members.

Then came the first move. The report for the 12th quarter, dated 15 September 1864, was published from No 1¼ Waterside South, very near to the High Bridge. Three months later the committee jubilantly reported that sales had risen to £613.14s.9½d and that "the rooms already occupied in the new store are rapidly becoming too small for the increasing business and the committee intend taking possession of the upper floor or floors immediately they can see the way clear for doing so. It is very necessary that this should be done as early as possible, in order (amongst other things), that the Society may have a room in which to hold its quarterly and other meetings".

Announcing that 14 new members had joined during the quarter, the committee asserted with confidence, "as soon as the principles of co-operation are known, Lincoln will be able to count its members by the hundreds". They were, in fact, far too modest.

The new store was part of an old riverside warehouse and whilst its position was very good, being so close to the High Bridge, it could hardly have been ideal as a shop, but it played an honourable part in the Society's development.

But the troubles were not yet over. Once more there

Waterside South looking west towards the High Bridge

was difficulty with a storekeeper. The local Weights and Measures Inspector had evidently called in to make a test purchase and although the scales were quite correct, the weight of the article purchased was not. As a result the storekeeper was called to appear before the local magistrates. What, from the Society's point of view, was much more serious was that he failed to notify the committee of his predicament and they were not unnaturally horrified when the first they heard of the matter was a report in the local newspaper.
The situation was explained to members in the next quarter's report, which also indicated that the committee's action in discharging the storekeeper had been unanimously endorsed by the members.

In some ways this event proved to be a blessing in disguise. Despairing perhaps of ever obtaining the right man from outside, the committee succeeded in persuading the Society's Secretary, Thomas Jackson, to become storekeeper. It was a move which paid dividends in more ways than one, for Jackson seems to have been a shrewd and capable man who showed a level of commitment which had clearly been missing in earlier storekeepers. Jackson was succeeded as Secretary by William Walker.

An interesting comment on the changes, as well as on the position of the Society generally, appeared in **The Co-operator** of June 1865, from the Society's President, Edwin Teesdale: **"We have hitherto been unsuccessful in salesmen. Now however, we have taken our Secretary. I believe our present salesman is as honest as possible and I am therefore now full of hope. As the Secretary is in the shop I shall now have to break in another Secretary and Treasurer and indeed, it is a difficult thing to meet with suitable people who will work hard for little money. Co-operation is really uphill work but we must keep up heart, I suppose. In Lincoln we have an abundance of shops and they are so well conducted** that members require very little indeed to draw them away. It is the women who stand so much in our way; while they are our greatest comfort they often bother us fearfully. Only ask Eve's daughters to work to a system and away they fly."

A most interesting reflection perhaps on certain changes which have occurred in society generally between 1865 and this day.

The shadow of the dishonest storekeeper came into play again in the succeeding report and balance sheet, when reference was made to the expense caused by removing him. But an even harder blow was a reduction of 6d. per lb. in the duty on tea. Members were told "this change in the duty took your committee, as well as every other grocer, by surprise and as our usual stock had been purchased, there must of necessity be a loss, if it were not made up by reducing the quality, which alternative was not adopted". One result was a small cut in the dividend from 10½d. to 9d.

At the January quarterly meeting of 1866 the members had unanimously agreed that the store should close at 7pm in the evening instead of 8pm as previously. With the new storekeeper firmly in office, he received £18 per quarter and with the help of a boy and a labourer, sales

Corn Exchange (to the left of the Exchange Arcade) site of the first annual tea meeting

and dividend both rose. Indeed the committee became almost lyrical in their usual comment on the balance sheet: **"The co-operative principle must stand, it is a growing power. Its future destiny is to raise the social status of the working classes and change the whole destiny of labour life. It gladdens the present and brightens the future."**

The autumn of 1865 was marked by the first of what was to become a series of annual tea meetings and festivals. These events were partly a reward to members for their loyalty and partly a propaganda exercise and were greatly valued by the Society and members alike. The first such event was held in November 1865 in the Corn Exchange and the Secretary described it as "large and enthusiastic". It was attended by "many hundred intelligent working men from the extensive engineering and agricultural machine works for which Lincoln is almost as celebrated as for its grand cathedral". Mr Teesdale, who presided, is quoted as saying that it was hardly possible for the poor to save anything from their scanty wages, but by joining a co-operative store they could save a considerable sum in a few years by economising their expenditure. "One shilling was the entrance fee", he said, "and then they can eat themselves into capitalists". These meals were often described as a "meat tea" or "knife and fork tea" and often had prominent co-operative activists from all over the country as speakers. Although these meetings started in Lincoln, they later spread to the country branches as that network developed.

An engineering firm in Lincoln had recently been made into a limited liability company and Mr Teesdale went on, "if the working men economised and saved (in the co-operative) they might become shareholders in the business at which they laboured". Speakers at this meeting in addition to Mr Teesdale included the Rev. F. A. MacDonald, a local Unitarian minister who played a helpful part in the Society's formative years, became one of its auditors and represented the Society on the committee which organised the first co-operative Congress, held in London in 1869. As a result of the meeting and the liberal distribution of co-operative propaganda, many new members were enrolled and a committee, reporting on the quarter ended 19 December 1865 declared: **"Four and a quarter years of experience has amply proved to us how easily the wealth of this country may be more equally distributed. £404.10s.9d which would have made the rich richer, has been retained during that period in the pockets of those prudent persons who joined the Society. Working men and women think of this large sum and remember that it may easily be doubled".**

By now Mr Teesdale was able to report in **The Co-operator: "We now hold our meetings at the store which is very convenient and will induce members to attend. I hope that in the Cathedral and hitherto old Tory city its hundreds of mechanics will soon become alive to the benefits of co-operation and that erelong we shall be able to have our own reading room, etc."**

The report of 20 March 1866 showed that sales had risen to £1,032.13s.11½d, capital amounted to £749.16s.10½d and a dividend of 1s.1d was declared. There was also an item of expenditure payable to Dr. Mason for attending the errand boy's broken arm. Members were reminded "The co-op store is only the first step, the rest will follow in due time. We want society levelling, not by pulling down the rich, but by lifting up the poor".

Three months later two new developments were announced. Arrangements had been made to supply members with coal, "quality and weight guaranteed", and for a local drapery firm, Messrs. Craps & May, to provide members with drapery goods. Members who made purchases in this way were able to hand in the receipted bills to the Society's store and receive dividend in return.

At the same time members were told: "There are one or two arrangements at the store which require improvements, to which the committee are giving attention. In the meantime it is hoped that members will be willing to bear some slight inconvenience, remembering that Rome was not built in a day".

An early reference to the Waterside store in **Co-operative News,** the national newspaper for the Movement, refers to it as being **"in a warehouse 20 ft. long by 50 ft. deep, with the drapery in a back garratt".**

Commission on coal sales in the first quarter brought in £4.2s.9d and on drapery sales £3.14s.6d and both agencies were reported to have given satisfaction. Rent of the store was £9 per quarter and 22s worth of gas was burned.

The report of 18 December 1866 shows that sales had gone up to £1,456.10s.7d and profit exceeded £100 for the first time. This enabled a dividend of 1s.4d to be paid and the committee were able to declare with some justification, "The principles of co-operation are daily becoming better understood and appreciated by the working men in this City".

An examination of the signatories to this report reveals that in five years the whole of the committee and

Metallic checks similar to these were issued to members as proof of purchase and enabled them to claim dividend - these examples are from the Rochdale Society.

officers had completely changed, not one of the original group remained, although Mr Teesdale, who was now Treasurer, had been associated with the Society from the end of 1862. This was partly because some people had moved away from Lincoln, but members were quite prepared to remove committeemen when faced with poor results.

Twelve months later the quarter's sales had risen to £2,459 and a satisfied committee were able to claim, "Our past and present success is a standing refutation of the assertion that co-operation cannot profitably be carried out by the working class". Some of the sales increase was due to the opening of a tailoring and clothing branch at 22 Spa Buildings, near the Wesleyan School where, members were told, they could find a stock of cloths, cords, moleskins, tapes, calicos, flannels, etc etc, and where Mr Britton, the tailor and cutter, is prepared to take orders for all classes of clothing and guarantees a good fit. Again dividend was to be given on every purchase. A sum of £59.19s had been expended on drapery stock and the shopman received wages of £17.11s.

In the same quarter the Society said goodbye to its pony and acquired a horse instead; clearly the delivery rounds were growing heavier with the rise in membership, which now topped 500.

Sales of £140.10s.8d were recorded in the tailoring department in the quarter ended 17 June 1868 and two or three months later the whole department was moved to No 6 Guildhall Street, "eight doors from the Stonebow" as the quarterly report proudly announced and within a year trade had risen to £365.16s.4d in the quarter.

By now the stores were closed at 1pm on Wednesdays "for the benefit of the employees".

In the early days, metallic checks were issued for the amount of purchases and these could be exchanged for copper ones of a higher denomination. These were metal discs which enabled members to prove the amount of their purchases and claim their dividend once it had been declared. This process soon began to occupy so much time in an already crowded shop that the committee had to make an appeal to members to exchange their checks as often as possible, "but not on Fridays and Saturdays on account of the pressure of business on those days". The Waterside store, which had served the Society well since 1864 was now bursting at the seams and there was no longer enough room to hold members meetings, which were transferred to various rooms in the City. In July 1870 one was held in the Baptist School, Benedict Square, three months later it was held in a large room adjoining the Butter Market, and still later in the upper room of the Temperance Hall in St Swithin's Square.

The first record of a "sale" being conducted by the Society occurs in the report for the quarter ended 6 October 1870. This announced that "having purchased a large quantity of blankets, flannels and calicos at a great reduction, the same will be offered at remarkably low prices (clothing clubs supplied)".

A picture of the volume of the Society's order trade at this time can be gained from an outline of the rounds which is given in the report of 2 October 1871. On Monday and Thursday mornings and Saturday afternoons goods were delivered to Waterside and Lock, Broadgate, Monks Road, Rosemary Lane, Spa Buildings, Croft Street, St Hugh Street, Baggeholme Road, John Street, Thomas Street and Winn Street. On Monday and Friday mornings the horse and cart visited Canwick Road, Melville Street, Newton Street, Flaxongate, Danesgate, Hungate, Mint Lane, Park Street and the Newland district. On Tuesday and Saturday mornings it was the turn of the Great Northern

Terrace area and the lower parishes, while on Monday and Thursday afternoons the Above Hill received its groceries. An indication here perhaps, where most of the co-operative members were living at the time.

Members were reminded that, "To ensure prompt delivery, orders should be sent to the stores the day previous. If it should occasionally happen that a member cannot conveniently send money with the order, the goods will be delivered providing he has sufficient capital to cover the amount, but in such cases the account must be paid during the week. 'No trust' is the central pillar of the Co-operative Structure and though such a rigid rule may seem hard it is a true kindness". Whether any members capital was ever taken in settlement of bad debts, or whether the Society had any legal authority to do so, is not known, but it was a threat which was to remain in place for the next hundred years. Again this is confirmation that there was, in fact, a weekly credit system in operation, in spite of the committee's apparent realisation of the risks of credit trading. How far it was seen as credit by the members, how far the advantages of having one's groceries delivered, and how far the general advantages of co-operation which appealed increasingly to Lincoln folk, the official records do not say. But this was a different kind of trading, they were, after all, using their own store. Things had changed for these working people like never before.

NEW COAL DEPOT.

The Directors of the **Lincoln Equitable Co-operative Industrial Society** (Limited,) beg to inform the members and the public generally that they have opened a **NEW COAL DEPOT**, where the following qualities will be kept in Stock, viz:— Firsts, Seconds, and Thirds; the Prices, including delivery, will be regularly posted up at the Grocery department.

Orders, **with the Cash**, must be sent to the Stores; if the Coals are required the same day, the order must be given before Half-past Ten o'clock. Bills shewing the quality &c., will be given to the Carter, and members will please ask for them. Cheques will be given, as on other goods, and non-members will be allowed the same bonus as that paid at the Grocery Stores.

The Directors promise their best attention to the quality, weight, and regular delivery of the Coals, and have confidence in the members making this branch—as they have the Grocery, Drapery, and Baking departments—decidedly successful.

This Society was established in 1861 by a few working men, who adopted as their mottoes—" Slow, but Sure." " Union is Strength,"—and determined that the central pillar in the structure should be "No Trust," "Cash Payments."

The Society has now 1114 Members, with a Capital of **£5343 12s 10d.** Since its commencement, Profits amounting to **£5116 11s 1d** have been added to the Members' Accounts, and **£723 16s 0d** has been paid for Interest on Capital, which is calculated at the rate of 5 per cent.

Co-operative Stores are not established for the purpose of opposing and injuring Merchants or Tradesmen, by creating monopolies, running down prices, &c., but seek in the First Place, to secure Un-adulterated Food, Goods of Pure Quality and Guaranteed Weight, at the regular Trade Prices: in the Second Place, to enable the Working Classes to improve their circumstances and position, by adding the legitimate profits of trade to the wages of labor. For this purpose, the Terms of Membership are adapted to the means of the poorest.

The Directors believe the above statements amply prove what the Working Classes entirely unassisted, may accomplish by care and thrift, and close this Notice by reminding the members that the present feature of Co-Operation in Lincoln, viz:—the distributive is but the first step. **Stores of our own, Houses, of which the Working**

At the end of ten years, in 1871, the Lincoln Society, which had faced opposition and criticism and also had to live down the embarrassment of a previous co-operative failure in the City, was able to record sales of more than £5,000 in one quarter and a dividend of 1s.6d was declared!

A bakery department had already been started and early in 1872 a new coal depot was opened, replacing the previous system by which a local private trader had supplied coal on commission. Promising "best attention to the quality, weight and regular delivery", the committee laid it down that "orders with the cash must be sent to the stores; if the coals are required the same day the order must be given before 10.30am".

In the same announcement "The Directors", as the committee now seemed to have been calling themselves, reminded members, almost prophetically, "that the present feature of co-operation in Lincoln, i.e. the distribution, is but the first step. Stores of our own; houses of which the working men themselves shall be landlords; mills, factories and workshops will certainly follow".

Before these ambitious projects could come about, a new store was urgently needed to cater for the growing membership and the committee were fully alive to the need. At the quarterly meeting on 5 August 1872, members were able to have a glimpse at plans for the Society's new store on Silver Street, an ambitious project which must have caused almost as many eyebrows to be raised in doubt as heads to be nodded in approval. The plans were a bold and confident assertion that the days of operating from back street doss houses and riverside warehouses were over. Lincoln's co-operators were going to town in a big way. They were about to join the premier league.

The following is an article which was carried in the report to members for the quarter ended 6 January 1873.

On Wednesday last, 29 January 1873, a deputation from the National Chamber of Trade waited, by appointment, on the Chancellor of the Exchequer, at his official residence. A paper was read by the Secretary and several speeches made. The Chancellor of the Exchequer in his reply went fully into the question of the Civil Service stores and in conclusion said: "It was not the Civil Service they had to contend with it was the principle of co-operation; it was the principle of allowing people much greater advantages who were willing to pay ready money for what they bought. They would find no want of people to compete with them when money was to be made by competing with them.

The success of the co-operative societies was due to the cheapness of the articles they sold. The deputation really put him in mind of the celebrated story of Sir Isaac Newton, who had two holes cut in a door one for the cat and the other for the kitten. They seemed to forget that if they stopped up the hole for the kitten, she could get out of that of the cat. He thought they were wasting their energies on this question. He was told that people made a saving of 30% in their expenditure by co-operation, and if that were so, were they likely to put it down? The only way to defeat these societies was by competing with them in the market, and if they were in a condition to do that let them do so and combine together, and offer to the public as good terms as these societies did. If they were not prepared to do that, let them make up their minds that these societies would drive them out of the market, for nobody would pay a high price for an article when they could buy it cheaper. He had been told that such societies had been founded by gentlemen in their clubs. They said that gentlemen in their clubs ought not to compete with them; but as long as people made large profits by turning over capital frequently in the year they would do so, as well as persons who turned it over less frequently and asked higher prices. He was sure if he were to propose any legislation on the subject to Parliament it would not succeed".

Robert Lowe 1st Viscount Sherbrooke Chancellor of the Exchequer December 1868 to August 1873 *reproduced by permission of The National Portrait Gallery, London*

The Silver Street store

'...in the short space of two hours the Society was removed from the foundation of sand to one of rock'

The decision which the Society took in 1872 to build a new store on a site which was, at that time, well within Lincoln City Centre, was largely an act of faith – faith that just as it had been successful in a small way, it would be equally successful in a big way. The move was also a matter of necessity.

As a writer in the **Co-operative News** of 1 May 1875, described it, **"No establishment was to be found which was conveniently situated in the City and the idea of building one for themselves seemed almost absurd"**. But the committee were in a difficult situation and their choices were clearly limited. They could not continue where they were and they had no intention of going backwards. Ultimately it was decided to proceed and a suitable site was soon found on Silver Street and acquired for £3,500. The site contained an old mansion known as Palfrey House, which gained its name from the original owner, a Mr Palfrey, who during the Civil War raised a troop of soldiers to defend the Royalist cause. It had a frontage of 200 feet on Silver Street and 180 feet on Free School Lane. The Society was little more than ten years old, when on 6 May 1872, the committee decided to buy this "eligible site". On this day 10% of the purchase price, £350, was paid as a deposit. On 2 October 1872 the members meeting approved plans for, "a very substantial and beautiful building, Gothic in style, three storeys high". It was left to the committee to decide how to raise the funds needed to proceed with the project and a very

difficult decision it must have been. Members' capital at that time amounted to little more than £5,000, all of it withdrawable on demand. We must remember too, that when a period of what we would now call recession, (they called it depression in those days), struck the city's industries, members' capital provided a source of ready cash which was always on tap. The action of the Committee at this time seems risky, almost reckless. It does not appear to display the level of prudence which has been such a feature of the Society's character throughout its life. This is possibly the only time in the whole history where there is any suggestion of caution, if not being thrown to the wind, certainly being pushed aside.

But fortune, as they say, favours the brave and the committee tackled the situation courageously. A special meeting of members was called for 25 November 1872 to deal with the capital situation. According to a report in **Co-operative News, "this was no Quaker's meeting"**. There were apparently three resolutions before the meeting, (1) that each member should hold two transferable shares, (2) that each member should hold one, (3) that 20% of all capital held should be transferable only. It was reported that when the votes were taken there was "a tremendous majority" for the one share option, the other resolutions being greeted with laughter. But this was not all. Approval was also given to a motion, proposed by the committee,

Silver Street store, opened in 1874

increasing the limit on capital to be held by each member to £200 and to the addition of a new clause to the rule governing the withdrawal of capital, giving the committee power to suspend the withdrawal of capital, "if such cause be necessary for the safety of the Society". Yet another resolution, that 5s be deducted from each member's account and that the first 5s of interest and dividend earned by all new members, should go to the building fund, was carried without dissention. When reporting the outcome of the meeting the **Co-operative News** commented: **"Thus in the short space of two hours the Society was removed from the foundation of sand to one of rock. As might be expected there are some who cannot rise to the dignity of having a share in such a handsome building which will be an ornament to the City and an honour to these working men. A few have, therefore, withdrawn and rumour has not been idle, a rumour said sixty had withdrawn. In fact there were sixteen, five of whom had left the City".**

Tenders were invited for the erection of the building and eventually one was accepted at a price of slightly less than £7,000. Shortly afterwards the builders started to clear the site and dig the foundations and on New Year's Day 1873 the foundation stone of the Silver Street store was laid, accompanied by massive celebrations, including a tea party and a public meeting.

Funds had started to accumulate. As a result of the measures taken by the committee, the building fund had started, but there was still a significant shortfall and the main financial problems remained. In one respect the Society had been fortunate. The vendor of the Palfrey House site, Mr W Rudyard, JP, far from being one of the enemies of co-operation, was very much a supporter and offered to lend the Society substantial sums at 4% interest, but the Society decided to make a direct approach to the Co-operative Wholesale Society (CWS) of which, at that time, it was not a member. On 13 May 1873 the committee sent a small deputation comprising George Hartley and Thomas Jackson to be interviewed by the CWS Directors in Manchester with a view to obtaining a loan. Seven days later the CWS Board agreed to lend £3,000 on mortgage, on condition that the title deeds of the whole of the property were deposited with them. Later, a further £1,000 was borrowed from the CWS at 5% on a promisory note. A local man known only as Mr Brogden had been a tenant in the old house. Not being able to give up possession until April 1874, Mr Brogden offered to lend the Society a sum of money if they would allow him to continue to live there in the short term. A document sanctioning the proposal was drawn

Main entrance of the store on the junction of Silver Street and Free School Lane.

up and agreed by all of the parties concerned and Mr Brogden remained in residence, paying rent, but the Society took from him, on loan, only £1,000 of the amount offered.

In the meantime the building work proceeded rapidly and members were promised, in two reports, that when the new store was completed, it would be "a credit to the Society and an honour to the working men of Lincoln". On 4 August 1873, the building of the central stores was proceeding so well that a roof-raising supper was authorised and enjoyed by the committee and many members. On the eve of the opening, the committee ventured into verse in their report, with the following (author identified only as O.J.S):

The Good Time Comes

There is a tide in man's affairs
Which taken at the flood
Leads on to long progress of years
Of usefulness and good
Then drop your oars into the wave
And make each stroke the stronger
Nor be to idle dreams a slave
Nor wait a little longer

E'en while we sleep the tide may flow
And leave us far behind
Then let us now resolve to show
Our broad side to the wind
Nor stay for flood, nor stay for tide
Action makes men stronger
And gives us power the storm to ride
Without the little longer

Free School Lane frontage of the new
central premises

Exactly a year after the laying of the foundation stone,
the new co-operative store on Silver Street was opened.
New Year's Day 1874 was chosen, perhaps symbolically
as the date for the formal opening of the new store and
what a day it must have been. The account given in the
Co-operative News seems to capture the mood of the
moment very well: **"On New Year's Day the store of
Lincoln Society, the foundation stone of which was
laid twelve months ago, was opened with a tea-party
and public meeting. It is one of the largest buildings
in Lincoln and arrangements have been made in it
for conducting on a large scale the grocery, boot and
shoe and drapery business. The business rooms are
very commodious and the building is an ornament to
the town. At the top there is a large hall capable of
holding from 1,000 to 1,200 people.**

**Much had been done during the year by the
tradesmen of the town to weaken the confidence of
the members but corresponding efforts were put
forth to meet these attacks and the replies to their
allegations were successfully dealt with. The room
on this occasion was decorated with evergreens,
banners and mottoes. The tea meeting commenced
at an early hour and there were several sittings down**

**before all present were supplied. At 7 o'clock the
public meeting was held when there were present
about 1,200 persons. Mr Hartley, President of the
Society occupied the Chair. He said their trade had
steadily increased. At the end of 1872 it was £26,000
and at the end of 1873 it reached £29,000 and he
hoped their success in the future would be of such
a character as to justify the step they had taken in
increasing their facilities for business. The meeting
was afterwards addressed by three of the Directors
of the CWS, Manchester, Messrs Crabtree, Allen and
Whiley, all of whom delivered forceable addresses.
Songs and recitations were given during the evening
and one of the most successful gatherings they had
held was brought to a close by votes of thanks to the
Chairman, the ladies and the speakers."**

Before the actual opening took place it is evident that
some business in bread and confectionery was being
carried out in part of the building. In July 1873 the
committee reported on the successful installation of new
ovens, "a patent never worked in Lincolnshire before",
and other plant which enabled 1,200 loaves per day to
be turned out. Bread from this plant, it was claimed
was, "equal in all respects to home made". But if the
more optimistic members of the committee, as well as
ordinary members of the Society, imagined that with the
new building, utopia had arrived, they were soon left in
no doubt that a long struggle lay ahead. Capital
remained a problem for some time and it seems clear
that some members, small in numbers perhaps, became

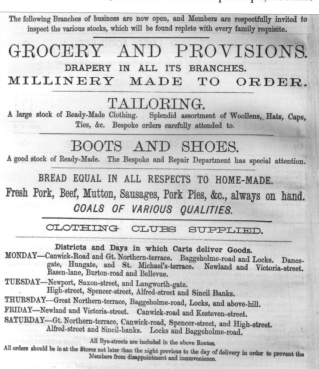

Society
advertisement
from 1876

Detail of a surviving section of Central Premises. The beehive with the motto 'Crescit Paulatim' (growing little by little) was a favourite co-operative symbol of the time.

nervous about the security of their shareholding, as a result of rumours spread by local tradesmen. According to Mr E T Trenery, a member of the Society's Education Committee, in the course of a paper he read to a co-operative conference, the Society had not attracted much local attention until the new store was opened. "As the work progressed", he wrote, "the private tradesmen became somewhat alarmed and asked if we were going mad". Attacks were mounted by private traders and other enemies of co-operation, both verbally and in the press, but the committee responded each time. Some of the exchanges were quite bitter. On occasions these 'enemies' displayed posters on billboards around the City with lies about the financial stability of the Society and the committee retaliated in kind.

When capital was needed to buy stocks, the CWS again came to the Society's aid and it is not surprising to find, on the agenda for the quarterly meeting of 3 May 1875, an item, "to consider the propriety of becoming members of the Wholesale". The discussion was, in fact, adjourned to a meeting on 6 July of the same year, where it was then approved.

Sales in the first full quarter in the new store amounted to £9,397 and the committee were able to report to the members meeting on 3 August, the first to be held in the new store, that profits were sufficient to pay a dividend of 1s.1d but that they preferred to pay 1s and pass the balance to reserves. Prudence had returned.

The problem of credit raised its head again as a result of increased demand for bread which was largely sold by roundsmen. In order to meet this demand the committee hit upon the idea of issuing bread checks, which could be bought for cash at the store. The scheme, described later by a member of the committee as, "perfection itself", initially proved successful. A special meeting of members approved this method of dealing with the growing bread trade on 24 February 1875. However, some years later the scheme led to a complication which nobody had foreseen at the time. In 1887 when bread prices fluctuated widely, many members bought excessive supplies of checks speculatively when the price of a quartern loaf was 4d. They not only bought them at the central stores but also at branches and even persuaded friends to buy checks for them. The result was two-fold. Other members were frequently unable to

Local children promote the Penny Bank - still going strong in the 1920s

obtain bread checks, whilst the speculators used the checks to buy bread at the old rate long after the price had gone up. Offending members were warned that, "not withstanding the precautions they take to conceal their action, they are well-known and should the course they are taking be persisted in, their names will be submitted to a general meeting". Also at about the same time, credit for coal and meat was completely banned.

A penny bank was started on 7 November 1874 and deposits, though small when compared with the Society's overall capital needs, no doubt played their part in expanding the Society's services and in cultivating a spirit of thrift amongst members' children. The year 1875 saw considerable reductions in trade. The report for the quarter ended 6 July recorded a decrease of £237 on the previous quarter, whilst there was a further fall three months later. What was worse, dividend slumped from 1s.2d to 8d and £716 was paid out to members who withdrew from the Society. The committee voiced regrets at the poor returns in the drapery, millinery, tailoring and shoe departments and

counter-attacked by issuing lots of pamphlets, "bearing upon the benefits flowing to the working classes by co-operation". Perhaps rather more practically, they held a clearance sale in the drapery, millinery and tailoring departments which, "whilst they have cleared us of a large quantity of inferior articles, have been a serious loss to the amount of £194.11s.11d". To meet the loss £100 was withdrawn from reserves and the dividend rose to 1s. "Since the sale", the committee reported, "a choice assortment of new goods have been purchased".

At the annual festival held in the new hall on 12 January 1876 George Hartley, who presided, warned members about listening to reports started in the city, "by persons who had a very great dislike of the Movement". He reported that some trademen were offering a discount of a shilling in the pound.

One of the weaknesses in the Society at the time was the relatively small average amount spent by each member. During the quarter ended 4 July 1876 this amounted to

£4.17s and the **Co-operative News** commented that this was only equal to **"one half of the amount that is ordinarily spent by working men's families in the articles supplied by the stores during the quarter. The other half, we presume, goes to private trade."**

This was perhaps a little harsh in view of the still limited range of goods carried by the Society, but the **News** in the role of a candid friend returned to the attack in the following January when they made the suggestion that **"Our friends at Lincoln have over-built themselves"**. The average spend per member during the next quarter rose to £5.6s.2d, which the **News** described as **"An improvement but scarcely deserving of commendation yet"**.

In 1875 James Cunliffe was appointed Cashier. Later he was described in some reports as 'Manager' and then reverted to Cashier. However, it is clear that he was head of the paid workforce and looked after the accounts.

One result of the appointment seems to have been a tightening up of the Society's affairs, for whilst sales did not immediately go back to their previous levels, the committee reported on 4 April 1876 that, "the net gain, notwithstanding a decrease in trade, is £692.18s.2d, a larger sum of profit than has ever been realised in one quarter since the commencement of the Society".

Sales fell again in the next quarter and 21 members withdrew, mainly through leaving the City. Throughout 1877 the committee reports continue to speak of "depression in the City", but trade slowly recovered,

aided no doubt by dividends which averaged 1s.2d and when 1878 dawned the Society was able to announce that sales in the quarter had exceeded £10,000 for the first time.

Boldness and confidence were beginning to pay off and the Society was making better use of its assets in the new store. Reports called members attention to the "large and beautiful hall and very convenient ante-rooms connected therewith, which are let upon very reasonable terms for lectures, balls, concerts and entertainments". The assembly hall could be hired for 17s.6d for a lecture or entertainments; a ball, with ante-rooms, until 2.00am, cost £2, including gas until 10.30 pm, and 2s an hour afterwards. Dimensions were given as 60 feet by 50 feet, 27 feet high, with a good, movable platform.

The hall became the scene of the popular tea meeting and festivals, held in the first few days of each new year. In 1877 the event had to be postponed for almost two months because of serious flooding in the City and county, the worst for over forty years. The banks of the Fossdyke, the Witham, Brayford Mere and Sincil Bank were breached and water stood on the Brayford Wharves three feet deeper than in the 1852 floods, which had been thought bad enough at the time. The City Council provided carts to enable folk to reach their homes in the Ripon Street and Canwick Road areas. Homes in Great Northern Terrace were isolated and work stopped in the Stamp End engineering works. So far as records show, the postponement of the festival was the only loss suffered by the Society at this time.

Contemporary illustrations
of the Lincoln floods of 1877

Saxilby store under construction
(photo courtesy of Saxilby and District History Group)

EXPANSION

'..the Society has been of really substantial service in alleviating the sorrows of many who unfortunately, have been distressed through circumstances for which they had no control'.

From the mid 1870's onwards the committee reports regularly speak of "depressed trade in the City", but the membership continued to grow, and with regard to sales, although they were sometimes up and down, the overall trend was positive. The confidence of the committee never seems to have been in doubt and they continued to develop and expand the Society's activities.

Responding to requests from members living outside the centre of Lincoln, the first branch store was opened at Bracebridge, on 26 May 1876. At that time Bracebridge was very much a suburb of Lincoln. Very soon, a second branch was opened, which was called Newport, but was actually in Gray Street, off Burton Road and in 1877, the committee, "having found the opening of branch shops conducive to the Society's

No. 4 Branch
RIPON STREET, LINCOLN.

No. 1 Branch: BRACEBRIDGE.

good", opened a third branch in Shakespeare Street on 1 August. These branches met with steady success from the start and as a result branch number four was opened in Ripon Street in 1878. The following year yet another branch was opened, this time on Burton Road and from its designation as "No 2" branch we can safely assume that it replaced the shop in Gray Street known as Newport branch.

In 1880 patent medicines were announced for sale, including painkillers, Solar Elixir and soothing syrup. Perhaps some of these painkillers were needed to relieve the heartache experienced by so many members because of the acute shortage of work in the city reflected from time to time in heavy withdrawals of capital. "In this respect", the quarterly report stated, "the Society has been of really substantial service in alleviating the sorrows of many who unfortunately, have been distressed through circumstances for which they had no control". In another way too, the Society helped to

relieve distress by making a gift of bread to a local soup kitchen.

In the October report of 1880 Mr Cunliffe's name as cashier appears for the last time and is replaced by that of Fred Stephenson. In 1881 the work of developing the Silver Street/Free School Lane site continued. For many years the Society's vehicles had been washed down in the public street and the horses groomed there, "much to the inconvenience of passers by". To avoid this, stables were built with an open yard behind the shops.

Members in the Great Northern Terrace area were now pressing for a branch store and their wishes were granted in 1882 with the conversion of a house. This year was however, principally celebrated by the committee for the fact that the mortgage on the Silver Street premises had been paid off, at the end of the Society's 21st year. At that point, the reserve fund stood at a mere £210. The year also saw a decision taken to convert part of the Free School Lane premises into a butcher's shop with accommodation for bacon curing. Another event in 1882 which proved to be very significant for the Society, was the appointment, as Secretary, of Duncan McInnes.

By 1884 the Society was offering furniture for sale, including pianos, harmoniums, watches, clocks and jewellery but, lacking room to stock the larger items, invited prospective purchasers to inspect the piano recently bought, for £29.8s by the Education Committee for use in the large hall. Two more branches had been added in the city, one in Baggeholme Road and another in Newland Street West. By this time it must have seemed that these amateur tradesmen could do nothing wrong.

So far as capital was concerned the position was now completely reversed, much to the embarrassment of the committee. Loans were made to members for house purchase and the Society launched out into the house building business, but the committee found it necessary to warn members that shortly "We must either refuse to receive more loan capital or we must find employment for it. In this contingency the most natural employment for any surplus, it seems to us, would be the production of articles for which we have a regular demand within the Society. We can use our money, therefore, either in buying shares in co-operative productive societies that manufacture goods we can sell, or in purchasing land which we could let or by employing the need for labour, cultivate to produce a portion or the whole of what we consume". This is clearly a reference to the possibility of going into farming, but it was to be some years before that actually came about. The Society at this time had invested £1,146 in the CWS, £50 in the Co-operative Insurance Society (CIS), £20 in the Hebden Bridge Fustian Society and £50 in Leicester Hosiery Society. The committee also had to warn members that interest rates might have to be reduced to stem the flow of capital and they soon were.

By 1884 the crowded rooms at Silver Street were calling for attention and the Society made an important decision to buy a block of property on Waterside North,

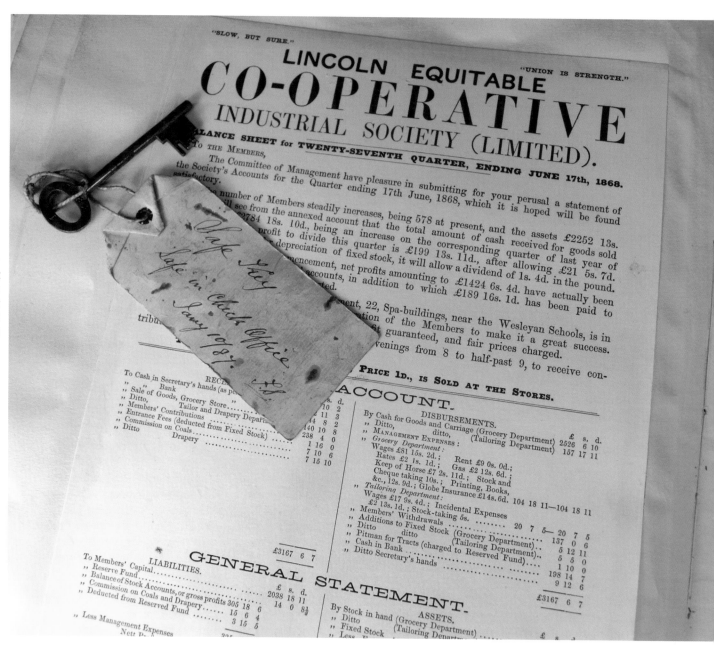

Balance sheet for the 27th quarter ended June 1868

consisting of a warehouse, malt kilns and cottages for conversion into a corn mill, bakery and stabling, the intention being to move the bakery and the stabling to Waterside, so as to make more room for furniture and crockery on Silver Street. The desire to mill co-operative flour was clearly still there as it had been 40 years earlier.

There had been some reckless buying at Silver Street, through weak control of the buyers by the committee. Large quantities of drapery goods and boots lay piled up on the floors covered in brown paper. One general manager, in absolute defiance of the committee, almost filled the cellars with cheese and tea and was dismissed immediately. It took some time to dispose of the tea stock but the cheese was cleared more quickly. His successor applied the same principle to the buying of currants and dried fruit and was suspended; his ultimate fate is not recorded. In 1886 the keeping of accounts was made a separate department under the cashier, and departmental committees were set up for the first time with a manager for each department. Two important decisions were also made in this year. One was to buy land for the Society's future needs and the other was to end the metallic check system which had operated from the start and replace it with a less cumbersome book based system. When the metallic checks were called in before the end of the year, they amounted to £4,000 more than the sales for the quarter and resulted in a reduced dividend. Apparently some members working in the engineering factories had taken to making their own checks and more £1 checks were returned than had ever been issued. The whole stock was eventually buried on Hykeham Farm, which was eventually sold to D. W. Bocock and is now the Dale View Estate. One wonders whether a resident on the Dale View Estate has, buried in their garden, a quantity of century old co-operative dividend checks.

In their report of 6 January 1886 the committee announced:-

The "reliable" flower and vegetable seeds of the Co-operative Agricultural Association may be obtained in penny packets at the central stores and all branches – also penny packets of fertilizer.

And in 1887 "concentrated garden manure" was added to the offer.

By now it had become clear to the committee that a firm decision was needed about the future of the Silver Street site and members were told in July 1887, "either the central must be enlarged or cleared out and reconstructed, or a new site must be obtained and suitable buildings put up". Action was again quick in

coming, for the very next members' meeting approved a decision to buy for £1,100, four houses and a joiners yard in Free School Lane. Very soon, plans were drawn up for a large-scale extension consisting of a three storey block to provide accommodation for furniture, crockery, tailoring and boot and shoe departments, with stock rooms, etc, and a library and reading room for the education department.

The opening of the first part of the extensions on 2 November 1889, was marked by one of the largest co-operative demonstrations ever held in the city. An exhibition of productive co-operatives was opened by Frederick Harrison, proprietor of the Lincoln Malleable Iron and Steel Co., whilst the Archbishop of Canterbury, Dr Benson, opened the new library and reading room. A tea in the Corn Exchange for 2,800 people was another feature of the event. The whole of the extensions were completed by the end of the year and trade flowed in so rapidly that the premises had to undergo extensive remodelling, the old reading room was incorporated into the general office, while the pork butchery was transferred to the other side of the road.

These were years of expansion in every sense. The city was growing rapidly and many new houses were being erected in the St. Peter-at-Gowts area. A small branch which had been opened in the summer of 1889 in High Street, was soon doing so well that the committee felt

35

Sub-Central
branch
on Lincoln
High Street
opened in 1893

there was room here for a "sub-central" branch. The members meeting agreed and the Society bought for £4,000 property in High Street with a frontage of 80 feet and access from Tanners Lane. The laying of the foundation stone of the new branch on 2 December 1892 by William Coulson, President, was the occasion for another great demonstration, the event being combined with the annual festival, normally held in January. It included a procession headed by the Malleable Iron Works Band, a tea in the Corn Exchange for 4,500 people and a concert meeting at which the artists were Nottingham Co-operative Choral Society, winners of the first prize at the National Co-operative Festival. They arrived, with other visitors, by train which had been especially laid on for the occasion. The new store was opened in September 1893 and was the first branch to be connected by telephone to the central store. It stocked groceries, greengrocery, pork, mutton, beef, pork pies, veal and sausages, as well as boots, drapery, bread and confectionary. Its first three years of operation brought in £36,078 and furniture was added to its stock in order to relieve congestion at the central store. At a later date van deliveries had to be started from the High Street branch. When the new branch was opened a local newspaper expressed serious doubts as to whether the Society had, indeed, gone too far and some members also had their doubts about the building of branches too large for immediate needs, but the policy proved to be absolutely correct.

The pages of the Society's magazine, The Record, which made its appearance in 1886, contained many interesting articles on life in the 1880's and 1890's in the form of advertisements for clothing, furniture and other household goods. They also provide an interesting picture of the fashion of that era. The well-dressed

Lincoln male co-operator of 1886 might take his Sunday morning walk in a black coat and vest with worsted trousers at 12s.6d, or a suit, made to measure at £1.15s. He had the assurance of the tailoring department that the fit would be perfect, "especially our French cut trousers, produced upon the recently discovered scientific principles". Sadly, no detail is given as to what these exciting scientific principles were. He had a choice of a hard felt hat at 2s.3d, or a new shape in silk hats from 10s.6d to 12s.6d. His wife would have been smart in a home-made outfit of black cashmere at 6½d to 2s.11d a yard, or a coloured cloth jacket with the newest shaped sleeves at 6s.11d and a skirt of striped material at 9½d to 2s.9d a yard, and high-leg boots, button or lace, at 5s.11d.

Newly-weds setting up home could acquire from the Society's newly established furniture department an imitation walnut suite in brocaded crimson plush, just the thing for the smart parlour, costing only £8.15s. Mahogany easy chairs with hair seating were available from £1.9s, and single chairs from 8s.9d to 10s.6d. The walnut over mantel with bevelled glasses was apparently a necessity and cost only £3.12s.6d. For the bedroom a painted maple wash stand and dressing table was available from 15s.9d, French bedsteads from 16s, flock beds from £1.8s and blankets from 6s.6d a pair. Fireirons, indispensable it would seem, included fenders from 1s.4d to £1. Kidderminster carpeting, one yard wide, cost 1s.10d, whilst a dinner set was available at 15s, a tea set from 12s, nickel silver teaspoons from 2½d to 4d each and table knives and forks from 6s.9d a dozen. When the children started to arrive a wicker cradle could be bought at the Society's store for 6s.3d, wash tubs in pitched pine cost 4s.9d and dolly pegs 1s.4d, but there was relief in sight for the housewife who had to use these kitchen essentials. The Society had become agents and later, manufacturers of "The Knuckle" washing machine, a real labour saver. "It works easy and does its work best with the operator sitting on a chair or high stool. While washing there is no bad smell nor steam rising to the face, the whole being confined to the machine", prospective purchasers were informed. "It will wash six or seven shirts or a good-sized bucket full of wet clothes at one time in six or seven minutes and they only require rinsing afterwards and putting into the blue water, then they are ready for drying. It is suitable for the mansion or the cottage and at 30s, brings it within the reach of both".

The Society had, in fact, become almost the universal provider, although many other services, including a milk service, were still to be developed.

TAILORING DEPARTMENT.

We have just received a large consignment of Goods, including all the latest Novelties in

OVERCOATINGS, SUITINGS, and TROUSERINGS, suitable for the coming season.

READY-MADES.

We wish to draw your special attention to our large and splendid collection of

GENTS' MELTON AND BEAVER OVERCOATS,

Cut in the latest style, also a choice selection of

Cape Overcoats, Nap and other Chesterfields.

BOYS' and YOUTHS' OVERCOATS in ever variety.

NAP REEFERS! NAP REEFERS!! NAP REEFERS!!!

THE CELEBRATED

MANDLEBERG WATERPROOFS.

Ready-made or to Measure, in any style.

A choice selection of READY-MADE, including

THE CAPE OVERCOAT,

THE INVERNESS,

And THE CHESTERFIELD.

FREE FROM ODOUR.

Gents' Outfitting and Fancy Department.

GENTS' SILK and FELT HATS in all the leading styles.   MEN'S and BOYS' CAPS of every description.

MEN'S and YOUTHS' CARDIGAN JACKETS, FOOTBALL JERSEYS, SHIRTS, COLLARS, GLOVES, TIES, HANDKERCHIEFS,

MUFFLERS, UMBRELLAS, &c., &c.

A rich assortment of GENTS' SOLITAIRES, CUFF LINKS, SCARF PINS, STUDS, &c., in all the newest designs.

By Royal Letters Patent.

THE

"KNUCKLE" WASHING MACHINE.

"A REAL LABOUR-SAVER."

Since we last called attention to this Machine, we have arranged with the Patentee to make it ourselves; this enables us to offer it at **30/-** which makes it the cheapest washer in the market.

Everything for the man about town in the 1890s

Wragby branch in 1947

6

ONWARDS AND UPWARDS

'The Society enters upon the 20th Century with bright prospects for prosperity, excellent corporate spirit and ample resources'

As the 19th Century entered its last decade the committee were still looking for fresh worlds to conquer. In 1892 they rented a shop in Gresham Street for a butchery branch and members in the above hill area were asked to be on the lookout for a suitable site for a second general store in that part of the City. They bought at auction the whole of the slaughterhouses on Sincil Bank after many years seeking a suitable location within the City for such activities. Obstacles had constantly been placed in the way of the Society by other interested parties.

Perhaps it was the memory of this continued opposition which led to a special meeting of members being called on 29 September 1892, to consider a proposal that the Society should be represented on the Town Council (sic). Mr Benjamin Hayes, who proposed a resolution pledging support for such a move, said no party politics were sought to be introduced into the matter. "The requisition had been signed by men of all shades of politics, teetotallers and red republicans among them", he said. As illustrations of alleged bias against the Society, he claimed that they had had to give up land when building in Free School Lane, without being paid for it; they had been refused permission to install a hoist and a licence had been refused for a slaughterhouse in High Street, although one had been granted to a private butcher. In spite of this powerful case, an amendment that the Society should take no part in nominating any member as a candidate was carried.

A general fall in commodity prices in the years 1893, 1894 and 1895 brought anxieties and in some quarters a decline in sales was recorded. The **Record** commented that the prevailing agricultural depression was more lasting than any of its predecessors and that the majority of landlords, farmers and all those connected with the land were sitting down **"in a state of hapless despondency under the feeling that the era of prosperity for British agriculture is gone forever....."**. Members were reminded however, in another issue, that **"the Co-operative Movement in Lincoln is now powerful enough to sweep all outside foes out of its path. The only foes we have to fear are within our own household. But our hope is in the patriotism and prudence of the wiser members......"**.

An interesting development in 1896 was an arrangement by which the Society carried out painting and decorating for members using its own painting department workforce.

An analysis of share capital holdings by members in 1896 showed that 5,467 members had £5 or under, 2,218 had between £5 and £30, 706 between £30 and £100 and 152 had over £100.

In the following year land was bought for a branch at Winn Street and a decision was taken to build new joinery and cabinet workshops at Tanners Lane. The first competition from multiple firms was noted by the **Record** in 1898, when the comment was made **"But the result has not been a domination of co-operative trading. On the contrary, the stores are more firmly established than ever"**. A provident club (an early kind of savings and loan scheme) started in 1898 soon had 1,000 members and another step forward was the purchase in 1898 of the Lincoln Coal and Coke Company on Canwick Road, Lincoln. A year later local building firms were protesting vigorously because the Society's building department had secured a large building contract to make and fit fixtures for a local bank and to erect new offices for Robey & Co.

Publication of the balance sheet for the quarter ended 3 January 1898 was delayed by the illness with influenza of the cashier and other members of the office staff. Work was in hand on alterations at the Burton Road

Winn Street branch - opened 1898

branch and property had been acquired on Ripon Street to enable extensions to be made to that branch which were opened on 13 December. By now the Society had 476 employees and was producing goods of various kinds to a value of £60,000 per year. Winn Street branch was opened in October 1898.

The Society's 40th anniversary gave the **Record** the opportunity to say that **"the Society has had many ups and downs in this period, but it enters upon the 20th Century with bright prospects for prosperity, excellent corporate spirit and ample resources. We are now worth more than double what we were even so recently as ten years ago. Members are increasing in numbers, share capital is growing in amount and our trade for last year exceeded that of 1899 by £20,884. From 1861 to 1870 the average dividend was 11¾d in the £, there were no reserves of any kind and members could not withdraw any capital below 25s, even if they had to leave Lincoln and were forced to sever their connection with the Society. From 1870 to 1880 the average dividend was 1s.3d and by that time there was a reserve fund of £263. From 1880 to 1890 dividend averaged 1s.5¾d and from 1890 to 1900 it reached 1s.7d and we now have a reserve fund of over £7,000"**.

The Society ended its first 40 years with 510 employees who were paid a total of £27,067 in wages, capital amounted to £108,067 and goods had been produced to the value of £82,983. The Society owned 77 horses and 75 vans and lorries.

The early years of the 20th Century were not easy ones. For three years the annual sales showed only small increases. The **Record** for January 1902 reported that **"The trade in the City has been experiencing greater slackness than at any period since 1879"**. Three months later the trade's slackness was blamed for a decline in sales of £711 and in July a reduction of dividend from 1s.4d to 1s.3d was attributed to a loss in the butchery department, smaller returns from the mill and increased working expenses generally. Amongst the latter was higher taxation "on account of the late war" (the Boer War) which had imposed an additional 7d on income tax, 1s a barrel on beer, 2d a lb on tea and 3d per cwt. on imported corn. Industrial unrest was growing and a local engineering trade dispute in 1902 caused the Society to lose many members who left the City to find new jobs elsewhere. This was reflected in a withdrawal of £46,751 from capital. There was pressure to keep the expenses under control, restrictions were placed on the size of the workforce and it was necessary to dismiss two female employees in the grocery department, what we would now call redundancies.

Duncan McInnes, Society Secretary from 1882 to 1902

Fortunately the situation in the country branches was less acute: the strength of Lincoln Society is its diverse portfolio, when one part of the business is suffering, it is balanced by others which are doing well. This clearly operated in the late 19th and early 20th Centuries as between the City and country branches.

The annual festival held on 31 January 1903 provided the usual rallying cry for members. It began with a song sung by the audience, "forward all ye workers, in one cause combined", probably sung to the tune of "Onward Christian Soldiers" and the artistes included Madame Stuart Cummins, soprano of the Hallé Concerts, Manchester, Madame Barker of Manchester Vocal Society, Thurgate Simpson and G H Ditchbarn, of Manchester Cathedral. Vocal items included the quartet "Regular Royal Queen". Speakers were members of the Midland Sectional Board, George Woodhouse, Derby and W J Douse of Nottingham. At the children's festival on 5 February, Dan Hatfield, described as Lincoln's Dan Leno and his "famous troupe", provided a programme which included the ballad by Master Clapham, "the Voluntary Organist". The long association with the Society of Duncan McInnes was broken in 1902 by his resignation from the Secretaryship. He was succeeded by William Turner.

The Society's meat trade had been under fire in 1902 and at one quarterly meeting a member called for the resignation of the buyer and the butchery committee. Another member demanded that the department should be disbanded and the manager dismissed. It was agreed to form a fresh butchery committee and give them a free hand.

Another controversial issue amongst some of the members was the Society's electoral system and in August 1903 a special general meeting decided to amend the rules to provide for all elections of officers to be held by ballot, carried out from noon to 9.00pm on quarterly meeting days. Previously voting had been at the meeting only. Some years later the rules were changed again to provide for voting at the sub-central, Winn Street, Gresham Street, Newport and Bracebridge between 3.00 pm and 8.00 pm on Saturdays before the quarterly meeting, voting papers being available on production of pass cards. Gradually the impact of new ideas and new methods were beginning to be felt. Electric lighting was installed in the millinery, tailoring and office sections at the end of 1903. Around the turn of the century a typist, Miss Mitchell, had made an appearance. Her successor, Miss Taylor, took over in 1902 on a salary of £1 per week. Two adding machines were bought for office use in 1906 and the book check system was abandoned in favour of the Climax check system in 1907. With this system, every time a member made a purchase they were issued with a small chitty, bearing their share number and the amount of the purchase. Each page of the Climax check book contained maybe 20 chitties and they were in triplicate, the second page going to the check office to enable the member's purchases to be calculated each quarter and the third copy being retained for record purposes.

A fine new branch store was opened in Canwick Road in 1901 replacing the old Great Northern Terrace property which had been in operation for 19 years. Gresham Street branch opened on 25 May 1907 and a property adjoining Newport Arch was opened for business in August 1908. A year later the managers of Gresham Street and Canwick Road branches were told that they could expect no pay increases because their sales did not warrant it. No 21 branch on Monks Road was opened in April 1911 and a new branch on the corner of Tealby Street and High Street became branch No 22 when opened in December 1912.

The Canwick Road branch which opened in 1901

Gresham Street branch - opened in 1907

Alterations, refits and refurbishments were constantly taking place on the Silver Street and Free School Lane site. One of the bigger schemes of extension involved the purchase, in 1907, of a piece of land from Mr Rudduck for £2,725. The development, when completed in 1910, included additions to the drapery, millinery and fancy goods departments, work rooms and the building of a first-class cafe, occupying a considerable portion of the Silver Street basement. The grocery and confectionery departments took up ground floor space above the cafe with access from Free School Lane. The total cost of the scheme, carried out by the Society's own Works Department, was £14,524. At about the same time it was decided to build new stables for 60 horses on Newland as the Society was paying out substantial amounts of money for the external stabling of horses. The new stables were completed in 1912.

The Society's works department had an unfortunate experience about this time. Developed out of a joinery department started in the 1890s, it had carried out a great deal of building for the Society as well as for outside organisations. There had been criticism in

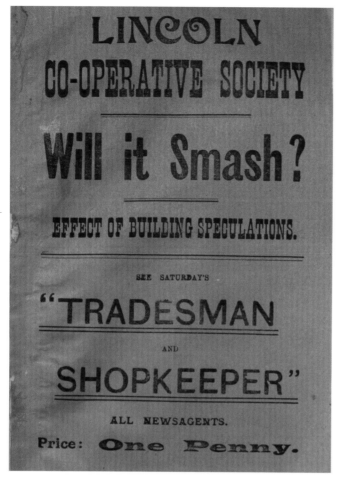

LINCOLN CO-OPERATIVE SOCIETY

Will it Smash?

EFFECT OF BUILDING SPECULATIONS.

SEE SATURDAY'S

"TRADESMAN

AND

SHOPKEEPER"

ALL NEWSAGENTS.

Price: **One Penny.**

and work held up until the department hired a motor pump. Delays were also caused by the late delivery of stone. The committee wisely decided not to accept any further tenders until the Post Office job was finished and at the quarterly meeting in February 1904, members received a report on the department's losses and agreed, not without much grumbling, to these being met from the reserve fund. A limit of £1,000 on the contracts which the department could undertake was imposed and existed for a number of years. A special report on the department was also called for and this was presented to the members in December 1907, by Thomas Broderick, later Sir Thomas, who was then Chief Accountant of the CWS. Losses in the department over a ten year period amounted to £2,849. Changes were made in the management of the department and members' confidence restored.

The Society was subjected to a vicious attack in the autumn of 1905 when a leaflet was issued by a periodical, **The Tradesman and Shopkeeper,** which was the voice of a private traders' organisation. Taking advantage of the situation of the Society's building department, the organisation named the Society and demanded in a leaflet "will it crash – effect of building speculations".

The committee acted at once. A statement of the Society's position and financial stability was published in the local press, posters were issued and arrangements made for a mass meeting in the Corn Exchange, an event which, in fact, was never needed. Subsequently **The Tradesman and Shopkeeper** was successfully sued for libel by Plymouth Co-operative Society and Lincoln Society bought 5,000 pamphlets giving details of the case.

What sort of days were these for those engaged in co-operative employment? Hours were long by today's standards, yet the Directors' reports claim that conditions were better than for those employed by most private traders. In 1893 the **Record** had commented that **"The example set by the Society 30 years ago of closing all its places of business for half a day a week, is slowly being followed by private traders"**. A year earlier the shops had been closed at 9.00 pm on Saturday nights instead of 9.30 pm, whilst working hours in the mill and bakery had been reduced from 58 to 54 without any reduction in pay. In 1906 clerks in the office worked from 9.00 am to 6.00 pm and girls in the tailoring and dressmaking workshops had an 8.30 am to 7.00 pm day, with an early finish on Saturdays at 6.00 pm! As early as 1902 all branch managers were given 13 days paid holiday, starting on Tuesday mornings. But in 1905 the members meeting rejected a proposal to

1899, when the committee had referred to the working of a co-operative society's building department being "hampered by conditions that do not exist in connection with the business of a private builder". These included the necessity for quarterly stocktaking because of the need for quarterly accounts. In 1902 the committee had found it necessary to tell members that the department was based "upon a good business foundation" and to deny an assertion made in the City that, "our men will not do as good a day's work for their own Society as for a private employer". This it described as, "a gross libel, too gross for belief, circulated by interested parties for the express purpose of discrediting co-operation". The whole department suffered a reversal as a result of a decision to tender for the building of Lincoln's new Post Office in Guildhall Street. The tender, for £8,500, was accepted by the Ministry of Works in August 1903 and work began right away. Unfortunately the Government architect concerned altered the plans so as to carry the basement lower than was laid down in the original tender. No price adjustment appears to have been made for the additional work. During the excavations a spring was struck, the workings flooded

give all employees six working days holiday with pay after one year's service. Twenty years earlier a members meeting had turned down a plan for a bonus to employees. There was no superannuation fund for employees. The committee had voiced regret at this in 1899, but fairly early in the next Century, they began to pay small weekly pensions for life to employees with long service. Staff training through the Co-operative Union started in 1906, whilst building department apprentices who attended evening classes had their fees paid by the Society. In the trading departments, boys were not accepted as apprentices until they had served a probationary period and had reached the age of 15.

A number of social activities were provided for employees in the early 1900's. There was an annual outing and picnic to a variety of places including Blackpool and Scarborough. They raised funds for a sick club by such events as "a grand soiree", which included a dance in the Oddfellows Hall, for which an "efficient band" was engaged and a "meat tea and grand concert", with none but first-class artistes providing the entertainment. A football club was started in 1908 and in 1909 members were given the use of land in Boultham Lane for cricket, together with a grant of £8 a year and the use of a shed for dressing accommodation.

In 1908 a new carter who had started work in the butchery department received £1 per week; a new manager at Market Rasen branch was paid 32s per week with a rent-free house, whilst a new member of the office staff received 30s per week and the deputy cashier's salary was raised to £2.5s. At Saxilby the branch manager was paid £1.18s also with a rent-free house. The National Union of Co-operative Employees was actively canvassing societies to adopt a minimum wage of 21s per week for all employees. Congress adopted such a scale as the Movement's objective and in December 1912 the union was informed that Lincoln Society hoped eventually to bring its employees into line. In May of the following year, after further pressure, the committee decided to adopt the minimum wage from 1 July 1914 and stood firm against requests to bring the date forward by a year. Reaction amongst employees was a threat of wholesale resignations and a strike, with a deadline fixed; serious trouble seemed likely. The President and Secretary even had an interview with the Chief Constable and employees were told that any who withdrew their resignations would be reinstated. In fact, several employees went on strike for three days. A crowded meeting on 9 June 1914 repudiated the committee's policy and, at a meeting immediately afterwards, the committee decided to resign en block. Union officials were immediately

Newport branch opened in 1908.

called in and, according to the minutes, were "nonplussed" at the news and asked the committee to reconsider their decision. Discussions continued until nearly 1 o'clock in the morning. At their next meeting the committee met union representatives including Joseph Hallsworth, later Sir Joseph, who became General Secretary of U.S.D.A.W. and Chairman of the North Western Electricity Board, and terms were agreed. An emergency committee of five members were paid 10s each and cafe expenses for their services and the Chief Constable was formally thanked. The committee also rescinded their previous decision to resign on the grounds that their disagreement with the members had only been on one point and that the previous decision was reached by "questionable means".

The Society's jubilee celebrations in 1911 provided some of the most memorable events in the history of the City. Planning began two years before the event and a sum of £1,250 was allocated for the festivities. One of the most useful things that came out of the celebrations was the setting up of a sick appliances fund which provided a variety of nursing aids for many years. This preceded the creation of the National Health Service by nearly 40 years.

An exhibition of CWS products was arranged. Almost every available school room was booked for a gigantic tea party on the final day of the jubilee celebrations and a huge public meeting was held in the Drill Hall. Children using the Society's Penny Bank were given a picnic and all the employees were invited to a meat tea. In addition to these events it was agreed to distribute £250 to local charities.

At the end of its first 50 years the Society had 12,781 members, capital amounted to £192,209, sales were £344,764 and there was a reserve fund of £9,002. There were 21 grocery branches and 7 butchery shops.

year, they have agreed to come to Lincoln on the last Saturday in September, and it is to be held in the Drill Hall, when it is hoped that the Members of the Lincoln Society will attend and hear for themselves what a high standard has been obtained by these Choirs. Charles Jessop, Esq., of Sheffield, is to be the adjudicator. We have also engaged Nugent Harris, Esq., to Lecture on " Co-operative Small Holdings," on November 22nd, 1911.

TOM MATHER, *Secretary.*

SICK ROOM APPLIANCES.

PREPARATIONS for the Jubilee celebrations are proceeding apace, the whole scheme of events being well in hand.

A full and detailed account will appear in our next Quarterly Record of all that has been done, with the exception of the scheme for providing Sick and Medical Appliances for the use of our Members, of which, because of the information to hand, should appear in the present issue.

A committee, composed of Mrs. Doughty, Mrs. Gibbins, and Miss Turner, from the Women's Guild, Lincoln Branch ; Mrs. Alston, Mrs. Harris and Mrs. Trafford, from the Bracebridge Branch ; with Messrs. Coulson, Harley and Bell, from the General Committee, was appointed to formulate the best possible scheme, and after much thought and discussion, a very satisfactory workable scheme has been adopted. The Committee Room, formerly used by the Educational Department, and now no longer required, has kindly been given up by them, and, having been specially fitted up, will now be known as the Centre of the Sick Appliance Department. A very large number of articles have been selected, after much care ; a complete list of which is given below.

A list of rules adopted as below, and a Caretaker will be appointed shortly, who will be responsible to a Committee of five persons, one each from the Committee of the Women's Guild, Lincoln and Bracebridge branches, one from the Educational Committee, and two members of the General Committee.

The exact date of opening has not yet been fixed, but due notice will be given.

LIST OF ARTICLES.

	PER WEEK EACH.
6 Slipper Bed Pans, large	1d.
2 ,, ,, medium	1d.
2 ,, ,, small	1d.
2 Round Bed Pans, large	1d.
2 ,, ,, medium	1d.
2 ,, ,, small	1d.
2 Male Urinals	1d.
2 Female Urinals	1d.
2 Stone Hot-water Bottles	1d.
6 Indiarubber Hot-water Bottles, various sizes	2d.
12 Spitting Cups, loose lids	½d.
12 Feeding Cups	½d.
2 Nipple Shields, Indiarubber	½d.
2 ,, ,, Metallic	½d.
2 Breast Pumps	1d.
2 Eye Drops, Glass	½d.
2 ,, ,, Bottles	½d.
2 Nasal Sprays	1d.
2 Throat Sprays	1d.
6 Ice Bags, Indiarubber, various sizes	2d.
6 Arm Slings, Adults	1d.
2 ,, ,, Children's	1d.
2 Ear Syringes, 1 oz.	½d.
1 ,, ,, ball	1d.
2 Spirit Lamps and Kettles	2d.
1 Leg Rest	½d.
2 Enemas with disconnecting tubes	2d.
2 Douches, glass lined	2d.
6 Ring Air Cushions, various sizes	2d.
2 Air Pillows	2d.
2 Waterproof Sheets, 72in. x 72in.	3d.
3 ,, ,, 72in. x 36in.	2d.
6 ,, ,, 36in. x 36in.	1d.
1 Arm Chair Commode	3d.
2 Small Commodes	2d.
3 Bronchitis Kettles, large	2d.
3 ,, ,, small	2d.
2 pairs Adjustable Spring Crutches	4d.
2 pairs Ordinary Spring Crutches	1d.
1 Bellows Inflator	
3 Bath Chairs, medium, 1 small	per hour, 1d. ; per day, 6d. ; per week, 1s. 6d.
3 Bed Rests, with arms	2d.
3 Bed Tables	2d.
1 Water Bed	6d.

RULES.

1.—They shall be lent to members and employés of the Society for their personal use, or for their children living under the same roof.

2.—All applications must be made to the Caretaker, either personally or through the Store Manager, the full name and address given, and the Member's Share Book number, stating the nature of the case.

3.—The times for letting out are as follows :—

6 to 7 o'clock each evening, and 1 to 2 o'clock each Friday, for the convenience of Country Members.

4.—Any person having had an article for three weeks, and wishing to retain the same for a longer period, must renew the application.

5.—Members borrowing will be required to pay the charge for loan on application for the articles, and will be held responsible for any damage done to same while in their possession, and must see that such articles are thoroughly cleansed and disinfected before being returned. If any article is required for a case of infectious disease, it must be stated on application, and the Committee will arrange for disinfection by the Public Health Department.

6.—The Committee trust the members will take great care of these articles, and return them as soon as done with, or within three days after a written application has been made for them. In no case must they be lent by the person borrowing.

PARTICULAR POINTS.
Extract from C.W.S. Directors' Report.

The Directors of the Wholesale Society, in their Quarterly Report, state that the total sales for the thirteen weeks amount to £6,401,819, an increase of £108,214 on the corresponding period of last year. The total supplies from the various productive works for the quarter are £1,729,072, an increase of £113,932. The deposits and withdrawals in the banking department for the thirteen weeks amount to £34,460,783, as compared with £32,889,808 in the corresponding period, an increase of £1,570,975.

The supplies from the productive factories for the thirteen weeks are as follows. The comparison, is, of course, with the corresponding period :—

	1911. £	1910. £	£
Crumpsall	45,927	38,790	7,137*
Middleton	91,575	68,646	22,929*
Irlam	157,523	160,418	2,895†
Silvertown Soap	44,494	37,958	6,536*
Dunston Soap	38,071	26,371	11,700*
Dunston Flour	177,292	209,942	32,650†
Silvertown Flour	125,626	164,044	38,418†
"Sun" Flour and Provender	240,935	232,947	7,988*
"Star" Flour	85,119	104,742	19,623†
Avonmouth Flour	107,570		
Tobacco Factory	171,702	165,412	6,290*
West Hartlepool Lard	26,382	31,647	5,265†
Longsight Printing	35,950	32,435	3,515*
Leicester Printing	5,026	4,269	757*
Pelaw Printing	5,011	4,263	748*
Littleborough Flannel	5,744	5,478	296*
Huthwaite Hosiery	26,168	20,520	5,648*
Desborough Corset	11,719	10,068	1,651*
Lower Broughton Shirt	24,436	21,879	2,557*
Batley Woollen	16,292	12,278	4,014*
Bury Weaving Shed	34,723	22,457	12,226*
Lower Broughton Clothing	10,717	11,110	393†
Leicester Boot and Shoe	128,843	116,989	11,854*
Heckmondwike Boot	20,224	20,854	630†
Rushden Boot and Shoe	28,851	32,897	4,046†
Lower Broughton Cabinet	6,003	5,928	75*
Leeds Brush	8,489	7,666	823*
Keighley Ironworks	4,583	3,792	791*
Dudley Bucket	5,992	5,993	1†
Birtley Tinplate	1,905	1,562	343*
Pelaw Tailoring	9,300	9,394	94†
Pelaw Cabinet	6,078	5,573	505*

* Increase.   † Decrease.

The Society's Sick Room Appliances fund preceeded the National Health Service by almost 40 years

Lincolnshire Agricultural Society
Show - Sleaford 1870

RURAL CO-OPERATION

'Wearing a drab smock...and speaking in a Lincolnshire Wold dialect...he testified that joining the stores had put £10 in his pocket'

There is no doubt that Lincoln Co-operative Society made a unique contribution to the setting up of co-operative stores in small rural communities, an area largely ignored by many 19th and 20th Century co-operative historians. Yet it is, in many ways, a very romantic chapter in Britain's economic history. To describe how, in the teeth of opposition from village tradesmen and the active discouragement of the squire and clergy, the benefits of consumer co-operation were taken into the very heart of village life is exciting and inspirational.

For over 100 years after the birth of the Lincoln Society many villages all over the UK remained the preserve of the private shopkeeper but there were fewer in Lincolnshire than in most agricultural counties, thanks to the determination and foresight of successive Lincoln Co-operative Committees in the 1870's and 1880's. It was in 1877 that the Society adopted a definite plan of propaganda and development for village co-operation and that plan was pursued without interruption for many years until a trading area of hundreds of square miles had been added to the Society's territory. Today it covers almost the whole of the historic county of Lincolnshire.

In taking the action they did, the committee were following in the footsteps of an almost forgotten body of men, mostly agricultural labourers who, as part of their trade union activity, set up small independent co-operative stores in many Lincolnshire villages. Unhappily, in almost every case, the enthusiasm of these rural pioneers exceeded their ability as traders and for the most part their endeavours ended in failure. Very few records exist about their activities but those that we do have paint an interesting picture of life in agricultural Lincolnshire at the time. The father of agricultural trade unionism, Joseph Arch, speaking in his capacity as President of the Agricultural Labourers Union at a meeting of the Market Rasen Co-operative Society in 1878, said he had had, "a thought for co-operation for 17 or 18 years....". Six years earlier, on 28 May 1872, Arch had been present at a meeting in Leamington Spa which had been convened to form a national agricultural labourers union and at which a Mr Butcher of Banbury read a paper on "co-operative stores in agricultural villages, how to establish and manage them successfully". In his paper, Butcher declared: "People may say, and they do say, that craftsmen can do these things but agricultural labourers cannot. At present it is almost certain that rural agricultural labourers will not of themselves adopt and carry out co-operative stores". This conference approved a resolution pledging itself "to do its utmost to spread a

The earliest rural co-operative stores were set up by agricultural labourers

knowledge of co-operation amongst agricultural labourers and to endeavour to put it into practical operation by encouraging the establishment of co-operative stores in every village".

According to the **Co-operative News** account of this conference, delegates were present from Lincoln. Whether these delegates had any association with Lincoln Society we do not know but in any event it is most likely that members of the Society's committee read about the conference in the News and the idea of village co-operatives began to simmer in their minds. Perhaps they were particularly attracted by the suggestion put forward at the Leamington conference that whilst agricultural labourers seemed incapable of beginning co-operative societies, craftsmen might do so successfully. And after all, were they not mostly craftsmen themselves?

For a time the idea did no more than simmer. Perhaps it was brought nearer to the boil by another item in the **Co-operative News** of 14 July 1877. This was a quotation from the **Labourers Union Chronicle** of 30 June of that year which made the comment: **"There is no reason why stores should not be established throughout rural villages; groups of 6 or 8 villages might be supplied from a central store to reduce the cost of management expenses. There would no**

longer be the fear of exposure or the dread of a county court summons. The tyranny of the village shopkeeper is often as great as that of the farmer".

There were two points in this comment which were calculated to appeal to the leaders of Lincoln Co-operative. One was the idea that, instead of separate co-operative societies for individual villages, there might be branch stores. The other was the picture which it gave of an urgent need that existed: to establish in the countryside the system which had served them so well in the City. In fact, at a conference held in Lincoln in the same year, the Society had been taken to task for its failure to move into the surrounding countryside, a criticism which must have seemed a little unkind to a body of men who had done so much to further the idea of co-operation. Rex Russell of Boston collected a great deal of information about the activities of the agricultural workers co-operatives, which were started by branches of both William Banks' Agricultural Labour League and Joseph Arch's National Agricultural Labourers Union and which he published in a book entitled "The Revolt of the Field in Lincolnshire". Both of these bodies appear to have been extremely active throughout the county between 1871 and 1880 and both

Joseph Arch - President of the National Agricultural Labourers Union

carried out a number of co-operative activities as well as organising large-scale emigration from the county. The first of these small societies appears to have been set up by Alford Members of the League in 1873, although the supply of coal to members seems to have been started before that time. Their store on South Bridge was opened in July 1873. Another seems to have been opened in Binbrook at about the same time and its success apparently encouraged league members at Caistor to venture into co-operative activity for themselves.

A decision taken by the Louth labourers in October 1874 led to the opening of a store in Answell Lane in May of the following year. In 1876 a co-operative store was opened in Spalding and in July of the same year the Labourers Union delegates held a meeting of members in market place, Market Rasen, at which the idea of opening a store was put forward. Amongst those who were present at this meeting was George Hartley and other representatives from Lincoln Society. Hartley urged the labourers to begin their own society, thus backing up advice which had previously been given in answer to a request from Union members at Rasen for a store to be opened there.

By 1878 there were, according to the Registrar's returns, 15 co-operative societies operating in Lincolnshire and some of these were undoubtedly those created by the farm workers unions. Without exception the life of these small societies was short and McInnes, in his jubilee history of Lincoln Society, attributes their failure principally to mismanagement, rather than dishonesty. McInnes claims also that the union members were misled by the leadership. "The labourers were led by the promoters to believe that the establishment of a co-operative store must follow the opening of a branch of the League and that from subscriptions and from profits of trading the outgrowth would speedily be farms worked co-operatively all over the agricultural counties", he writes. "Although no such speedy growth was possible, pioneers went from village to village preaching it as gospel, establishing branches of the League, opening co-operative stores, renting or buying land. Some of the stores were registered, some, whilst doing a substantial amount of business, never got as far as that. In at least one of these cases, the savings of a lifetime of hard work were invested by a number of poor, thrifty men and dividends were declared, although practically no accounts were kept. The treasurer, a League official, took in contributions towards shares and paid out withdrawals from his trouser pockets wherever he chanced to be when a member applied to him. This patriarchal procedure was varied by another of the officials, an office-bearer of the League, taking an occasional trip to Canada in charge of a party of emigrating labourers. One of these stores, whilst drifting steadily towards ruin from a similar lack of management, established branches in four distant villages, placing each under the control of incompetent men, farm labourers and collectors for the League. Of the extravagant household management of these storekeepers it was said in the villages that their bread was buttered on both sides and ham and eggs were always frying on the fire. Confidence began to be shaken and ruin steadily followed. The stores failed, the members lost every penny of their capital, the branches of the League were closed and its agents and collectors were discredited. The predicted labour affluence proved to be but a mirage in an industrial desert and, whilst a whole countryside was strewn with the wrecks of co-operative societies, the small pieces of land fell either into the hands of the more astute of the collectors or were disposed of to the highest bidders".

19th Century woodcut of an early
co-operative store

This is an interesting and, no doubt, accurate enough general picture. We can however identify the society which established branches, whilst itself "drifting steadily to ruin", as that at Market Rasen, which opened shops in Ludford, Nettleton, Binbrook and Howsham.

So what were the difficulties which stood in the way, not so much of the formation of rural co-operatives but which prevented them from being operated successfully? Was there some truth in the criticism that agricultural labourers were incapable of running co-operative stores for themselves? McInnes suggested that the conditions of life in the country resulted in the mind of the agricultural worker being slower in its

working than that of the town worker. "He is secretive and watchful and has not in as great a degree as the townsman, the faculty of language for unburdening and defusing his thoughts, nor has he so many facilities for meeting with fellow workers. In introducing co-operation to them, one has to contend not only with the sluggishness of ignorance and the apathy of despair, but with the suspicion of being actuated with a desire to over reach them, in order to obtain some object that does not appear on the surface", he claimed.

From one of the principal architects of Lincoln Society's country development programme, this might be considered a fairly objective assessment of the situation, although from this distance in time it does appear a little harsh.

It is, however, largely corroborated by some statements made by George Hines from Suffolk, in a paper presented to the 1879 Congress on "co-operation in agricultural villages, its difficulties, and how they may be overcome". In his paper Hines declared: "There is little chance of our getting any very rapid relief by political action. The landlords, the idlers, the power-lovers, the military glory hunters and the tax-eaters generally are far too powerful for the masses of the people to make much impression upon their position. But we have in our co-operative movement, the power for accomplishing far greater things than we have yet attained".

So far, he said, co-operation had hardly penetrated into agricultural villages. "There are many difficulties in the way, the difficulty of finding men in agricultural villages with the necessary qualifications for becoming secretaries is perhaps the greatest of all. Then there is the repugnance on the part of their employers, the farmers, probably also the minister, to upsetting the existing order of things in the village. One or two little shopkeepers must be displaced and old systems must be broken, to attempt to do which would raise a storm of indignation against the initiator, unless he happens to be one of the village magnates. Again, I would earnestly urge our co-operative friends in the towns and the agricultural districts to hold out their hands to the labourers in the villages. I am persuaded that many successful branches might be established in the various villages around these towns with some little effort. At the same time", he added, "I would not say start stores anywhere and everywhere, but wherever a reasonable chance appears of making a store pay". In the subsequent discussion of the paper, George Hartley of Lincoln admitted there was a difficulty in finding men capable of managing stores in agricultural villages and said he had a scheme which to some extent would overcome this difficulty. The first need was to establish a co-operative store in each large market town and move out in different directions working from that as a centre of action. If independent stores could not be established in the villages, let them establish branches. They had gone out into the villages ten miles from Lincoln and established a branch. A manager with a horse and cart worked the district, endeavouring at the same time to educate the agricultural labourers into a perception of their position and a realisation of the benefits of co-operation. He believed that agricultural co-operation would be successful if it were "preceded by co-operative propaganda and a central board should work in this direction, getting men for love or for pay to lecture to the villagers and distribute co-operative literature".

On the work of the Labourers Union, Hartley said he believed it had done some good "by raising the tone of thought amongst the men and inspiring the hope of improving their position". This latter view was not, it appears, shared by another delegate at the congress, W. H. Hall of Newmarket, who, in a paper on "the spread of co-operation in rural districts", after speaking of the difficulty of finding "the honest and capable manager", included amongst the hindrances to the spread of co-operation in rural districts "the present influence of the National Agricultural Labourers Union, which seems now powerless for good except in the furtherance of migration, but very powerful for evil".

The rural branch to which Hartley had referred as having been established by Lincoln Society was that at Welbourn, 13 miles from the centre of the city.

When writing the 100 year book, A Century of Achievement, Frank Bruckshaw and Duncan McNab, commented "even in these days the country worker is still amongst the lowest paid and life isn't always easy, but few people can have any real idea of the living conditions which existed amongst vast numbers of dwellers in rural Britain in the 1870's and 1880's. To farm workers, cottagers and small farmers alike the possibility of co-operative trading, with the prospect of accumulating small sums by way of dividend, which could be utilised for a variety of purposes in times of need, came like a ray of hope. Lincolnshire in even greater measure then than it is today, was an agricultural county par excellence with a strong squirearchy, and village traders saw the credit they allowed as the chains which bound the customer to them for life. By the determination of men like McInnes and George Hartley, himself a country man and a former farm worker, the chains were in time broken but it was a slow and often discouraging process".

(photo courtesy Mr Bill Goodhand)

Welbourn branch - opened in 1878

Writing in the **Co-operative News** of 27 March 1880, of the calls which had been made by Lincoln Society for a county-wide drive to develop co-operation, McInnes declared: **"If there is a district which needs thoroughly missioning it is this. There are market towns and villages in which agriculture is the only industry, where co-operation has never been heard of and where parish relief and the workhouse are the inevitable jail of the toiling underpaid labourer. It was ignorance of the first principles of store management which wrecked, quite recently, co-operation in Spalding and the same thing contributed to bring to an end two young societies in Boston and Stamford".** Enthusiasm for village co-operation did not blind McInnes and his colleagues to the risk which small and weak village societies might run. As early as 1883 in a paper given to the Lincoln District Conference Association on "branch stores versus independent societies", he strongly advocated the development of branches of existing societies instead of small societies being formed. Writing a little later he commented that some of the things connected with the management of the small societies in agricultural villages and small towns in Lincolnshire were "almost incredible". He quoted the case of one society which had been doing a trade of nearly £30 a week for two or three years with nearly 100 members. It had not been registered, had no books of account, the treasurer received contributions in the street and kept the cash in his pocket. "This is the avenue through which a large number of poor agricultural labourers lost the savings of years in the name of co-operation. Nobody actively connected with these quasi-co-operative ventures could be accused of dishonesty, they simply lacked business capacity. What is required in districts such as this, is that large societies should open branches. I feel that there is a most urgent need for the extension of co-operation to the agricultural class of workers, but it had better not be attempted at all than attempted on unsound lines. To establish small independent societies is to court dismal failure in this district, whatever it may be in others". This was clear and unequivocal; it was a policy which proved to be unquestionably the right one. Numerous examples could be given of the way in which poorly paid farm workers benefitted. At a co-operative meeting in one area an agricultural labourer asked permission to speak and was invited to the platform. Wearing a drab smock, armed with a formidable walking stick which he used to emphasise his points and speaking in a Lincolnshire Wold dialect, similar to that used in Tennyson's "Northern Farmer", he testified that his joining the stores had "put £10 in his pocket".

A writer in the **Co-operative News** of 15 November 1890 describing some of the ways in which country members were helped by the Society, pointed out that many of them withdrew share capital to buy seeds for their allotments and in an even larger number of cases, to buy pigs, whilst some had been able, from their dividends, to buy cows. **"Such facts as these, publicly contributed by local members themselves at the meetings, do more to promote co-operation in the villages than anything besides. The results indicated must be as satisfactory to co-operators as they are to the Society which has for 13 years indomitably persevered against the greatest natural obstacles, in planting co-operation and making it a business success among a class that needs it almost more than any other."** In an unexpected way the branches helped the Society, for in times of depression in the City the country branches often maintained their sales. There are many illustrations in the records of the forms taken by opposition to the movement in the countryside. One of the most common was the refusal by religious bodies to allow their school rooms to be used for co-operative meetings, on a variety of grounds, but chiefly because school managers or trustees were local tradesmen. As late as 1890 for instance, a meeting at Brant Broughton had to be held in the club room of the Generous Briton Inn and the club room of the Sun Inn at Caythorpe was hired also for a meeting. In both villages the use of school rooms had been refused "by interested parties". The Horncastle branch festival was held in the Masonic Hall and that of the Saxilby branch in the Sun Inn club room. Sleaford's gathering took place in the Corn Exchange, but Metheringham was able to use the church school room at Scopwick, "kindly loaned by the Rev. C. Hall"; not all of the clergy were antagonistic to the Society. Evidently Mr Hall had come to the rescue of the Society when it was denied the use of the Wesleyan

Horncastle's branch festival was held at the town's Masonic Hall

School, which it had hired for the previous six years for festivals and meetings. There was some correspondence with the Rev. R. Dillon, then Methodist Superintendent Minister, as to why the school could no longer be let. His reply was "I understand there was something objectionable in the character of the entertainments".

This point was taken up by Duncan McInnes in a letter to the Rev. W. I. Rawson, vicar of Metheringham, when applying for the use of the church school. In it he said: "This statement admits of several interpretations. We deny that anything morally objectionable had been done at any time and we venture to attach a degree of competence to our judgement as to what are the real causes". Mr Rawson replied: "I see no reason against you, but I feel I must consult the other managers". He did so and they refused permission, hence the switch to Scopwick nearly three miles away.

When an attempt was made to hire the school room for a tea and public meeting at Caythorpe, near Grantham, this was met with a refusal on the grounds that three trades-people were members of the Board and would not like the meeting to be held there. At Bardney, prejudice which prevented the Society from hiring the school room led to its building a meeting room of its own. Later records show that "more tolerant views prevailed" and the school room was loaned.

From their foundation until 1937, the annual festivals held in connection with the village branches were notable events. They generally took place at the end of the harvest in October and served a triple purpose, as a form of harvest festival, as a friendly get-together and as occasions for propaganda. For the members of the committee who went round to all of them they must have been something of a trial, especially when they involved lengthy journeys, usually by train and then lengthy walks along unlit country lanes. The "knife and fork" teas must have been generous affairs; admission usually cost 1s. There were occasions when to some, at any rate, the tea was more important than the meetings and speakers were sometimes interrupted unexpectedly. Often of more value than the set speeches were the "naively related experiences contributed by some of the local members". Equally interesting and even more amusing were the impromptu contributions to the concert programmes which were made by local people who were "prevailed upon" or provoked into singing. The records tell of the "demonstrations of satisfaction" with which a Saxilby festival greeted the humorous song "Kidney Beans", contributed by a Mr Gilbert. Another popular contributor at festivals was Mr E Hallam, for many years one of the Society's auditors and a member of the education committee who gave Yorkshire sketches including "How owd Stoansnetch's dowter got wed".

The official entertainment at these festivals was of a very varied nature and on occasions some of the artists, notably the singers of comic songs, were the cause of criticism and their efforts were alleged to be of such a character as to keep people away.

One branch committee member had to ask that more care should be taken in the choice of songs, some of which contained "things which were objectionable for children to hear and repeat". The official reply to this complaint was that every possible care was exercised by the committee, but that when the artists were encored, they would transgress occasionally. A bigger cause of complaint on some occasions was the way in which boys and youths not connected with the Society crowded the tearooms, whilst members, who had sometimes walked several miles, were unable to get places. One critic complained that more Metheringham people attended the festivals for the tea than anything else: "they cared more for filling their bellies than the music, the main thing was to provide, once a year, a good tea". A similar criticism was voiced when a suggestion was made for a branch library in the village: "they were more for eating than reading there".

Saxilby festivals in the 1890's were often disturbed by a noisy element and on one occasion a policeman had to be stationed at the door of the Sun Inn club room to keep order, although this did not prevent one of the audience denouncing the Society and complaining of higher prices. Metheringham also suffered from the efforts of "a certain class of young men", who created disturbances.

Even in the smallest villages, a tea festival attendance in excess of 250 was not uncommon. On two or three

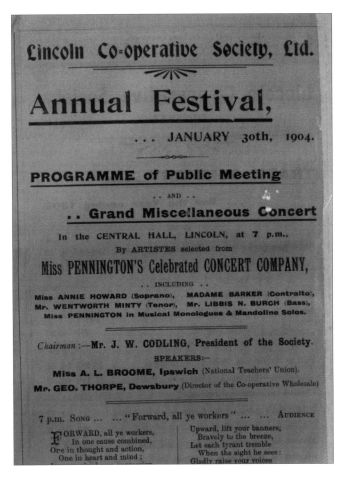

occasions the festivals were also combined with sales of goods from the central store. An interesting general account of these festival gatherings appeared in the Society's **Record** in January 1910. **"Concert meetings, beginning with a meat tea, at which considerably over 3,000 have sat down, have been held at 15 of our villages and small towns and the impressions made on those present will not soon be forgotten.**
The festival party, prepared for all kinds of weather, arrived at a place of meeting when tea is about to commence. Here we find (thanks to the local committee and a host of ladies, members of the Society) tables groaning under a load of good things and for the space of an hour and a half these good women, with their helpers, are working might and main. By almost superhuman effort the room is cleared so that the meeting can commence by 7 o'clock and by this time the place is packed with a most interesting audience. How shall I describe the people present to give a real word-picture, so interesting, so bright, so intelligent, so thoughtful. The old and grey are here who have travelled a long way and know so well what the movement has done. The horny-handed son of toil and his buxom wife

are here by the score with a light in their eye and a brightness on their faces that makes one glad to see and it is easy to perceive they are partakers of the benefits that come by co-operation; and youths and maidens are here who have not yet learned to take life seriously and the boys and girls in good number make up our meeting. And then the story is told once again, what the movement can do and is doing, but it does not need illustration, for here are living witnesses all around as to its efficacy and power to lift up and to help. As the meeting breaks up and a rush is made for the train home, one feels devoutly thankful for the wise forethought of those who, years ago, remembered our comrades in the country. Do I hear someone say, "does it pay?" Pay? We shall not see all the results this quarter or in a year; we are doing business today as the outcome of meetings like this held years ago."

Two years after this account appeared, another describing the previous autumn's festivals also appeared in the **Record** and spoke of 5,350 having sat down to tea at various places. **"The meetings were most of them crowded in the extreme, not only was every inch of standing room occupied, but in some cases a good number standing outside peering through the doors and windows. The principles of co-operation have been explained to willing ears, what CWS means and why we should do our business at our own shop. Those about to set up housekeeping have been reminded of the advantages in joining the store and making a good start; and last but not least, the young have been interested and seed sown that will doubtless bring forth good fruit."**

Those who remembered them in the middle of the 20th Century had pleasant memories of these bygone events but since those early days greater sophistication had reached the countryside and it was concluded, around 1935 to 1937, that a tea followed by speeches and a concert would no longer have the same appeal.

Fairly early in the history of country branch trading there took place an innovation which contributed greatly to its success. Scattered throughout the Society's area were many smallholdings, the traditional three acres and a cow perhaps, as well as larger farmers, whilst many cottage dwellers kept a few chickens. Often more butter was made than its makers and their families could eat and there was often a surplus of eggs. Some unknown co-operative genius, at a time which is equally unknown, hit upon the idea that this surplus produce could be acquired by the Society for direct sales to its members, whilst the farmers and cottagers received goods in exchange. It was a return to the oldest trading system in the world, bartering, and it worked extremely well for very many years. The Society's van men collected the eggs and butter and delivered them to the central warehouse. Prices allowed for the produce were based on those applicable in the Lincoln Butter Market and van men were issued with a standard price list from the warehouse each week. They took round groceries and other goods which had been ordered by the country members and any difference between the cost of the produce and the goods bought from the Society was made up by cash payments. Sometimes in spring, eggs would cost only 1s for 20. In 1902 purchases of butter and eggs by this method amounted to £7,770. There were of course, as one might imagine, some snags in the system. Greatest of these was that of obtaining uniformity of colour and quality in the butter; some of it turned out to be rancid. The barter system continued until the mid 1930's. The control and accounting must, on occasions, have been quite challenging by today's standards.

The men who worked the country rounds must have been tough and loyal workers. Day in and day out, regardless of weather, they and their horses made lengthy journeys along lonely fenland roads from early morning until late evening. A list of rounds from 1896 gives a good indication of what was involved.

Bracebridge
Monday to Lincoln for bread, calls at St Catherines, Bracebridge, Bracebridge Low Fields, Waddington Low Fields.
Saxilby
Monday, one cart to Lincoln, one to Saxilby Moor, Wall-Rudding, Harby, Wigsby, Thorney, Kettlethorpe Lodge, Broxholme, Tillbridge (fortnightly).
Market Rasen
Monday – Linwood, Lissington, Wickenby, Snelland, Wickenby Station, Faldingworth, Buslingthorpe.
Bassingham
Monday – Norton Disney, Stapleford Moor, Stapleford, Broughton, Clays, Carlton-le-Moorland, Stragglethorpe.

Staff at the Welbourn branch
pose for the camera in 1910

(photo courtesy Mr Bill Goodhand)

ESTABLISHMENT OF RURAL BRANCHES

8

'Living...away from any village, neither church life nor social institutions bring her into touch with others. The store's cart goes across rough fields to her door'.

The Society's first country branch was at Welbourn and was begun at the request of a few labourers and cottagers in the district, who had made an approach to the management committee of the Society. They responded by sending a deputation to the village, with the objective of explaining the working and constitution of the Society. No-one was prepared to rent them a room for the gathering and, in almost biblical fashion, it took place under a tree by the roadside, with a heap of stones as a platform. There are still a few people in the village who will point to this place, not because they were there, but because it was pointed out to them in their younger days.

A later meeting was held in the Joiners Arms when a promise was made that a weekly delivery of goods would be made by van from Lincoln to supply all those who became members. An almost immediate result was that many of the new members of the Society, who were heavily in debt to local tradesmen, found themselves issued with County Court summonses. When the cases came before the Registrar however and the situation was explained to him, he fixed a monthly payment, sufficiently low as to enable the dividends on the member's trade with the Society to be paid directly into court as they became due until the debts were cleared.

The ability of co-operation to free men from hopeless indebtedness which was demonstrated by this act did not go unnoticed by other villagers and the volume of orders soon made it necessary for shop premises to be rented, which, in turn, served as a centre for further van deliveries, thus increasing the depth of co-operative penetration into rural Lincolnshire.

The branch at Welbourn was opened on 2 May 1878. The new branch made steady progress except for one short period in 1879, when the spectre of excessive credit raised its ugly head once again and almost destroyed that which was designed to keep indebtedness at bay. Upon discovering that there was a problem, McInnes and Joseph Hartley, together with "an efficient staff of stocktakers", descended on the branch without prior notice and dismissed the manager "on the spot". There were clearly no issues around formal disciplinary procedures at this time. McInnes and his team took stock of the goods and held on to them and the business part of the premises for the remainder of the day and throughout the next night, until the manager, his family and household effects had been removed altogether. So the branch manager not only lost his job, he lost his home as well. Later in the day another branch manager was appointed and the shop opened again for business. The incident did one thing, if nothing else: it made the committee aware of the

(photo courtesy Mr Bill Goodhand)

This view of Welbourn dates from 1900 - the light area next to the tree is the site of the first co-operative meeting

possible dangers of remote control and led to the institution of a system under which new branch managers deposited a sum of £50 in cash, as a bond against eventualities of this kind.

Six years after it was opened the sales of the branch had reached £918 in a quarter and it became clear that the branch, as it now stood, was operating at or near capacity. Lack of accommodation was inhibiting any further growth, so the committee did not hesitate to purchase the shop, its dwelling house, three cottages and a paddock for £370. Rebuilding was quickly carried out to provide what was later described as "one of the most comprehensive and perfect country stores that it is possible to design". A little boastful perhaps, but indicative of the confidence of the Lincoln committee. To have done this much by way of pioneering rural co-operation was a significant accomplishment, especially in view of the record of earlier failures by the trade unions, but it was only the beginning. With the possibilities of village trading fully confirmed, the committee embarked on a long term plan for bringing huge areas of the outlying countryside into the co-operative orbit and undeterred by opposition and criticism, as well as sometimes by the threat of failure, this plan was carried out rigorously over the next 20 years. No wonder that when J. T. W. Mitchell, a CWS director and one of the best known co-operative advocates of his generation, gave evidence before the Royal Commission on Labour on 25 October 1892, he chose Lincoln Society as affording the best illustration of co-operation in an agricultural district.

After Welbourn the committee turned their attention to the north and two months later opened a small branch in the tiny village of Owmby, which lies just off the great Roman highway known as Ermine Street, now the A15. For some years the village had been visited by the Society's delivery vans every fortnight and it was evidently felt that this order trade provided the nucleus for a successful store. A cottage was taken over and a member of the Society, a shepherd, was appointed branch manager. His wife looked after the shop during the day while her husband was out in the fields and he took over in the evenings. The van delivery from Lincoln was also continued. Unfortunately, contrary to the committee's hopes, most of the members preferred to receive their goods at the back door than travel to the shop which, they complained, was not sufficiently well stocked to make a visit worthwhile. After a chequered career of just under two years the Owmby branch was closed in June 1880. Its takings had never reached £200 in any quarter and the highest quarterly profit achieved was only £1.7s. The decision to close an uneconomic branch once again demonstrates the committee's firm grip on reality and their financial prudence.

The choice of Welbourn and Owmby might appear to us now to be slightly unusual, but life in rural Lincolnshire was obviously very different in those days.

Three years were to elapse after the launch of Owmby before the Society ventured again into the countryside but on this occasion the choice of venue seems more logical. Metheringham was then, and still is, a significant Lincolnshire village from which the Society still operates. On this occasion the approach came from a number of agricultural workers, who signed a requisition for the holding of a meeting in the village, at which the principles of co-operation could be explained. On 23 April 1881 a deputation from the Society's general and education committees travelled out to Metheringham by train for a public meeting in a local hall which according to the **News** account was: **Well filled by an audience of adults and addresses on co-operation were listened to with great attention. Afterwards, on the Chairman requesting the audience to ask for any further information they might desire, two or three very pertinent questions were put to the clergyman of the parish, a Mr Curtis, who was present throughout the whole of the meeting. At the close of the meeting 15 persons signed the declaration book, paid the deposit required by rule and were duly accepted and enrolled as members. The will of many others was good enough but, the means were not immediately forthcoming owing to the loss of wages experienced during the severe weather of last winter. A decision will be come to by the management at Lincoln, whether to open a branch in the village or to supply members by weekly van. The clergyman was the first to come up to the platform to join the**

Society and his action seemed to quicken the confidence of the people in co-operation which the addresses from the speakers had evoked. It is a significant fact, showing forceably what the movement has to contend with in agricultural districts that 4 out of 15 new members and these not elderly men, could not even write their names. When this is added to the few facilities for meetings and the scattered dwellings, some idea may be formed of the obstacles which Lincoln Society are successfully overcoming. This meeting terminated at 10 o'clock although it had been intended to bring it to an end at 9 o'clock, but one of the audience rose and asked for more speaking, observing that as there were some upon the platform who had not yet addressed the meeting, they felt as if they did not like to give over supping till the mug was empty. The meeting was prolonged accordingly and was pronounced by all present to be one of the most successful ever held by the Society.

No. 6 Branch : METHERINGHAM.

Afterwards, on this April evening, the "deputation" made their way back to Lincoln, deliberating no doubt on all they had seen and heard. A month later a branch store was opened in Metheringham, with a membership of 47, in rented premises from which deliveries were made by van. Five weeks trading brought in £209.9s.10d. Before the year was out the Society had bought its own premises and the site was further enlarged by the purchase of a private house in 1893. The branch has been extended, re-modelled and rebuilt many times over the next century and remains one of the Society's finest offerings. Metheringham had its own branch committee practically from the start and these active members made a considerable contribution to the success of the branch over the years. Seven years after the opening of this branch, McInnes was able to

The first Saxilb[y]
store, opened
in 1883 , can b[e]
seen towards t[he]
left of the pictur[e]

report to the annual branch festival, held in the Wesleyan Schoolroom and at which 300 people were present, that the most notable feature of this branch was the amount of money standing to the credit of its members, who numbered 178. "The whole of the profit made by this branch has been left in the Society as a savings bank", he said, "accumulating until it has reached £2,183, an average of more than £12.5s. per member". Over 100 years ago this must have seemed like a small fortune to the humble folk of Metheringham to whom it belonged.

Two years later a third country branch was established at Saxilby, on the banks of the Foss Dyke. Once again there had been a request from local people for a public meeting and members of a deputation from the committee spoke at a gathering in the club room above the Sun Inn. The unusual factor in this case was that one of those calling for a co-operative store to be opened in the village was a local tradesman, who had found himself in difficulties through allowing too much credit. He had a simple solution to the problem. The Society should take over his shop. It did so in July 1883 and duly appointed him as manager. His reign, however, was not a long one, as in little over a year he had resigned. There was trouble too with his successor, who had the confidence of the local committee, but not of the Lincoln management committee. Eventually

Lincoln committee's assessment proved to be correct, because in 1889 the official had to be dismissed and his bond money was seized by the Society. This led to an action at the Lincoln Assize Court for the return of his deposit, but the verdict went in favour of the Society. Since those days the branch has played a substantial part in the general progress of the Society and has been relocated twice in recent years, the current branch being a model for 21st Century rural co-operative trading.

For their next rural adventure the committee chose the ancient village of Bardney, lying peacefully on the banks of the Witham and crossed at that time by a ferry. The initial move for a branch here came from a Mr Parks who had been a member at Saxilby before moving to Bardney. He acted as missionary in the area and very soon a request was going to Lincoln for a public meeting to be held. Because of opposition, the only room available for this was in a local public house. Unfortunately the records do not say which one, but it was said to have been lively and well attended and soon led to a decision to buy a site for a shop at a cost of £125. On this site a store was built together with a managers house, at a further cost of £392. It was opened for business in January 1886 and at the same time a van service was started to serve neighbouring villages. The co-operative circle was once again being widened. 20 June 1888 saw the formal opening of a co-operative hall in the village of Bardney in order to put an end to the boycott which had prevented them from obtaining meeting rooms. Later this became a grocery warehouse, after the authorities agreed to hire the school room to the Society for its meetings.

The report of the committee for 5 January 1887 stated that they had purchased, at Horncastle, suitable premises in which a well-appointed and well stocked branch store would shortly be opened. In the meantime, they reported, 100 members were being supplied from a dwelling house. This dwelling house was the primitive first store of the short lived Horncastle Society, which had been started 18 months earlier by a number of working men in the area. In the face of considerable opposition, mainly from local tradesmen, (2 public meetings are said to have broken up in disorder), they pressed ahead and called on the Lincoln District Conference Association for help. William Reynolds, a member of the Lincoln Society's Board and Duncan McInnes, Secretary of the Society, met the challenge of the opposition at a meeting in the Masonic Hall so effectively that a provisional committee was formed right away. Rules were later drawn up and registered and a seal adopted with the device of a castle on which a man was standing blowing a horn. A small dwelling house was rented and fitted up as a shop with a counter and two shelves. Capital was not forthcoming in any useful quantity, possibly because of the renewed anti-co-operative propaganda of local tradesmen who placed pressure on employers to dissuade their workers from joining the Society. The two shelves remained largely empty and the counter unused and the one room shop became an object of derision. "A penny toffee shop", was one description, whilst a local barber generously offered to take it off the committee's hands and open it as "a penny shaving saloon". Once again an appeal went out to Lincoln, a public meeting was held, help was promised and a shop bought in North Street which was opened as a branch store shortly afterwards. At a later date a bakehouse was added and adjoining cottages and a warehouse taken over and incorporated into the store.

The idea of a Society in the busy market town of Sleaford had been suggested, two years earlier, by Mr C White who, in a letter to the **News** had drawn the attention of the Midlands Sectional Board, and Lincoln District in particular, to the need for a society in this town of 5,000 people. **"There are many working men in this small town who would rejoice at the thought of a co-operative society in their midst. The secret is here, wages are low and many of them are nailed to the pauperising counters of the small shopkeepers,**

No. 13 Branch: SLEAFORD.

always a week behind in their payments and are constantly pursuing that they have lost which co-operation alone can pick up for them." This brought a reply from McInnes, who said: "If we had gone to Sleaford unsolicited, to advocate co-operation, the first question asked would have been 'what do these men want to get out of us', and the answer would have been, 'money in some way or other'. If we were solicited by a few working men residing there who wanted to learn about co-operation, we should certainly go gladly and the result would probably be the establishment of a small society with a directorate of labourers, which would be cramped for capital. It would start in a way which would ensure ultimate failure. Every shopkeeper would, immediately the store opened, have recourse to the County Court. As well as this, pressure would be brought to bear in other ways, hardly realisable by people living in large towns. An agricultural labourer who had all his life been a Methodist, told me not long ago, it was all over when he became a co-operator. A shopkeeper who had been his class-leader for years would not speak to him. Eventually he drifted into the Salvation Army where he was not thought ill of for being a co-operator".
An earlier attempt to form a separate society in Sleaford had, in fact, come to nothing, but as soon as it became clear that Lincoln was to set up a branch, a provisional committee was established very quickly and soon 100 members had been enrolled into the Society. The store at Sleaford was opened on 17 September 1887 under the management of Mr Webber, after two or three public meetings had been held in the town. Very soon van rounds were serving the surrounding villages and sales increasing accordingly. Most of the early members were agricultural workers with a few railway men and other workmen and it is recorded that half of the first members were heavily in debt to local

trades people. Trade at the branch in the first quarter amounted to £370 and very soon an old chapel nearby was taken over as a warehouse and bakery. The sale of bread stepped up sales very quickly and in two years time the output of the branch exceeded 900 4lb loaves every week and a larger bakery was considered necessary. In April 1889 the Society bought a block of property in Southgate, Sleaford, near to the railway station for conversion into a store and bakery. The new premises were opened later in the year and by October 1890 the committee were reporting that the new warehouse was already too small. Growth had indeed been almost phenomenal, particularly in view of the constant opposition which the Society met. Some shopkeepers, in their antagonism, referred to the railway workers who were strong supporters of the Society as "railroad swine". Another report was that some shopkeepers were threatening to withdraw their work from employers whose workmen became co-operators. Others complained of the smoke from the new bakery chimney and attempted, without success, to compel the Society to spend money on a higher chimney. In spite of this criticism and opposition the branch prospered and more extensions to the premises were completed towards the end of 1892.

The Market Rasen branch is the Society's only direct link with one of the many small societies started by the Agricultural Workers Movement. Co-operation here was several years old before it became part of Lincoln Society. Rasen in the mid to late 1870's was a strong centre of activity by the Agricultural Labourers Union. Joseph Arch, its leader, paid regular visits to the town, usually on a Good Friday afternoon when he addressed huge meetings in the Market Place. In 1876 an official of the union, Mr W Everett, is believed to have taken an active part in promoting a retail society. The advice of the Lincoln Society was sought and at a public meeting in the Market Place, George Hartley advised that an independent society should be started and this was acted upon. A provisional committee was formed, Mr Everett becoming Secretary; members were enrolled, contributions received and a manager appointed who had been an official of the union in Norfolk. Business was started in Queen Street in the autumn of 1876 with a membership of 29. By the end of the first quarter this had grown to 49. Sales reached £344, but total profit was only 7s.3¾d. Capital amounted to £194.15s. What followed seems to have been a sorry tale of incompetence and mismanagement, with the manager buying what he liked, credit being given recklessly and dividends being declared without being earned. There were changes in personnel without much change in the fortunes of the Society.

No. 15 Branch: MARKET RASEN.

Indebtedness grew and the situation was made worse by the opening of branches at Ludford, Nettleton, Binbrook and Howsham. As the Lincoln **Record** commented later, **"misfortune and mismanagement were twin currents in a stream of disaster that could not be stemmed"**. A desperate appeal was made to Lincoln to effect a rescue, but this was declined. In 1892 the Society went into liquidation, the members losing the whole of their capital while the bank, to which the Society was heavily indebted, received 18s.8d in the £. As its doors closed, however, Lincoln Society opened them again as a branch taking over the stock at valuation. Six years later the old brewery in Rasen was bought by Lincoln Society for £575 and a new store with a bakery and stables was built on the site. The laying of the foundation stone of the new branch by George Hartley on 29 May 1897, was preceded by a procession headed by the Rasen Town Band. The **Record** commented, **"The procession was due to a suggestion of the local committee, very few of whom, or of the local members were present to take part in it; but the tea held later seemed to be taken to more congenially, a larger number attending than had ever been served at previous teas at Rasen. It is only fair to add that the procession was held in unfavourable weather."**

Next on the list for development was Bassingham where, after the now familiar requests from members and potential members and the holding of propaganda meetings, a house and land facing the village green were bought in the autumn of 1891. Work on the new store was held up by severe weather and it was finally opened on 6 July 1892. Local traders immediately hit back by beginning to pay dividend and reducing their prices and for some years the branch faced difficulties and did not always earn the rate of dividend paid.

Another district which had been the subject of propaganda for many years was Reepham which was supplied by van from Bardney or from the central store. Towards the end of 1892 a request from 32 members and 55 non members in Reepham and Fiskerton was received, asking the Society to open a branch. They were told to hire a room and organise a meeting and in May 1893 a branch was opened in premises which were later to be described as "inadequate for their purpose as any into which the Society, during its most struggling period, was compelled by poverty to go". In the late summer of 1900 the Society bought, for £75, a house to be used as a shop and bakery and for £375 another house, stabling and a paddock and on 24 April 1901 a new store and bakery were opened.

The Hackthorn and Cold Hanworth Provident Society began operations in 1888. For a short time it enjoyed reasonable success but it was probably too small to survive long term. In 1899 its membership was 57, sales were £540, capital amounted to £274 and it paid a dividend of 2s. Hackthorn merged with Lincoln Society in the summer of 1900 and it was decided to hold propaganda meetings in the neighbouring villages before extending further in that area. It was to be 20 years before the Society opened its next country branch but in the meantime delivery rounds were extended and the existing branch premises were extended and modernised to meet growing demands. Even so, many of them remained simple village stores because of their remoteness. In 1902 for instance, the committee agreed that an oil lamp should be fixed to the Metheringham premises to light the street in front of the shop; neighbours agreed to pay for their share of the oil. When Saxilby branch was rebuilt in 1907 the committee debated whether to light it with acetylene gas and decided against. The new shop opened on 7 September. As late as 1915, a writer in the **Wheatsheaf**, a national co-operative magazine, who had spent a day on one of the Society's country rounds, described how there was one woman customer who might not see another woman for six months at a time. **"Living with her husband and children away from any village, neither church life nor social institutions bring her into touch with others. The store's cart goes across rough fields to her door".**

In 1918 a property was purchased in Washingborough, but war conditions and their aftermath prevented the development taking place immediately; the new store eventually opening on 5 March 1920. Almost as soon as it had opened, members were told that the new premises, "are not sufficient to meet the growing trade that is ours if we

No. 16 Branch: BASSINGHAM.

will take it". A new branch had opened on the main street at Branston just a few weeks earlier and in the same year furniture was added to the range of goods available at Horncastle. In the autumn of 1921 a branch was opened in a wooden hut at North Hykeham and served as a store for two years before being replaced in October 1923 by a permanent building. The hut then became a social room. In the summer of 1921 the first travelling shop was introduced to provide members in some of the country districts with a butchery service. In 1932, land was acquired at Tattershall and a branch was opened in that village on 9 July. Additional travelling butchers shops were introduced to serve the Bardney and Market Rasen areas. In 1935 an existing shop was purchased in Billinghay and started trading under the co-operative banner in July and yet another branch was opened in that year at Waddington. This was the conversion of a former Methodist chapel and school room.

Early in 1937 plans were approved for a new "Emporium" at Sleaford. This was opened on 28 May 1938 and was effectively a small department store including grocery, drapery, footwear, outfitting, furnishing and an optical service. At about the same time premises were bought in Wragby as a site for another branch. The site was cleared and a new store opened in 1939, but almost immediately it was taken over by the military and did not re-open as a shop until January 1947. It had been handed back to the Society shortly after the end of the war, but when application was made to the Horncastle Food Control Committee, a licence was refused. Very strong representations were made to the divisional food officer and the matter was taken up by the Co-operative Union. As a result the food licence was eventually forthcoming.

The Society's first development in Woodhall Spa was a chemist's shop, opened on 3 May 1947. An application for a food licence was refused at first but was granted on appeal and a grocery shop was opened on 18 October. Later, because of a shortage of qualified pharmacists, the chemist's shop became a drug store under the supervision of the grocery branch manager. A shop was purchased in Heckington in the autumn of 1946 but again, because of difficulties over the food licence, this did not open until 24 February 1948. A high percentage of the trade at this branch was said to be done not in the shop but on van rounds. The private grocery business of Larder and Sons at Nettleham, which included a post office, was bought on 25 August 1947. In that same year branches were opened in Spilsby, Ingham and North Kelsey. For many years the Society had had its eye on the small market town of Spilsby and a grocery and butchery business was bought in that town in the autumn of 1947. Despite being told that this was not a co-operative area the development went ahead and proved to be a success. The shop made history for the Society by becoming the first branch to have a wine licence, other than for medicinal wines. Private businesses were taken over and transformed to co-operative stores in Skellingthorpe on 1 May 1948 and in Ruskington on 12 September 1949.

A successful innovation in February and March of 1950 was a series of trade exhibitions in the country areas, each occupying two days. These were staged at Welbourn, Hykeham Institute, Nettleham Village Institute, Ingham Scout Hut, Spilsby Drill Hall, Market Rasen Corn Exchange, North Kelsey Village Hall, Saxilby Village Hall and hotels in Tattershall and Wragby. Large crowds were attracted to these events and significant increases in trade came about as a result.

Coningsby was the next target for the Society's expansion where a private grocery business was purchased towards the end of 1949 and opened on 2 January 1950. This proved to be an excellent acquisition with a great deal of its trade coming from members of the R.A.F. and their families stationed in the area. Also at the beginning of 1950 a block of four shops, one of which was already being rented as a butchery branch, was purchased at Bracebridge Heath. Another unit was quickly converted into a grocery branch and a third into a drug store. The fourth unit, the post office, remained in private hands for some time but was eventually brought under the Society's control. The flurry of activity in the first few months of 1950 continued with the purchase of a private grocery business in Welton and a gentlemen's outfitting

No. 17 Branch: REEPHAM.

business in Horncastle was acquired later in the year, when a furniture store was also added to the portfolio. Two further additions were made to the growing list of country branches in the autumn of 1951. On 1 September a small shop was purchased at Navenby and a grocery and bakery business in Helpringham on 10 October. Early in 1952 another rural outpost was established, this time in the village of Ludford, where an existing private trade shop was bought. Here again, as with so many of these very small branches, more than half the trade was carried out by van rounds. In the early days, considerable trade was done with camp dwellers in the neighbourhood. One camp was occupied mainly by Poles and an attempt to prevent the Society trading there led to a question being asked in Parliament.

In March of that year the Board announced a policy of expanding the non food trade into the country areas. The first step was the purchase of a small drapery business in Spilsby and this was followed in Sleaford, where pharmacy, fancy goods, radio, television and electrical departments were opened and the drapery section extended. Early in 1955 a new branch was opened in the old village of North Hykeham, in Lincoln Road on the site of two old cottages and later in the year a grocery shop and off-licence had been opened in George Street, Sleaford. In December 1956 a small branch was opened in the village of Martin and in 1957 another, this time in Ancaster. At the end of the Society's first Century the Board proudly claimed that "virtually no village of any size within the Society's trading area is out of reach of co-operative service and the dream of those who first started the Society along the path of village co-operation has become a reality".

Society coal lorry on Canwick Road in 1937

The buying of coal by working people had always been a problem. The worries were uncertainty about quality and short weight. People would stand around watching the coal men delivering orders and carefully count the bags to ensure they got 20 cwt bags to the ton. Even then, they could never be sure the bags contained the full cwt and the quality was very much an unknown factor. It is hardly surprising, therefore, that the Society got involved in the coal trade very early on.

In 1866 arrangements were made with an agent to supply members with coal and the annual report of June 1866 declares: three qualities sold, prices include delivery, quality and weight guaranteed, in addition to which checks are given (which meant dividend). By 1872 the Society was boasting its own coal depot at Holmes Yard and again stressing that quality and weight were guaranteed.

In 1873 the committee announced "arrangements have been made with some of the best collieries and members may rely upon being well served with coal". By the 1880's availability of coal was listed as follows:

Firsts - Wharncliffe and Strafford Old Silkstones
Seconds - Snaith & Main
Thirds - Riddings Bright and Screenings
Fourths - Bestwood Brights and Screenings
Old Silkstone Nuts
Hard and Engine Coal

In 1898 the Society bought the rolling stock, offices and trade plant of the Lincoln Coal and Coke Company on Canwick Road, Lincoln. With this acquisition the Society also obtained their coal yard, together with additional space for storing coal from the Great Central Railway Company. Members living in that area were asked, in future, to deliver their coal orders to the Canwick Road office.

From that point on, the coal department grew very quickly to the point when, as we approached the middle of the 20th Century, the Society had coal depots all over its trading area, mainly close to the rail network, including two in Lincoln, selling thousands of tons of coal every week.

As we moved into the second half of the 20th Century, coal usage was in decline as gas and electric fires grew in popularity and working people started to have central heating installed in their homes. In 1972 the Bracebridge depot was closed and all the Lincoln business transferred to Ropewalk. In 1975 the Lincoln depot was closed and all of the business was moved to Gainsborough. And then in 1980 the whole thing finally came to an end, when the Gainsborough business was sold to British Fuels.

The department had provided a very useful and valuable service to the members for 114 years and brought fair trading and trust to the coal business which was very much appreciated by the members.

Whitefriars House in 1967

The sale of watches, clocks and jewellery was first mentioned in the report 9 April 1884 although the committee commented that it was unable to display the stock "owing to want of room". Shortly afterwards the committee were announcing that clocks and watches and all kinds of jewellery could be supplied direct from the Co-operative Watch Manufacturing Society at Coventry. Illustrated catalogues were available from the cashier.

In 1920, premises which had been acquired earlier, at the corner of Silver Street and Bank Street were opened as a Jewellery and Fancy Department and the range now included rings, watches, clocks, barometers, cruets, biscuit barrels, cameras, little broches or novelties in the form of the Lincoln Imp, and an optical section, which included sight testing. The optical section was transferred into the pharmacy division when that was established in 1928.

In 1931 the department was moved, with others, to the newly built shops at the top of Free School Lane, a small unit, but the best so far.

Around the time of its one hundredth birthday, the Society had bought a 15th Century, timber-framed building in Lincoln, just south of the High Street level crossing, known as Whitefriars House.

The original plan was to demolish the building, but this met with considerable opposition from the conservationists and historians. There followed long drawn out negotiations with the local authority and

Government departments, many meetings in Lincoln and London and much correspondence. Eventually agreement was reached, the building was restored and opened, in 1967, on two floors, as a high class store for the sale of jewellery, glass and china. It was a very fine unit.

Whether it was due to its position, just outside the city centre, we do not know but, for one reason or another, "Whitefriars" failed to reach its potential as a jewellery shop and in 1979 it was moved back to the top floor of Co-operative House on Silver Street. This was a specially created unit, with high security, which presented as a sort of bank vault or strong room.

The department traded in this unit for ten years, then in 1989 it moved again, this time to the ground floor of Co-operative House for the sale of glass, china, clocks, watches and costume jewellery; the high class end of the jewellery offer was discontinued.

The department continued in this position until 1999 when the Society withdrew from the store and the 'gifts' section was first moved to the Corn Exchange and then to the Moorland Centre.

The sale of footwear started in 1874 as soon as the Society moved into its own store on Silver Street. The quarterly report of 6 October 1874 announces: "Boots and Shoes, a good stock of ready-made. The Bespoke and Repair Department has special attention". By 1878 they were offering "Ladies', Gentlemen's and children's boots and shoes, all ready made goods in the department are manufactured exclusively by the Co-operative Wholesale Society at their works in Leicester. Quality and workmanship guaranteed".

The quarterly **Record** of April 1889 clearly indicates that the Society was not only meeting the needs of its members, but also addressing a social problem. It states **"Working men and women support your fellow workers who earn fair wages, work in healthy shops and make goods that will wear well. Don't forget that the boots and shoes sold by the Society are made by Co-operators while tons of boots come into this district from 'SWEATING DENS' where men, women and children work eighteen hours a day at starvation wages. Support Co-operation – Fair wages and sound goods."**

Prices for boots and shoes ranged from 3s.11d to 7s.11d but slippers could be bought for 9d.

By the early 1900's the range of goods had been extended considerably and prices maintained or cut. The repairing department was also very extensive by this time and members were reminded that all repairs were carried out using "best English leather". Footwear in need of repair could be left at the Central, Sub-Central or any branch and would be collected from there on completion. When extensions were carried out in Free School Lane the Boot and Shoe Department was moved into one of those units, opposite the Central Library with the repair section above. At its peak 25 to 30 men worked in the footwear repair shop, dealing with thousands of pairs every week. Another indication of changing times came in 1976 when the repair shop closed due to lack of business. The retail side of the department continued in Free School Lane until Co-operative House was opened in the 1960's when it was relocated there. It traded well in that position for many years until changes in the market and the reduction in the number of co-operative societies, leading to a shortage of good co-operative footwear managers, caused the Society to franchise the business to Lilley and Skinner. That later changed to Shoefayre, a co-operative business of which Lincoln Co-operative was a shareholder. Shoefayre was later acquired by Stead and Simpson. When Co-operative House closed in 1999 the franchised operation was moved to two locations in Lincoln, Corn Exchange and Tritton Road where they continue to trade as Stead and Simpson. There is also a similar operation at the Home store in Gainsborough.

Santa arrives in style at Silver Street

The first mention of goods which eventually came to be sold in this department appears in 1895 when cycles are offered for sale in the furnishing department. The 'Federation Model C' is on offer at a price ranging from £10.2s.6d to £10.7s.6d depending on the type of tyres chosen, with the 'No 2 Model' slightly cheaper at £7.12s.6d to £8.5s.0d. These cycles seem expensive for 1895, equivalent to over £800 today. Prices had however come down by 1907, when 'Rudge Whitworth's' were being offered at £5.19s.0d, 'Harris' from £5 and Federation from £4.19s.6d.

Dolls were first advertised in 1900 and football boots, in the boot and shoe department, in 1901. The first reference to 'toys' comes in 1911 and from then on the range gradually increases. The business was carried on in the Silver Street/Free School Lane properties. By the 1950's the Co-op toy department was starting to have a much more substantial presence in the City.

In 1961 it was announced that the 'Christmas Toy Fair' would be moved to the 'Old Chapel' on Silver Street. In 1962 the sports and toys department moved to its new home on the first floor of Silvergate House where it enjoyed a good reputation and traded well. The next and, as it turned out, final move came in 1979, when the department was relocated to the basement of Co-operative House, on the other side of Silver Street. It was here that 'sports and toys' probably enjoyed their best years.

Throughout the 1980's and 1990's, the Co-op toy department was the place to be for toys, certainly at Christmas. 'Santa's Grotto' attracted huge crowds, children sometimes waiting their turn for over an hour. Records show that the busiest ever year was 1993 when 7,800 children visited Santa. The department was effectively wound up when Co-operative House closed in 1999, although a limited range of toys has been tried in the 'centres' at various points since then.

Ladies and Gentlemen's Hairdressing on the corner of Free School Lane, Lincoln in 1967

The hairdressing service started in the new block of shops on the east side of Free School Lane in 1931. The salons were at the top of the stairs above the tobacconists, ladies to the left, gents to the right. On average there were four hairdressers on each side, sometimes more on the ladies. Few who "enjoyed" the experience will forget Jock, "The demon barber of Free School Lane", whose reputation spread throughout the City. Jock was in the habit of making rather exaggerated hand movements whilst still holding the scissors, which led people to fear that they might not escape with their ears intact.

When the Free School Lane shops closed in the mid 1970's, the ladies hairdressing moved to a unit at the bottom of Free School Lane, on the ground floor, opposite the Central Library. The service for gentlemen ceased at the same time. By the mid 1980's the hairdressing service was moved into Co-operative House and then franchised to Kauffman's who later became John Michael. Hairdressing in Lincoln was discontinued when Co-operative House closed in 1999. John Michael also operated in Newark for a while. A service is still provided by them in the Society's home store in Gainsborough.

John Michael Hairdressing at Co-operative House in 1994

65

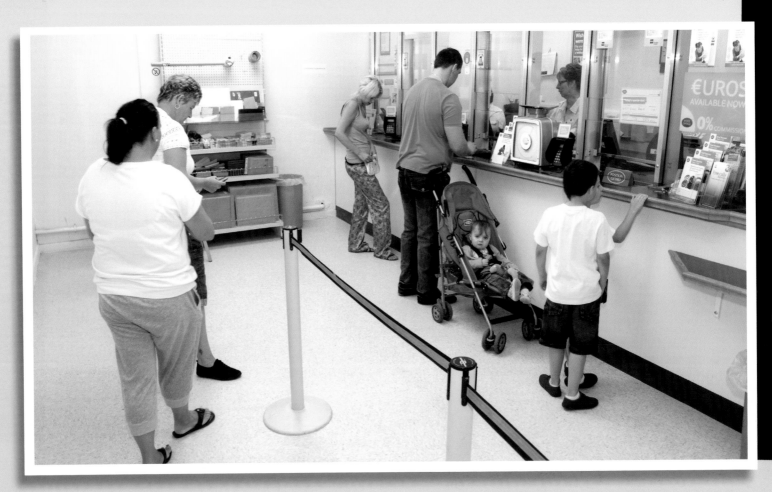

The Society's first post office acquisitions came in 1947 when food businesses were bought at Nettleham in August and Boultham Park Road, Lincoln in November, which both had post offices. A third was acquired in 1956 at Gosberton, near Spalding.

In the late 1990's the main Crown Post Office in Lincoln moved from Guildhall Street, a property built by the Society in 1903, to part of the Corn Exchange, a property owned by and rented from the Society. At the same time the Society opened a small sub office in the City Square Centre. In 2003 the Society took over the running of the former Crown Post Office in Lincoln and moved it into City Square Centre. The management of the former Crown offices in Gainsborough, Newark, Market Rasen and Spalding was also transferred to the Society.

During the late 1990's and early 2000's many small sub post offices were acquired by the Society, including quite a few in the Grimsby area, as part of the drive into Humberside. Most of these offices were transferred into the Society's food stores. When they were first bought these post offices brought in a reasonable amount of income, which helped to make the total operation more viable. They were also bought with a view to increasing footfall, as well as to assist viability.

Over the years post office income has come under pressure and decreased to the point where many offices are no longer viable and the food operation subsidises the post office. This is seen largely as a service to the community, which is often valued highly by the local residents, but there is a limit as to how far this can go. The Society currently operates post offices at:-

Carlton Centre, Lincoln
Lowfields, Brant Road, Lincoln
Metheringham
Horncastle
Mablethorpe
Billinghay
Waddington
Nettleham
Heckington
Skellingthorpe
Washingborough
Ruskington
Bracebridge Heath
Welton
Long Sutton
Monks Road, Lincoln
Holbeach
Gosberton
Chapel St Leonards
Trelawney Crescent, Lincoln

Misterton
Kirton Lindsey
Hykeham Green
Churchill Drive, Newark
Old Leake
Lincoln Road, Sleaford
The Willows, Grimsby
Coniston Avenue, Grimsby
Cambridge Road, Grimsby
Nunsthorpe, Grimsby
Whaplode
Convamore Road, Grimsby
Westcliff, Scunthorpe
The Riddings, Scunthorpe
Messingham
Market Rasen
Market Place, Gainsborough
City Square Centre, Lincoln
Spalding

In 2009 the Society was named National Partner of the Year by the Post Office.

Ballroom and stage at the New Hall on Free School Lane

The Society has a long and honourable record when it comes to feeding its members and customers. It all started in 1889 when a refreshment bar was opened on Silver Street alongside the library and reading room. Initially this was open only on market days and Saturday evenings, but the hours were quickly extended until by 1900 it was open from 8.30 am to 7.30 pm each day except Wednesday, when it closed at 1.00 pm. It did not of course open on Sundays.

The first move came in 1910 when what was described at the time as a "first class cafe" was created in the basement of an extension on Silver Street. This was a large and impressive operation which quickly became an important feature of the Lincoln social scene, catering for large and small parties, as well as the casual diner. Many Lincoln people will have fond memories of children's parties in the "Co-op Cafe". In 1949 the whole of the cafe business was moved to the New Hall at the bottom of Free School Lane. The Society's main offices occupied the ground floor but on the first floor a superb ballroom with stage was developed. Once again the quality and status of the catering/entertainment offering had been upgraded.

The room was very well used, for lunches and teas during the day and as a dance hall, concert hall or meeting room in the evenings. It could be hired for the evening by companies or charities or even individuals. A gentleman by the name of Mr Burdell, who lived in Toronto Street, ran a dance on Saturdays each week for many years, strictly as a business venture. Eventually the Society ran the Saturday night dances themselves on a commercial basis.

Regularly, in excess of 400 people crowded into the "Co-op Hall" on Friday and Saturday evenings, dancing to bands like "The Clubmen" or "Tommy Worth". Throughout the 1950's and early 60's this was the place for young people to be seen, it was the "Ritzy's" or Lincoln's "Stringfellows" of its time, oh happy days! Another sign of the changing times is that, whilst soft drinks could be bought, alcoholic refreshments were rarely available. It was very difficult to obtain a licence for such a bar.

In 1964, the main offices having relocated to Silvergate House, the catering/entertainment facility was extended and upgraded once again. The Society was now offering "a first class restaurant, fully licensed", which was available for dinner parties or dinner dances. The dance hall remained upstairs whilst the restaurant moved to the ground floor. The Silvergate Restaurant was able to cater for up to 200 and the St Swithin's Room 30 to 40. The Board proudly declared "any function, large or small can be catered for".

In 1972 the Silvergate Restaurant and St Swithin's Room were refurbished in an effort to secure more high quality business and the ballroom and stage upstairs was upgraded and re-named the "Regency Room". The Board announced in their report of February 1972, "we now have a complete suite of banqueting rooms in the centre of the city, which add to the prestige of the Society". But it was not to last and by 1983 the pattern of the entertainment and catering business had changed considerably. A snack bar facility which had been started in Co-operative House some time earlier was extended and upgraded to restaurant quality and the day time trade transferred, but functional catering was discontinued.

The Society's current catering offer takes the form of five coffee shops situated at Corn Exchange, City Square and Tritton Road in Lincoln and also Gainsborough and Long Sutton, where a range of hot and cold meals, snacks and drinks can be obtained.

Business as usual after
the Great War -
Horncastle staff pictured at
Easter 1919

WAR AND PEACE - ONE

9

*'I have often wished I was still with
the Bracebridge bread cart driving
a good horse about the county'*

War clouds first appeared on the horizon in March 1912, when it was decided to register ten horses for the Army "in case of an emergency", at a retaining fee of 10s. per horse. Eleven months later it was agreed that the necessary steps should be taken for placing horses at the disposal of the Government "for mobilisation purposes in case of war", at a retaining fee of 10s. per year for light horses and £4 per year for heavy horses, for the military. Two days after the declaration of war in 1914, a Major Wilson attended a meeting of the committee on behalf of the Government, "with a view to obtaining rolling stock to meet the emergency". He was allowed to buy two sets of harnesses for £16, two carts for £44 and two horses for £80. Members were warned that delivery service had to be curtailed and a few days later the horse committee sold a dozen more horses to the Government. The quarterly meeting agreed to place £500 at the disposal of the committee to meet emergencies and very soon the Society's first motor vehicle appeared. The possibility of adopting this new fangled method of transport had been under consideration since 1908, when the committee enquired about other societies' experience with it and found that "no economic advantage would be derived from the change", although a car had been hired from a local firm on contract to enable the cashier to collect cash from the branches. Three months before the war began an order was placed for a steam wagon for delivery purposes and in August 1914 a motor van joined the Society's rolling stock, one of the horse drivers being given driving tuition in order to operate the new vehicle.

An early decision was that men called up or volunteering should be reinstated at the end of the war and that a grant should be made to their dependents; 10 shillings per week for married men, the cases of single men and dependents to be considered on their merits. In November 1914 Belgian refugees appeared in Lincoln and the committee agreed to grant three loaves of bread per week to each of five families. Free storage was also provided for a quantity of cheese in the grocery warehouse to be distributed as relief to other refugees. The quarterly meeting held in the same month approved a suggestion that one of the refugee families should be adopted by the Society and provided with a furnished house, whilst it was agreed to loan two further houses in Coulson Road to the employees, who would accommodate two more Belgian families. In December 1914 the Moortgat family of six from Antwerp was housed on Newark Road, an allowance of 30s per week granted for maintenance, with coal and gas allowed free and Monsieur Moortgat was offered a job in the Society's warehouse. A little later two families each with mother, father and one child, the

Mattheys and the Van Gaevers, moved into the other two houses.

In February 1915 the possibility of aerial damage caused the committee to carry extra insurance on the central premises, the mill, building department and sub central and in March another motor vehicle was bought whilst members of the rolling stock committee combed the countryside in search of horses. Reference is made in the January 1916 report to the difficulty in providing "adequate labour" to cope with the growing demands of the business and shortly afterwards it was decided to employ female labour in the grocery shops, while a chaff-cutter was hired to the Government for £1 per week and land at Boultham Park Road was allocated for allotments. The committee generously undertook to pay fines imposed on two departmental managers for infringing black-out regulations and decided immediately afterwards to black out skylights and windows.

In 1914 the Society provided food and accomodation for Belgian refugees

The Society was represented at a meeting in Lincoln, called to consider the provision of mosquito helmets to the 6th Lincolns at the Dardenelles and the committee also decided that their right to take rabbits in "the butcher's field" should be given up and that any member and friend should have the privilege of doing so. It was also in 1915 that the Society's shops first began to close for lunch, for one hour on each of three days per week, whilst Saturday night closing was brought forward to 8.00 pm.

At their meeting on 2 May 1916 the committee were interrupted by a buzzer alarm indicating that enemy zeppelins were in the district and the meeting was hastily adjourned until the following evening. Soon afterwards 10,000 cards and posters were ordered for "the purpose of regulating the sale of sugar to members": rationing had arrived, if only in an unofficial form. With restrictions in so many directions, it is perhaps surprising that the Society was able to continue developments, even in a limited way. The new Boultham branch, on Coulson Road was opened in October 1915. Early in 1916 the St. Edmunds property at the corner of Bank Street and Silver Street was bought and orders were given for the construction of a new abattoir at Brayford to replace the one used for many years on Sincil Bank. The old premises were then used as a munitions factory.

One of the war-time casualties was the Society's motor barge, Co-operator. This had been purchased in 1912 for £1,200 and was skippered for many years by George Richardson who had the help of a mate and an engineer. The barge, which carried grain from Hull to the Society's mill, had its first trip in March 1913 and made regular voyages until 1915 when it was sold to the

For King and Country - both men and horses from the Society served during the First World War.

Admiralty. Subsequently it was used as an ammunition carrier on the Thames and Medway. Another effect of the war was the decision in July 1916 to close down "for the duration" the butchery branches on High Street and at Bracebridge.

By April 1917 the Society's Role of Honour contained 234 names and more than 300 appeared on it before the

peace treaties were signed, many of them men who had lost their lives during the war. No record seems to have been kept of the Society's horses which were commandeered, but in all, more than 70 were mobilised and many probably saw foreign service. A former van driver of the Society no doubt typified the feelings of many of his colleagues when in a letter to the Record from France he wrote, "I have often wished I was still with the Bracebridge bread cart driving a good horse about the country. I often wonder where poor old Laddy got to. I did used to think something about that horse, we were just like two brothers together".

With the coming of Government controlled food rationing, the Society had cause for serious dissatisfaction as, although it served half the area's people with bread, it was allowed only one representative on the food control committee. The local authority refused to receive a deputation on the issue and the whole question was taken up nationally through the Co-operative Union. In the closing year of the war, a determined effort was made to restrict credit trading and a regulation was adopted to abolish credit altogether in the first and last months of each quarter. This resulted in a considerable saving of labour in the office and, as a consequence, it was decided to adopt "cash trading only" once again in the boot and shoe, drapery, millinery, outfitting, and furnishing departments from the beginning of 1919. In the summer of 1918 the Society acquired the land and buildings in Silver Street belonging to Dr. Carline for future extensions. When the war came to an end the Society's membership had risen to 18,195 and total trade amounted to £732,000.

With the war over and men coming back from the front, it was still some time before the Society got back into its old stride. One early revival that was appreciated by the members, however, was the annual festival which had been suspended for the duration of the war. This was held in the Corn Exchange on 15 February 1919, after a gap of five years. The village festivals recommenced the following year.

Many plans that had been in cold storage were now brought out and the committee considered how services to members might be further extended. The former pork butchery in Free School Lane became a wet fish shop whilst the newly acquired premises at the corner of Silver Street and Bank Street were opened as a jewellery and fancy goods shop in 1920.

The following year, Fred Stephenson, who had been associated with the Society for 46 years and had carried a heavy burden during the war, retired as cashier to be succeeded by Charles Mackinder.

In April 1921 a hut on the Swanpool estate was converted into a shop and soon afterwards another temporary shop was opened on Wragby Road. The first travelling shop to provide members in the country districts with a meat service began in the summer.

But the big event of the year, however, was the Society's diamond jubilee. It included an exhibition of co-operative products held in the Drill Hall from 13 to 20 August which was attended by many thousands - a special treat, details of which are not recorded, for all members of the Penny Bank aged under 14 and a giant tea party for all employees on one of the days of the exhibition. Also to celebrate the jubilee, additional articles were added to the stock in the Sick Room Appliance Department. But these celebrations, although successful, took place against a sombre background. The first of the post-war depressions had already started to affect the City and many members were out of work. The Society made a grant of £1,000 to assist them, but this was soon exhausted and the committee were authorised to grant a further £500. The grants were issued in the form of vouchers which were exchangeable for small quantities of groceries, but the full amount of the grant was expended within three months. In their report for 5 October 1921 the committee drew attention to the serious position that had developed. "For a long time we were able to withstand the aftermath of the war", they reported, "but it is now so great that our turnover in some departments shows a marked reduction. In food stuffs many more tonnes have been sold for less money than the corresponding period last year". Sales for the quarter showed a decline of £42,747 which was attributed to unemployment, trade depression and a heavy fall in prices. Further decreases in sales were reported in January 1922 when the committee commented: "the markets have been swamped with huge quantities of goods of all kinds causing a drop in prices. It has meant heavy losses in reducing our stocks down to market value". Successive quarters repeated the same gloomy tale. By July 1922 dividend was down to 3d and 1,290 members withdrew from membership. Nevertheless, the committee remained optimistic commenting: "turnover amounted to nearly £400,000 at a time when prices are about 20% less than a year ago. The silver lining encourages us to believe that the tide has turned and that one of the most difficult periods in the history of the Society is behind us". Sales decreases continued however, in spite of a gesture of increasing the dividend to 9d, and it was not until the last quarter of 1923 that an increase in sales was again reported. This was one of £2,134 and the committee hailed it as "the last peak of the depression".

The Employees Superannuation Fund started on 1 January 1924 and 7 employees benefitted immediately. All of them were between 70 and 76. Another employee event in 1924 was a full day trip to the Wembley Exhibition for which the City shops were closed on 27 August. With the City's industries on a more even keel and prices more stable, trading figures continued to improve. For the last quarter of 1924 the increase was £18,144 and dividend went up to one shilling, whilst the next quarter was described as the best for some time.

Earlier on in 1924 the Society, along with the rest of the Co-operative Movement, had mourned the death on 23 March of Duncan McInnes, at the age of 76. He had been living in retirement in Lincoln and had maintained his keen interest in the activities of the Society and in co-operation generally. Another long association with the Society was broken early in 1925 by the death of William Coulson, who had been active in the Society since 1869.

In January 1926 the committee reported, "We are doing a very large business in wireless equipment. We can do the whole business ready to switch on, fitted with loud speakers or headphones". Soon afterwards the business of charging accumulators for radio sets was begun.

Radios were "a very large business" in 1926

Before the end of the year a new branch was opened on Wragby Road, replacing the temporary shop opened some years earlier. This branch had meeting rooms above, which were available for dances and other social events. A chocolate and sweet shop at the corner of Free School Lane and Silver Street opened in time for Easter 1927 and on 19 November of that year a big crowd gathered for the opening of the new branch at the corner of Moorland Avenue and Skellingthorpe Road. A tea party and concert was held on the premises following the opening ceremony.

Enlargement of the sub-central premises in High Street enabled the footwear and drapery department, which was frequently overcrowded, to be moved out of the old shop early in 1928 and room made for hardware, furnishing and building materials. Work also began on pulling down the old premises at the corner of Free School Lane and Silver Street for the construction of a new suite of shops with offices and board room above. A new and highly successful event was a gladioli show held in the reading room on 25 August 1928. The blooms had to be grown from bulbs bought from the Society and proof of purchase was required. Members of the public were admitted for one penny each. The

event was extended the following year to include tulips, daffodils, narcissi and anemones. The Society promoted a large stock of seed potatoes the following spring.

An electrician had also joined the staff and electrical work was being carried out for members for the first time, including the fixing of wireless sets supplied by the furnishing department.

Unfortunately, 1929 saw the start of the Great Depression and sales started to decline once again. A new secretary, John English Harrison, who came from London Society, took over at the beginning of April 1930 in succession to George Harris who had been associated with the Society for 30 years.

The new Free School Lane shops, which included butchery, tobacconist with ladies and gents hairdressers above, jewellery, fruit and florist, fish and game were opened on 14 February 1931. A new board room and offices were also provided on the first floor. Sadly, sales decreases continued to be reported throughout 1931 but dividend was held at 1s.3d. Because of the economic situation the Board reluctantly decided to cancel the festivals that year in both the City and the districts.

1929 view of Society shops on Free School lane - these were demolished shortly afterwards and replaced by the units in the picture below.

Free School Lane shop units (shown here in 1967) were opened on 14th February 1931.

They were never revived. There were, however, some bright spots. One was the award of a gold medal for the Society's exhibition of flowers at the Lincolnshire Show and another was the success of the Society's new Trading Club which recruited 2,529 members in its first year.

1932 saw little relief with sales decreases again recorded in spite of a "great shopping fortnight", which ran from 27 June to 9 July and included a trade exhibition in the large hall involving various departments. Free membership of the Society was offered and 320 new members were recruited. During the year the Society's boot and shoe repairing

department had been refitted with the latest machinery and was claimed to be the finest in the county. Four new cubicles had been added to the ladies hairdressing department. At this time men's tailor-made suits were on offer from 63s to £6.6s, women's tailor-made coats at 57s.6d and costumes at 63s.

Further sales decreases were recorded in 1933 but again the dividend was maintained at 1s.3d. More than 15,000 members, together with members from other societies, signed an unsuccessful petition which was presented to Parliament, to protest against any further taxation on co-operative societies.

The National Government's measures to deal with unemployment, which included proposals for the direction of labour, came in for some fierce criticism during the winter of 1933/34 and at the Society's February meeting in 1934 members approved a resolution promising moral and financial support to the "Lincoln Protest Marchers reception committee". A sum of £5 was granted to the committee for the purpose of providing food for the City's "hunger marchers", who took with them to London a petition with 10,000 signatures to protest against "the concentration camps and conscription of labour which now threatens the whole country by the new Unemployment Bill". Although the prospects for so many of the Society's members seemed bleak, especially for those who were normally employed in the City's basic industry of engineering, the committee seemed to have more reason for confidence. For the first time since 1929 an increase in sales was recorded in the quarter ended 3 January 1934. It amounted to only £2,558 but was seen as a sign of better times to come. By October the half-year's sales had risen by more than £20,000 and dividend was increased to 1s.4d. Six months later it rose again, this time to 1s.6d. The time had come for further expansion.

In the first quarter of 1933 the Society purchased the old General Dispensary premises adjoining the central store in Silver Street and they were earmarked for development. Soon afterwards workmen were demolishing old property in Free School Lane for the erection of a new hall and public office. A ten year plan of development was also embarked upon in anticipation of the centenary of the Rochdale Pioneers which was to be celebrated in 1944. A target fixed for 1936 was 800 new members and a sales increase of £25,000. Some interesting figures are quoted in the half year report for April 1936. Sales for the half year included 15,230 tonnes of coal, 381,535 gallons of milk, 108,469 lbs. of butter produced in the Society's dairy and 1,733,048 2-lb. loaves of bread.

Newport branch
rebuilt in 1938

In July there was a modest celebration of the Society's 75th anniversary with a CWS exhibition attracting more than 80,000 people. The new hall and offices were opened on 4 July 1936 and in October the report showed that the sales and membership targets had both been comfortably exceeded. During the year, 985 new members had been recruited and sales rose by more than £70,000. This enabled the sales for the half year ended 7 October 1936 to exceed half a million pounds for the first time in the Society's history. Since 1928 they had been within striking distance of this figure on several occasions, but the repeated trade depressions had held back the accomplishment. Total trade for the year was £1,018,000, a landmark achievement to celebrate 75 years of co-operation in the City and County of Lincoln. A new and more menacing shadow on the horizon was heralded by an appeal from the Co-operative Union for its Spanish Civil War relief fund. A sum of £25 was granted in cash and £10 worth of food was also sent.

For some time it had been increasingly evident that the central premises, planned for the requirements of an earlier age, were unsuitable, in many respects, for the task they now had to perform and in July 1938 the committee announced that following "lengthy and careful deliberations" it had been decided to go ahead with their reconstruction and an architect had been instructed to prepare plans. But when the war came, a building scheme of this nature was out of the question and the whole proposal was put on hold for an indefinite period. For more than a year before the war began a sub-committee of departmental managers had been involved in a scheme for civil defence precautions for the whole of the Society's premises and these were to prove of enormous value. The rebuilding of Newport branch, to include a modern hall with seating for 200 people, was completed in September 1938 and this too was to prove a valuable development.

The Society invested £70,000 on behalf of members in a "Wings for Victory" week in 1943

WAR AND PEACE - TWO

'When the Society's "Aid to Russia" fund was wound up in 1945, a sum of £3,702 had been sent to Russia and more than £1,000 was raised for the "Aid to China" fund'.

When the war began in September 1939, the Society was better prepared to meet eventualities than it had been in 1914, but there were inevitable difficulties for the committee, management, staff and members. One immediate problem was occasioned by the commandeering of many motor vehicles by the local authority and a shortage of petrol for those remaining. This meant an immediate curtailment of delivery services. This time, however, the first world war's difficulties over rationing were not repeated. The Society was represented on food control committees throughout its area and on the fuel control committee and its butchery manager, C. P. Appleton, was area meat agent. An air-raid shelter was built in the central store and there was a core of employees who had been trained in various aspects of civil defence. The new hall in Free School Lane was taken over by the military authorities within a very short time of the war starting and was not handed back until 1946. In the meantime many of the functions normally held there were transferred to the Society's cafe, which had been renovated during the first winter of the war. A welfare and comforts fund for employees serving in the forces was also set up with the aim of sending monthly parcels to all of the Society's servicemen and women.

In July 1940, with Dunkirk a very recent memory, more motor vehicles were requisitioned by the military and in October the first fire-watching rotas were being drawn up. The house of the Horncastle branch manager, Charlie Ullyatt, had the doubtful honour of being the first of the Society's properties to suffer damage from enemy action. In an incendiary raid it was almost completely destroyed and had to be rebuilt by the Works Department. Other damage was sustained later by Baggeholme Road, Waddington and Moorland Avenue branches. These all received the attention of the works department which had also been concerned with

St Swithin's School on Baggeholme Road March 1941 (photo courtesy Lincolnshire Echo)

converting Newport Hall into a decontamination centre on behalf of the authorities.

Increasing difficulty was being experienced by the end of 1940 in obtaining supplies, particularly in what were described as the "dry goods" departments, which meant non-grocery, and this same problem was to occur in many other sections of the Society before hostilities were finally ended. Earlier closing was introduced because of the black-out and the risk of air raids. The same factors had led to a decision in the autumn of 1940 to hold the November quarterly meeting on Saturday afternoon, whilst the branch quarterly meetings were cancelled altogether. This situation continued for the remainder of the war. When air raid alerts were given it was the practice in the central store to ask shoppers to take shelter and to suspend trading operations until the all-clear was sounded. With typical British courage, or maybe bravado, many customers complained that this was an unnecessary interruption and in April 1941 the committee announced that, in future, only when the 'danger near' signal was sounded, would customers be asked to take cover. "We appeal to members to pay due regard to this warning and immediately leave the departments to take shelter and so liberate our staff, as danger really is imminent and our first duty in all our services, is to avoid becoming a casualty, however brave we may wish to appear", the committee commented somewhat mournfully.

Staffing problems were gradually becoming more acute and in mid 1941 the directors had to report that since the outbreak of war, the whole of the dairy office staff had been replaced, "only with great difficulty has the manager and several senior members of staff been temporarily reserved", they complained. At this time 302 employees were in the forces, 8 on munitions work, 10 in the A.F.S. (Auxiliary Fire Service), 8 in the Police War Reserve and one on the land. With petrol supplies further reduced in the late summer of 1941, a complete revision of all delivery rounds had been carried out. The next committee report contained an appeal to the owners of 500 pairs of boots and shoes, lying in the central boot department after repair, to take steps to collect them! The Society's "Aid to Russia" fund had been set up in 1941 and at the end of the year share number 9001 was set aside so that dividend on purchases made on this number could be allocated to the fund. When the fund was wound up in 1945, a sum of £3,702 had been sent to Russia and from the same share number, more than £1,000 was raised for the "Aid to China" fund.

In January 1943 the quarterly report announced under the heading ARP - Air Raid Precautions that "Our staff on duty have had their baptism and their action in co-operation with the N.F.S., is calculated to have rendered invaluable service to the City. The individuals concerned are to be congratulated on their prompt action and preparedness which has enabled immediate action to be taken and the damage very strictly limited".

Three months later, the directors were proudly pointing out that, although they were now in the fourth year of the war, under difficult trading conditions, the Society had shown remarkable progress. Sales in the preceding twelve months were the highest in the Society's history. The Society invested £60,500 in a "Wings for Victory" week on behalf of the City members and £9,500 in the name of the country members, making a total of £70,000 in 3% savings bonds. A year later in a "Salute the Soldier" week, a further £20,000 was invested. Perhaps because of unhappy experiences in other societies, members were warned in mid-1943 to take special care of their dividend checks. They were told: "should the Society's records suffer damage as a result of enemy action, your checks would be invaluable in proving your claim to dividend".

As well as the armed forces, some employees joined the Auxiliary Fire Service.

The Society played its full part in celebrating the Centenary of the Rochdale Pioneers in 1944 with two major events. The first was a service in Lincoln Cathedral on 2 July, conducted by Archdeacon A Warner, when the singing was led by the Society's choirs. Then for the following week, the pageant play, "Pageant of the People", was performed before large audiences in the Society's garage on Newland, which

had been temporarily converted into a theatre, quite a common occurrence in the 1940's and early 50's. At this time the Society's milk registrations numbered 54,700. (During the war, people had to 'register' with a milk retailer in order to obtain supplies.) At the end of five years of war, 435 employees were in the forces and 90 were away on work of national importance. Sadly, 9 employees had lost their lives and 14 out of 26 who had been discharged from the forces had returned to their old jobs. For most of the time, a special committee under the chairmanship of Frank Grainger, a director of the Society, had been at work to deal with staffing problems, reservations and the recruitment of substitute labour. This had been a major headache as more men were called up and untrained, and often unskilled, labour had to be obtained in the face of huge demands by local industry which was heavily engaged in providing materials for the war effort. In all £23,147 was paid out in grants by the Society to serving employees or their dependents. Shortly before the war came to an end the directors acquired the old Silver Street chapel and school room as well as the house numbered 15 Silver Street, for post-war development.

Commenting on the end of the war in their report of 4 July 1945, the directors anticipated with pleasure the return of the Society's absent employees and voiced thanks to them for the service they had rendered. Many had been away for more than five years, 16 had lost their lives and 4 were still reported missing. At the same time, thanks were given to those who had carried on the work of the Society and to the members who had accepted "some of the deficiencies in services forced upon us by wartime conditions". They added, "We hope the future expansion of our co-operative services will become possible as we gradually leave behind wartime conditions of scarcity and restrictions". They were not, of course, to know that several years would go by before rationing, licensing and shortage of supplies would end. But when they spoke of expansion, they could hardly have dreamt of the massive changes and developments which have occurred in the Society since the end of the Second World War.

One change which was made with reluctance in the autumn of 1945 was the retirement of Charles Mackinder, who had been cashier, sometimes described as accountant, of the Society for many years and an employee for nearly 55 years in all. His retirement, which had been postponed for 4 years by the war, was accompanied by another change in the Society's administration. John E. Harrison gave up the secretaryship and A. R. Chance, who came to the Society from

Chipping Norton Society, became secretary and chief executive officer. At the end of the war, sales for the half year were £793,243 and the dividend was 1s.9d.

The necessity for building licences, as well as food licences, to be obtained in the post-war years for new businesses limited the Society's progress and it was many years before any new premises were built. To a large extent this difficulty was overcome by purchasing private businesses and expanding them to meet growing trade and ambitions, this being particularly so in the Society's country branches. At the same time a policy of renovating old shops was pursued, whilst van rounds were developed rigorously as new rolling stock became available.

The sub-central furnishing shop at 141 High Street which had been requisitioned during the war was handed back to the Society in the spring of 1946 and by the end of the year 346 employees had taken up their old posts and the rehabilitation committee was disbanded. A memorable event in 1947 was the widespread flooding in the spring, following a winter of heavy snow. Many incidents of delays and breakdowns were reported, but in the main the food service was maintained. The biggest burden was borne by the coal workers, who were called upon to carry coal under conditions never before experienced. In spite of all the efforts which were made, deliveries did fall into arrears, the position being complicated by the large number of members who wished to collect extra coal after having used their allocation and the large number of licences for extra coal issued by the Fuel Office. After the snow came the floods. The Society's dairy was completely surrounded by water for 18 days, but although the dairy offices and messroom were flooded and had to be evacuated, the water was prevented from entering the boiler house by a barrier of board and clay and the work of pasteurising and bottling was continued. Three grocery branches, Ripon Street, Canwick Road and Washingborough, together with more than 3,000 homes in the City, were flooded and the Society contributed £250 to the Mayor of Lincoln's relief fund. Tales of heroic deeds by employees struggling through first the snow, then the floods, to deliver coal, milk and food orders were recalled for many years to come.

The Society's first female president, Annie Williams, left the City in May 1947, to return to Cheshire. Her membership of the Society went back to 1897; she first joined the board in 1928 and was president in 1934/35. A. R. Chance, secretary and chief executive officer, tendered his resignation in 1947 after he secured the position of general manager with the Oxford Society. His successor, Duncan McNab, a Scot, was recruited

Dairy staff Fred Ogden and Jack Taylor carry on regardless during the floods of 1947

Duncan McNab (left) became
Managing Secretary in 1947

from the Leicester Society and was given the title of Managing Secretary.

A private grocery shop in Boultham Park Road owned by Mrs Bransgrove, which also had a post office, was purchased in November 1947 and plans were announced for the opening of two greengrocery shops in Gresham Street and High Street. Another very important and significant change took place towards the end of 1948 at the sub-central branch in High Street, where a new method of trading was to be piloted. Workmen were busy adapting the old grocery store to self-service. Breaking this news in their report the Board commented, "it remains to be seen how Lincoln people will respond to this very latest method of shopping, but where tried in other parts of the country, it has greatly increased sales". There was, however, no cause for apprehension. Lincoln people did like the new idea and sales in the first quarter of its operation increased at that branch by 25%. It was the first step locally of a national revolution in trading and the committee decided to go ahead with similar conversions at Bracebridge, St Giles and Baggeholme Road. The Board were soon able to tell the members that self-service was here to stay and that there was no longer any argument on that subject.

Two travelling grocery shops for service in the country areas were ordered at about the same time and the first of them was brought into use early in 1949. A plan for a quick-service tea-room adjoining the cafe was abandoned because of licensing difficulties, but a decision to transfer the whole of the cafe business to the new hall was implemented in the summer of 1949. These were good times for the Society: in March 1949 dividend rose to 1s.6d. and McNab was congratulated on his management of the business. In 1950 a long-standing ambition of the Society was fulfilled by the acquisition of a grocery shop in Swift Gardens on the St Giles estate, where trade grew so rapidly that extensions were needed in less than a year. A big scheme for the modernisation of the millinery and drapery department, carried out in the summer of 1950, was the first in a series of changes made to the old Silver Street premises to bring them more in line with modern trading standards. The Board claimed that the new department was the finest in the county and the changes were rewarded with substantial increases in trade.

Perhaps the most memorable event of 1951 was the Festival of Britain exhibition on the South Bank in London. The Society's own celebrations of the Festival included two dances for employees, tea and concert gatherings on three days for members with more than 45 years' membership of the Society and a tea and film show for children holding penny bank accounts.

The report for September 1951 showed that sales had exceeded £3 million for the first time, a target set three years earlier. Changes planned at Silver Street included the conversion of the former cafe annexe in the basement to a children's department. Expansion also took place on the St Giles estate, where another small private business was purchased in Lamb Gardens and had to be enlarged almost immediately to cope with the growing volume of business. A butchery shop in Macauley Drive, St Giles, purchased in December 1951 was said to have become one of the Society's most prosperous butchery units.

Mobile butcher's shop from 1952

In the early 1950's the Society declared an aim to have a trading unit strategically placed in every major centre of population and to provide a service in the remoter areas by van or travelling shop. There were still problems in securing building licences but where it was possible to build new premises this was done. In other cases existing businesses were purchased from private owners. Members were informed in the report of March 1952 that the Board intended to modernise the whole of the central premises as soon as licences were available and that the electrical department would be extended to take in the offices known as Palfrey Chambers. Another important board decision was that future property purchases must be in the main shopping area of the City. Trade was given a big impetus by a large exhibition of CWS products, staged in the Society's garage on Brayford from 5 to 12 July 1952. A small temporary branch was opened on Richards Avenue on the Doddington Road estate and this was replaced by a better, permanent structure on Wetherby Crescent some years later. It is interesting to note that the original

Shoppers queue at the newly opened Queen Elizabeth Road branch.

plan for the Doddington Road estate was quite ambitious and included two blocks of shops with flats over, a meeting hall, public house, children's playground, two blocks of lock-up garages, eight homes for the elderly and 268 houses. That sounds like a kind of modern shopping centre and somewhat ahead of its time. Why did it never go ahead? Maybe they were beaten to the start line by the Forum at North Hykeham, just a few hundred yards away. In 1962 the Society was offered a supermarket on the Forum as it was being developed. As they already had this site surrounded by shops, the offer was declined. With hindsight that was an error. Neither the Board nor the officers could have foreseen the success which was to greet such centres. Shopping was about to change from a mere chore to the nation's number one leisure activity.

On Coronation Day, 1953, large numbers of old age pensioner members took advantage of the Society's invitation to witness the event on television sets in the new hall.

The stop/go nature of the planning for the restructuring of the central premises continued, but a significant event in 1954 was the provision of a passenger lift for the first time and the opening up of various passages to give access between departments. In June 1954 a branch was opened on Woodhall Drive on the new Ermine Estate in Lincoln with provision for footwear and drapery. Another new food shop was opened in De Wint Avenue in September 1956 and in November 1957 two new branches were opened, St Margaret's Gardens on Hykeham Road and Queen

Elizabeth Road on the Ermine West, both stocked with what was then a novelty, pre packed meat. Both shops also had full off-licences. At that time very few branches had liquor licences and applications were frequently refused by the licensing Justices. Opposition in Lincoln was led by a Methodist lay preacher who was a former branch manager and he argued that it was against the co-operative principle of teetotalism. All that gradually changed over time to the point where it is now a normal part of a food store. The cafe in Free School Lane obtained its first licence in 1962. Early in 1959 a grocery, wine and spirits store at 62/63 High Street, Lincoln, formerly known as Gordon's, was taken over.

The major event of 1960 was the opening of Silvergate House at the corner of Silver Street, Flaxengate and Clasketgate, on the site of the former AEU (Amalgamated Engineering Union) club, which the Society had acquired some time earlier. The club had been used regularly by co-operative members and was a popular meeting and drinking place. A variety of plans had been drawn up over the years but not proceeded

with for a number of reasons, including difficulty over licences and planning consents. Now though, on 8 September 1960, exactly 99 years after the Society opened its first shop, it opened what was then its flagship store, housing furniture, hardware, electrical, glass and china, carpets, sports goods and records with offices and board room above. It was said at the time that the Society went from the worst furniture department in the Movement, to the best in the county. As the curtain fell on Lincoln Co-operative Society at the end of its first Century, sales exceeded £6 million, having doubled in the last decade, it had over 55,000 members and dividend was 1s.4d in the £. There were 71 grocery branches, 30 butchers, 10 chemists and over 30 other non-food stores. Members were also told of a major decision by the Society's board. This was the complete rebuilding of the whole of the central premises in three stages over a five year period. The first step in the scheme, the demolition of the oldest part of the Silver Street store started in the Society's centenary year.

(photo courtesy Lincolnshire Library Service)

Silvergate House -
(above) under construction in 1959
and (left)
open for business in 1960

Former main Post Office on Guildhall Street (now the Varsity) was one of many building projects completed by the Society.

HOUSING FOR THE MEMBERS BUILDING FOR THE CITY

'Lincoln Society cannot be reproached for apathy in respect of...better housing for the working classes...'

It is not always readily appreciated what an important and practical role the Society played in housing its members. Many hundreds of Lincoln and Lincolnshire people have been enabled, through the years, to own their own homes with the help of mortgages from the Society. In some cases the houses were built for sale by the Society's own workforce, in other cases the transaction was a straight loan at a low rate of interest.

Once again, it was the enthusiasm for all things co-operative of Duncan McInnes which set the Society along this path in 1883.

Many years earlier a few members of the Society had advocated starting a house building department and enquiries were made about the conduct of building societies. Probably because there was insufficient capital available for such a development, a members meeting turned down the proposal, but the idea of a separate society for house building did not go away and the Lincoln Permanent Co-operative Building and Land Society Ltd. was formed early in 1872. It was registered under the Industrial and Provident Societies Act on 18 May 1872. Shares were £1 each, all transferable and to be taken up at any time, payable at once or in monthly instalments of 1s per share, per month. On the first subscription night 42 members were enrolled and 345 shares were allocated. Several of those prominently connected with Lincoln Co-operative Society were amongst the first committee of the building society. Its first building venture was a group of six houses on land in Ripon Street. Subsequently the Building and Land Society extended its activities to house mortgage and developed a banking business. It continued to play a useful part in the life of the City and the surrounding area until 1958, when it was incorporated into the Leicester Building Society. The Leicester Building Society later merged with the Alliance to form the Alliance and Leicester, which de-mutualised along with some other building societies in the 1990's and when that all went wrong, it was taken over by the Spanish bank Santander. One wonders what those early co-operators would think of that.

In 1883 the capital position of Lincoln Society was such that earlier objections to the development of housing had been removed and there was such a surplus of cash and labour that a decision was taken to build and sell to members, on mortgage, good quality houses at affordable prices. The advice of E. V. Neale, General Secretary of the Co-operative Union, was sought and a plan for advancing money on mortgage, on the basis of monthly instalments, was adopted.

The first adventure into house building was a block of 20 dwellings in Chelmsford Street and these were

offered to members, on mortgage, at a price of £165 each. So keen was the demand that the houses had to be allocated by ballot. The report of 9 July 1884 records that the Society's surplus capital was now chiefly invested in houses and land. Most of the houses were sold to members on mortgage but a number in Sincil Terrace were retained as an investment. Sites for 22 houses had been bought in Boultham Avenue and before a brick was laid 6 of these had been sold. A year later, all of the first group of houses had been bought by members and keen interest was being shown in the second group. This new venture was popular and a further success for the Society. There were occasions when, because capital was required for some other large-scale development within the Society, the mortgage department had to suspend its activities, but fortunately these occasions were rare.

HARTLEY STREET, MONKS ROAD
(Built by Society).

Soon country members were able to reap the benefits of modern housing with the Society's help. In 1896 Caythorpe members were pressing the Society to build houses for the benefit of the ironstone miners in that area and the **Record** reported that from the tone of the meeting, **"There can be no doubt that most of our members at Caythorpe will be ready to enter houses built by the Society as soon as such can be had".** A year later land was bought in Metheringham, part to be used for house building, while when land was bought in Winn Street for a branch shop, enough was purchased for the building of 18 houses by the Society's own building department. In 1898 another plot was acquired for 22 houses in Monks Road and soon afterwards members were taking up occupation of houses in Belmont Street, Florence Street, Waterloo Street and New Boultham, whilst additional land for housing was bought near to Welbourn branch. In 1899 two plots containing ten acres each were purchased at

Bardney and the **Record** was able to claim, with some justification, that **"Lincoln Society cannot be reproached for apathy in respect of the question of better housing for the working classes, for we have been engaged in this work for the last sixteen years. Now fresh fields are opening up before us in villages where small houses with insufficiency of room, insanitary conditions and defective water supply are the rule. The question now being asked is; can the Society do anything to alter these conditions? The important question 'will it pay?' can be answered affirmatively."** The report added that ten acres had been purchased at Bardney for houses and 28 one-rood allotments to let at 12s.6d a year. The estimated cost of 12 houses was £200 each. The fact that village houses were desperately needed is evidenced by a report in a local newspaper of a case at Bardney where a man, wife and seven children were living in one bedroom and it was reported that in an adjacent village, people were drinking "diluted sewage". When the Society started house building in Bardney it was necessary to sink a well to provide fresh water.

By 1900 Lincoln was growing so fast that the Society came to the conclusion that: "it has become worthwhile for us to consider the advisability of purchasing a large tract of land for houses with gardens outside the City. The forces of progress and the march of events are yearly becoming more favourable to this co-operative development. The bicycle, the motor car and the tram will play a much greater part in the future than they do now", the committee reported, once again demonstrating the quality of their vision - even trams are making a comeback in some major cities. At this time the Society had advanced £68,445 to 288 members, of which £47,438 had been repaid and it had not been

necessary to foreclose on any mortgage. The combined record of Lincoln Co-operative Society and the Building and Land Society in 1900 exceeded 1,000 houses built.

Carefully, the committee continued their policy of land purchase. In 1901 additional land was bought at Welbourn, bringing the Society's holding there to more than 13 acres and in 1904 houses were built in St. Catherines in Lincoln. At this time the Society was engaged in selling all its cottage property, but the building department continued to build houses for sale to members. One of the most substantial developments was at Monks Road, where in 1909 streets were re-named Hartley Street and McInnes Street, in tribute to those two officials of the Society and another active worker was remembered when his name was given to Coulson Road on the Boultham estate. This too was a very large scheme where development continued for many years.

At this time the Society's building committee were meeting every Monday evening in the building department's office in Tanner's Lane to receive applications for property from members. Houses in Scorer Street and Monks Road were snapped up almost before they were completed and, as an experiment, two pairs of cottages were built at Welbourn and Metheringham at the request of country members. The building operations created a stir in the two districts, the report commenting, "cottage building being much of a novelty in many country places".

Operations at Coulson Road continued well after the start of the First World War and there was also housing development at Boultham, but in 1916 the committee reported that building was almost at a standstill, "advanced prices for labour and materials making it practically prohibitive". When building came to a halt, 102 houses had been built at St. Catherine's Grove and Newark Road, 136 at Hewson Road, Fleet Street and Howard Street, 61 at Coulson Road, 32 in Scorer Street and 47 in Monks Road, Hartley Street and McInnes Street.

Loans for members' house purchase were not resumed until 1924, although the Society's works department had recommenced house building fairly soon after the end of the war. Sixteen houses were completed in St. Andrews Drive in 1924, but the largest post-war venture was on the Moorland Park estate where, in 1926 and 1927, 66 houses were built. Purchasers made a deposit of £25 and paid a similar sum on completion; the repayment rate was 2s.6d per week for each £100 owing. A show house at Moorland Park with furniture made by the Society's own works department was a great attraction

ST. CATHERINE'S GROVE
(Built by Society).

and the furniture, "was sold several times over". Further housing at Moorland Park in 1928 and 1929 added 108 more dwellings to the Society's total. Those in Harris Road cost £500, others in Bell Grove, of a non-parlour type, were sold for £445, the lower price having been made possible by a Government subsidy. When the estate was completed in 1931, a total of 204 houses had been built. Land fringing the Society's farm at Branston was developed in the early 1930's and 31 houses were completed between 1934 and 1936 on Rookery Lane, adjoining the Boultham estate. Not only had the Society afforded its members the opportunity of owning their own homes but, at a time of general trade depression, had provided very much needed employment for building trade workers in the City. Later developments were at Skellingthorpe Road, Lincoln Road, North Hykeham and three bungalows were erected in Station Road, Branston in 1959. Early in the 1950's 74 houses were erected for sale on the Doddington Road estate, the streets being named after some of the Society's directors, (Leonard B) Clarke Road, (Mary) Richards Avenue, (Sid) Buttery Close and Constance (Brooke) Avenue, although the Society did not actually build any houses on Constance Avenue. The Society's house building activities came to an end when the remaining part of the Doddington Road land was sold to Barkers, a local building firm in 1961, save for one final adventure in 1976, when 4 houses were built on Brant Road, no's 122 to 128. This was a plot which had been earmarked for a grocery branch but with changes in shopping habits, the Society decided to join other retailers on the Lowfields Shopping Centre. When house building by the Society's works department came to an end, a total of 1,144 homes had been completed, a figure which includes a number of individual houses built by the department to the member's own specification. A very small number of mortgages are still held by the Society but these are gradually maturing. Even in difficult days, the Society adopted a very tolerant attitude to those buying their homes on mortgage and in periods of unemployment was content to receive interest only, until such time as the mortgagees were employed again.

Quite apart from its house building activities, the Society's works department has, over the years, undertaken some major building contracts in the City and surrounding area. Amongst large-scale contracts carried out by the Society have been extensions at the Lincoln County Hospital; an extension to what is now Lincoln College; new public swimming baths at Boultham; a new infants school on Skellingthorpe Road; a new school on Bristol Drive; a new children's library in Free School Lane; a new craft block at the then

Lincoln Girl's High School and the building of the main post office in Guildhall Street. Many offices and other business premises were built for private sector firms. During the Second World War the department carried out several hut camp schemes for the War Department and built petrol and ammunition stores, air-raid shelters and defence barriers.

COUNTRY COTTAGE, WASHINGBOROUGH (Built by Society.)

LINCOLN, THE HIGH SCHOOL.

Another of the many contracts carried out by the Society was a new craft block at Lincoln Girl's High school

The Co-operative Mill
opened in 1886

MILLING AND BAKING

12

'Gadsby's now supply a first class range of bread and confectionery products, not only to the Society's own food stores but to a number of other stores and many private businesses'.

As was recorded in Chapter Two, the first organised form of co-operative activity in Lincoln was in flour milling. This ended in failure in 1857 and it was to be almost thirty years before co-operative flour milling was attempted again in the City, this time as part of the activities of Lincoln Co-operative Society. There were, no doubt, good reasons for the long delay, not the least being a reluctance to embark upon a venture which had previously proved unsuccessful. Yet in the 1870's co-operative thought all over Britain was once again turning to the desirability of co-operators milling their own flour, possibly within a federal organisation. Conference speakers were constantly promoting the idea and the pages of the Co-operative News were commending it to the attention of societies.

In Lincoln, bread baking had been started as early as 1867 and a bread and confectionery bakery got underway in the new Silver Street store in 1873, at least six months before the official opening.

In the spring of 1879, at a Lincoln District Conference, a Mr Jubb, from Gainsborough, presented a paper on Co-operation in Lincolnshire in which he advocated the idea of a corn mill, preferably in a central area with each society in the district taking up shares in proportion to their membership. In the same year there were reports of co-operative corn milling at Harwich, Chelmsford and Airedale. At Lincoln Society's annual festival in January 1881, William Reynolds, President, said the Society had so increased its trade that it would be necessary, in a short time, to build a mill to grind flour for the members. The Society was conducting so much business that they now had a market for any flour they could produce.

From the autumn of 1876 the Society had been grinding barley meal for sale to members with the help of an eight horsepower portable engine and mill. Country members in particular were often pig keepers and they had been pressing for some time for the opportunity to buy feeding stuffs from the Society. It was this angle of the business, the ready market for offals which could be expected, as well as the actual demand for flour in the Society's bakeries, either at the central or the country branches, which no doubt persuaded the committee, eventually, in June 1884, to buy a block of buildings, including a warehouse, malt kilns and two cottages for conversion into a mill and bakery, with stabling for horses on Waterside North. Another important factor was the Society's growing volume of unused capital; the cash account in April 1885 showed £4,000 cash on deposit. In August 1885 the quarterly meeting gave the committee powers to go ahead with a roller milling system and approved capital

expenditure of £6,000. Members also carried a resolution urging that a wholesale department should be set up, although they were told by the committee that this might not be possible for some time.

In order to provide employment for as many of its own members as possible, the Society decided that the building work should be undertaken by its own building department, whilst contracts for milling machinery, engines and boilers were let to Lincoln firms which were, at this time, on short time working. The scheme was for a "four sacks an hour" flour plant in the mill, storage for grain and flour and a new six oven steam bakery. Building work was delayed by an unduly long winter, but the new mill began to turn out flour on 1 June 1886 and the committee were able to report in July of that year that "the expenditure on the Montague Street property amounts to but little more than last year's net profits".

They recommended that, for a time, profits should be set aside for a fire insurance fund. Coinciding as it did with the Society's silver jubilee, the opening of the mill on 7 August 1886 was made the occasion of a remarkable double celebration. The account of this, published in the **Co-operative News** on 14 August 1886, so well captures the mood of the occasion that it is quoted here almost in full.

"Shortly after midday, parties of bronzed agricultural labourers and others from the Society's village branches began to arrive at the mill, anxious to get an early chance of inspecting the machinery and ovens. The engine was stopped at 12 noon so as to avoid any danger of accident from the presence of large numbers of visitors, who rapidly poured in as soon as the doors were opened. City and country

members, male and female, young and old, mingling together, all wandered at their own sweet will up and down stairs, in and out, hither and thither, narrowing passages already narrow enough and crowding up and down staircases, until many suits of Sunday black began to take a lighter hue. Many a buoyant spirited and mischievous young penny bank depositor, disporting around flour sacks, enjoying sliding down stair hand rails and dodging, with floured clothes, past black dresses, came in for a muttered anathema. Only a half-angry one though, for pleasure beamed on every countenance and every step was light with a sense of part ownership. Outside, in the centre of the mill yard, where the band, in the trimmest of uniforms, was playing, the sun shone brilliantly and the music could occasionally be felt as well as heard. Around the dough kneader in the bakehouse, a crowd of critical housewives was continuously gathered, whilst swarms of curious children clambered up its sides and peered within to 'see where the works was'. Had any evilly-disposed unseen power suddenly set the machinery in motion, there would have been a unique blend of flour, finger ends, gloves, boys hats and caps, but no element of danger was present, except the ends of the bakers peels when they drew from the ovens the hot rolls that were being baked for the 'big tea', which was to take place later that evening. Bread and rolls cleanly and sweetly baked on plates above steam pipes and no fire visible, flour kneaded, not by perspiring hands and arms of flesh, but by combs of cool steel, water boiled by steam, to see these or the appliances for these, to say nothing of the roller mills or the centrifugals or purifiers, or the bewildering maze of spouts that seemed to lead all ways and to know that they were part owners and that simply one year's profits of the Society had purchased and paid for the lot and that this place was simply a toy to what some co-operative societies possessed, was something too much for the minds of some of the village members to grasp. One of these, evidently of older standing in co-operation, lustily endeavouring to pitch his voice higher than the cornets in the band outside, button holes two or three of the greenest and with great volubility explains to them their true position as members. His uplifted stick, emphasising his remarks is seen here and there, sometimes on one of the mill floors above and sometimes in the bakehouse below, wherever there is room for a knot of people to congregate, till by the time the procession is ready to start from the Central Stores, hoarseness supervenes. A committee-man, who had good-naturedly set himself to explain to all who are within earshot the

functions of each machine near to him, from a shade of delicate navy blue clothes, gradually changes to French grey and eventually develops into a counterfeit presentation of a veritable 'jolly miller'. In spite of constant mopping, beads of perspiration trickle down his forehead, like the streams of water in the thirsty land of the psalmist. But the programme must be adhered to and now the marshals form the procession. The penny bank children each receive a ticket for a tea to be held next week. The band heads the lorries, decorated and loaded with flour and bread, the crowds of children and members fall in, the music begins and away goes the procession, joined as it proceeds, by successive contingents of members and preceded and followed by idlers and sightseers. Leaving the 'Central', it approaches the Stonebow, where the narrow street is quite blocked. Many a medieval pageant has passed through its ancient portals; many a procession of guilds, of priests and friars, but they have never before echoed to the feet of a procession like this. Like the living present slowly evolving from a past that is dead forever, the co-operative host emerges from a partial twilight under the old Bow into the sunlight in the open street beyond and the (Corn) Exchange is soon reached. Within this hall is a sight most pleasant to behold. Forty two tables have been set out with flowers and plants by the forty two ladies who are to make tea, for is it not set forth in the programme that six prizes are to be given for the most tastefully decorated tables? The room has been cleared of everybody but the judge, who is now going round the tables to make his awards. Outside, kept

Contemporary illustration of the newly built mill

at bay by stalwart police and strong doors, are the processionists, hungry and eager to get in. High above, on the balcony at the end of the hall, the forty two ladies who are competing, together with as many more who are to act as waiters, anxiously await in silence, such, surely, as ladies never observed before, the decision of the judge. One by one he drops his prize cards, the winners names are read out, each lady takes her place, the doors are opened, the cornet leads the grace with the 'old hundredth', and in relays, soon sixteen hundred are provided with a splendid knife and fork tea. The room being cleared, the chairman, William Coulson, opened a meeting numbering over 2,000 grown up people and briefly reviewed the Society's history for the past 25 years. The secretary read letters of sympathy with co-operation and regret at not being present from the Marquis of Ripon and Joseph Ruston, head of the engineering company, 'Ruston and Proctor' and a former Mayor of Lincoln and MP for the City from 1884 to 1886. Mr G Bastard of Leicester spoke warmly and effectively and was warmly received. Songs and glees followed and Mr T Wilberforce from Leeds, making his first appearance on a platform in Lincoln, electrified the audience with laughter and moved them to intense enthusiasm in a speech alternately humorous, rousing and eloquent. Local speakers, representing the manufacturers of the milling machinery also took part in the meeting, which was brought to a close at 10.20 pm, having been in all respects, the most successful, as well as the largest gathering ever held by the Society."**

A proud committee were able to report in October 1886 that, "the first quarter's working of the new mill proved remunerative", and went on, "We have sold wholesale to neighbouring societies. A higher quality of barley meal is to be made and we await the directions of members before providing machinery for wholemeal flour". Arrangements were also made for large scale purchases of offal at the same rates as those offered by local corn factors. There was a startling incident a year later when the upper floor of the Society's grain warehouse in Free School Lane collapsed and carried with it its contents and those of the floors below into the confectionery bakery. One of the most important results of the Society's new found ability to produce its own flour was that it was able, very largely, to regulate the price of bread, not only in the City but in the country areas also. It kept down the price of bread in 1887, 1888 and again in 1889, when a 4 lb loaf was sold for 4d, despite desperate appeals by local bakers and even though this meant that the dividend was slightly lower

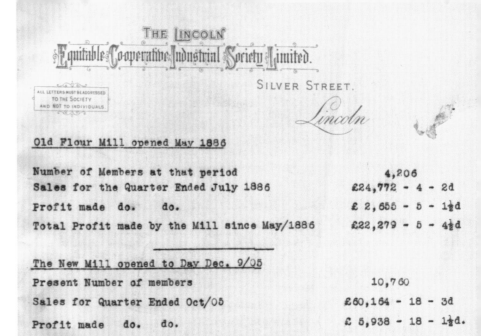

as a result. The advertisement for the Society's bread trade in Sleaford saw local tradesmen dropping the price of a 4 lb loaf from 4½d to 4d and the **Lincolnshire Chronicle** voiced congratulations to the Society on **"having broken down the ring of bakers which has so long existed here"**. Cartels were clearly not an invention of the 20th Century.

In 1889 members were notified that, because much of the previous season's wheat had been of an indifferent quality, it had been difficult to produce flour that was uniform in colour, strength and quality. But, the committee added, "we have determined to run the mill until this year's wheats are at hand, if need be without profit, using best grades of wheat only, rather than producing flour which does not do us credit". At the annual festival held on 1 February 1888, the president, William Coulson, told members they were highly satisfied with the mill which had been working about 18 months. "During the year", he said, "a trade of £11,000 had been transacted with a profit of about £800, thus falsifying the prophecies of those who said the mill would prove our ruin".

Soon the new bakery was inadequate for the needs of a growing membership and the committee reported in April 1892 that they had decided to add to the bakery the whole of the premises on the Waterside, then being used for stables, in order to provide several more ovens, a large cooling room and bread store. Adjacent land was bought to provide stabling. The new stables were finished in 1895 and permission was obtained from the authorities to place a gantry across the street so as to permit unloading from barges on the River Witham. A year later saw the bakery extensions completed and the confectionery bakery was transferred from the central stores to Montague Street.

By 1900 five country branches had their own bakeries, thus materially helping the output of the mill.

In 1903, seventeen years after the mill had been established, milling experts were called in and the committee accepted a recommendation to renew the milling plant, which had been made obsolete by new developments in milling technology. The plan adopted was to build a new mill adjoining the old one and to equip this with completely new machinery. The task was completed and the mill opened for inspection in December 1905. The old mill premises then became a warehouse. The cost of this latest development amounted to £7,000.

In 1911 a big scheme for re-building and modernising the bakery was adopted by the committee, involving the removal of the stables to Newland and the incorporation of the stable site into an extended confectionery bakery. One of the co-operative movement's first travelling ovens and automatic bread making plants was installed and a first class confectionery plant was also purchased. While this work was going on the flour milling plant was extended from a 4-sack to a 6-sack plant and the whole was driven by electricity instead of the now obsolete steam power. When the scheme was completed in July 1915, the country had already been at war for almost a year and the new plant proved to be of great value. This plant continued in operation until 1932, when the bakery was re-modelled and a new oil fired travelling oven installed. The completion of the work was marked by three open evenings when members were invited to inspect the plant at work. Fifteen hundred of them did so and were delighted with all they saw.

Horse drawn delivery cart manned by
Fred Sharp & George Walter in 1935

The milling machinery had been brought up to date in 1923, but in 1935 substantial alterations and additions were made. A bread wrapping machine was installed in 1939 and in 1950 an order was placed with Baker Perkins for a new uni-flow plant for automatic bread production and the installation of this was completed early in 1952. In addition to the bread sold in the Society's grocery stores there were many bread rounds both in the City and the country areas from the 19th Century through to the mid 1950's. These often comprised a man, a boy and a horse and cart, although in the City a one-man operation with a hand pulled cart was also a feature.

One of the most important changes at the mill in the 1950's was the installation of a suction plant for unloading bulk grain. Until that time all the grain delivered to the mill, most of it by river barge, was in sacks and three men spent a great deal of time handling it. The suction plant made light work of the task, drawing up the grain from the hold of the barge directly into hoppers. Most of the grain used at the mill either for flour or feeding stuffs was carried by barge from Hull, an average of two barge loads per week being delivered in this way in the 1950's. Over 100 stones of imported grain and 60 to 70 tons of home grown grain, most of it from Lincolnshire, was used every week at this time and bread flour, biscuit flour, brown flour and self-raising flour were produced. Flour for sale in the Society's branches was pre-packed at the flour mill. The price list from the mill in the late 1950's, containing nearly 50 items, would have astonished some of the farmers and cottagers who bought their barley meal from the Society almost 80 years earlier. There were 14 grades of poultry food, 5 of pig food and 18 types of cattle food. Antibiotics and vitamins were used to enrich some of the feeding stuffs.

During the 1960's sales in the mill and bakery started to decline, due to a number of factors. People's lifestyles were changing, families were getting smaller, they were eating less bread and fewer people had chickens and pigs in their back yard to feed.

By the 1970's, competition in the bakery market in particular was getting more keen with the emergence of national bakery operators. The Society was starting to incur losses in its own operation. In May 1971, after more than one hundred years of various attempts at milling and baking, some of them very successful and providing a valuable service to the members and the community, the Society sold its mill, bakery and confectionery operations to J. W. French, a new company formed by the CWS and Lyons. The new owners did not, however, enjoy any greater degree of success and the total operation was closed down in July 1971.

That was thought, by everyone, to be the end of the Society's involvement in the bakery trade. But that was not so, because in September 2000 the Society acquired a controlling interest in the family business of Gadsby's of Southwell Ltd, master bakers. Gadsby's now supply a first class range of bread and confectionery products, not only to the Society's own food stores but also to a number of Co-operative Group stores and many private businesses, with sales of over £3 million per year.

The Society's involvement in this business has changed greatly over 140 years, as society itself has changed and who knows what further changes lie ahead. The Society's record suggests that it will be ready to respond. On the retirement of Terry Gadsby, the son of the founder after 45 years in the business, the Society acquired the remaining shares, but the Gadsby family are still involved at the bakery.

(photo courtesy Lincolnshire Library Service)

Left: demolition underway at the old Co-operative Mill

Right and below: Gadsby's of Southwell Ltd.

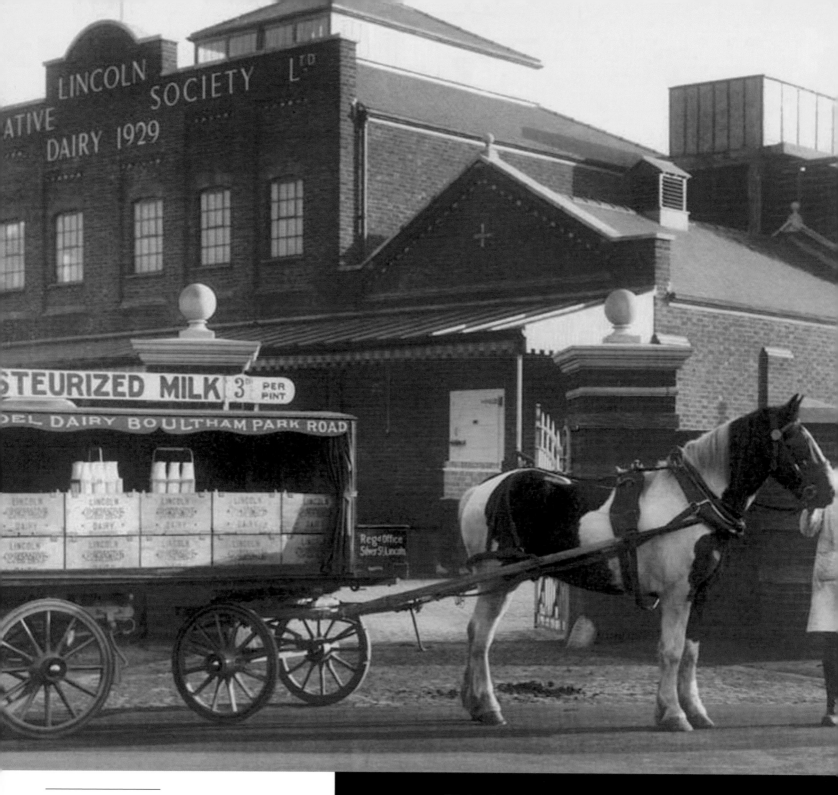

The dairy on Boultham Park Road
was officially opened on
2nd November 1929.

FARMING AND DAIRY

13

*'It is also clear that another factor
which influenced the Society's entry
into farming was an excess of
manure in the stables'.*

It is hardly surprising that early in its history, the Society made a decision to go into farming. Lincolnshire has, after all, some of the finest agricultural land in the country and many of the villages where the Society had shops in the early days, depended almost entirely on the farming community for their existence. Two factors were no doubt instrumental in driving the committee in this direction, one ideological, the other financial. Early in 1887 a paper on co-operative farming was presented to a conference of the Lincoln District Conference Association by Duncan McInnes, in which he argued that what co-operation had to accomplish was much the same in respect of land as it was in manufacturing, i.e. to devise some method by which the masses of the people or those so minded, should be permanently benefitted by carrying on farming in secure and more equitable conditions. "At a time when tenants are clamouring for lower rents and labourers are emigrating because they do not obtain sufficient from their labour to carry them decently to the end of life's journey", he declared, "our co-operative societies, such large consumers of farm produce, have not yet seen fit to utilise portions of their capital on our oldest and greatest industry. Societies would be not only landlord, farmer, money lender and labourer, but to a very large extent, consumer also". He went on to suggest that retail stores should then be planted in agricultural districts from which an educative influence would spread and which would act as receiving depots for produce. McInnes also had ideas for some sort of profit sharing. He suggested that only members of retail societies should be employed on the farms, that they should be paid wages only for two years and if at the end of that time they were accepted by the committee, they would be eligible to take part in a profit sharing scheme. He also advocated making plots of land available to any individual co-operator requiring them. What a bold and imaginative vision.

Clearly the germ of the idea for the Society's farming ventures was in the mind of the Society's secretary for at least two years before the first definite step was taken. It coincided with a period when the Society had ample funds and was looking for new outlets in which to employ them. It is also clear that another factor which influenced the Society's entry into farming, was an excess of manure in the stables.

In April 1889 a start was made with the purchase of a farm of 11½ acres at North Hykeham. (At that time the North Hykeham area was solely agricultural. Once a tiny village, since 1973 it has officially been a town, with its own town council and now has a population in excess of 10,000. There is now no green space between North

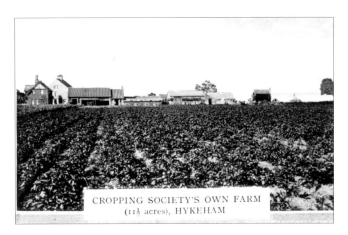

CROPPING SOCIETY'S OWN FARM
(11½ acres), HYKEHAM

Hykeham and the City of Lincoln.) At first the farm was run as a small market garden with a number of fruit trees and pigs were also kept and bred on the farm. By the 1960's it was being run as a small arable farm with one acre set aside for tomato and flower growing under glass. Over the years the Society either leased or bought various plots of land, sometimes small farms, sometimes little more than smallholdings, in the North Hykeham and Bracebridge areas. As with all the farms the results were up and down. In March 1897 there was an attack of swine fever followed by a succession of dry seasons causing disappointing results. By 1968 it had become necessary to discontinue farming at Hykeham because of an attack of eel worm. Planning consent was obtained for the change of use of Hykeham farm and the land was sold to D W L Bocock, a local builder, and this now forms the Dale View estate.

In April 1910, the committee instructed the cashier, Fred Stephenson, to attend the sale by auction of Branston farms with authority to buy up to a maximum of £10,000. He was able to report to the committee at their next meeting that Ashfield House estate had been purchased for £10,000. The house itself was leased to a tenant, whilst the Society took up the task of farming 360 acres of arable and 51 acres of grassland. Branston was completely rural at this time and while it still remains a country village, it has grown substantially. This purchase was warmly welcomed by the next members' meeting as one of the most satisfactory deals the Society had entered into and arrangements were made for members to visit and inspect this new asset.

The next big adventure into farming took place in 1915. The area chosen was Welbourn, the site of the Society's first country branch, which still held a very warm place in the Society's affections. Two small farms had been acquired here earlier, but they were let to tenants and it is possible to imagine the excitement of, what was then, a very active local committee, as they discussed the

The Society's award winning herd of Ayrshire cattle

ASHFIELD HOUSE.

ENTRANCE TO ASHFIELD FARM ESTATE.

possibility of having their 'own' farm as a complement to the village store. The Society eventually purchased a 350 acre estate which was run solely as a dairy farm, initially with Lincoln Red cattle but replaced by pedigree Ayrshires in 1948. Was this because the new Chief Officer was a Scot, or was that just a coincidence? Over the years many animals bred by the Society at Welbourn farm have won awards at some of the most important County Agricultural Shows and in 1971 the Society's prize winning Ayrshire cattle won the best of breed award at the Lincolnshire Show and the highest award in all classes at the East of England show, held in Peterborough. In the early days, milk from the farm went straight to the Society's shops and was sold directly to members.

In 1950 a farm was purchased at Welton, a small village at that time, which had not yet seen the rapid expansion of house building which has taken place in recent years. The farm comprised almost 300 acres and like Welbourn, was almost solely a dairy farm. A few cash crops were grown, but the main business was the 200 head of pedigree Ayrshire cattle, which have again won many awards at local agricultural and county shows.

The Society made co-operative history in 1908 when a members' meeting approved a resolution altering the rules of the Society, so as to include amongst its objectives the furtherance of the provision and successful cultivation of smallholdings and allotments for its members. The committee were given authority to invest surplus capital in acquiring land for these purposes. The decision followed the passing of the Small Holdings Act and is reported to have 'aroused the keenest enthusiasm of members'. Two years later the committee reported that they had received very few applications for assistance and in respect of those applications which had been received, nearly every one had had to be refused, because no security could be given. Later the Society purchased land in various parts of its area which was rented to members as allotments. Some allotments were still occupied on the Doddington Road estate and in Branston until the early 1960's.

In the summer of 1918 the Society purchased for £14,000 the Grange and Tile House Beck farms at Bardney. These consisted of 433 acres of which half was arable and half pasture. The Society's first tractor, a 25 horsepower Titan, and a three-furrow plough was bought in October 1919. By the end of the year, 150 acres had been ploughed by it and 3 horses had been sold; farm mechanisation was on its way.

Profits made on the various farms fluctuated considerably over the years. In the early days some substantial losses were incurred and it is perhaps significant that substantial profits were shown during and immediately following the two World Wars. This is noticeable from a glance at the accounts for the 1914-18 period and again at those for the period 1939-1945. In between the two World Wars profits were small or non existent. The early days of the 1920's were bad for all of the farms, but particularly Bardney and a quarterly meeting early in 1924 instructed the committee to dispose of this holding. When it was offered at auction the reserve price was not reached and it continued to be worked until 1926, when it was sold.

The co-operative movement has, for a variety of reasons, almost always experienced difficulty in making farming pay and in this respect, Lincoln was no different. The Society had rarely received a satisfactory return on its investment. In November 1976, when the Farms Manager resigned on the grounds of ill health, the decision was taken to sell. The timing could hardly have been better - farm prices were high as were interest rates. Because of the heavy capital programme which was just around the corner, any liability for capital gains tax could be 'rolled over' onto these new assets. Farms which were bought for thousands or in some cases even hundreds of pounds, were sold for £1.2 million, and the Society's reserves went from £2.8 million to over £4 million. A nineteen acre field at Branston which was retained at the time was later sold equally profitably for housing. The Society had always known, and the committee often told the members that, despite poor revenue results, the assets could always be turned into capital profit.

So McInnes' dream was not realised. In the end it proved too difficult to manage farms at arms length, but it had not been a disaster: employment had been provided at a time when it was desperately needed, members had been supplied with some produce and financially the total deal was well in the black.

With the Society's close association with the countryside and its extensive farming experience, it must have been almost inevitable that, at some stage, it should turn its attention to the dairy business. In fact it was not until 1918 that this came about, although the idea had been in the minds of the committee and officials for many years previously. As early as 1908 the committee decided to advertise for a dairy supply of up to 200 gallons of milk and to visit Peterborough, where the local society had already begun dairying. At the beginning of 1909, after the farms committee had visited Peterborough, Leicester, Derby and Long Eaton societies, they decided to adopt a milk supply system on the lines of that at Leicester and to ask members whether they would take their supplies from the Society. Evidently the result was not one to give the committee any incentive to go ahead and the next we hear is a decision to start the milk business in May 1918 – no delivery, standard prices, best quality, discount on purchases, were promised. Milk from the Welbourn farm was sold from a shop adjoining the sub-central branch in High Street, Lincoln. Nine gallons were disposed of on the first day and this had gone up to 43 gallons at the end of eight weeks. A year later the committee reported that, because of the heavy demand, another depot had been opened adjoining the

The Society's first tractor was a Titan- similar to the example shown here

Baggeholme Road branch and that new standings for 60 cows were being fixed on the Welbourn farm.

From then on progress was continuous. By January 1920 milk shops had been opened adjoining the branches in Baggeholme Road, Canwick Road, Newland and Newport and others were soon to follow at Bracebridge, Tealby Street and Ripon Street. Deliveries did not begin until 1925. The first round was in the West End of the City from Gresham Street branch and milk tokens were introduced. Members purchased the plastic milk checks at the grocery branch and exchanged them for milk from the dairy roundsmen, thus reducing the amount of cash carried by the milkman. Within a year the business had expanded so rapidly that plans were in hand for a fully equipped dairy providing for the scientific treatment of milk. A suitable site was hard to find, but by the beginning of 1929 a first class dairy was being built at the corner of Dixon Street and Boultham Park Road and this was equipped with a 600 gallon per hour pasteurising plant. In their report of 17 October 1929, the committee advised members: "On the 14th of October, the sale of loose milk by the Society was discontinued and the distribution of bottled milk was commenced. The dairy is now in full working order and the efficiency of the plant, which is the most modern of its kind, is reflected in the rapidly increasing demand for this new grade of milk which the Society consider is the best and cheapest obtainable. At the dairy, the whole process is carried out without the milk at any time being exposed to the atmosphere. The milk is pasteurised in accordance with scientific principles which leave no doubt that pasteurised milk is nutritious and beneficial to young and old; that it is free from harmful germs. The re-organisation of the milk supply is proceeding a pace and very shortly the whole of the City will be covered".

Within two years of the opening of the dairy, sales had reached 9,000 gallons a week and the service had been extended to Sleaford and to other country areas. In 1933, increasing trade necessitated the installation of a new bottling plant capable of dealing with an output of 6,400 bottles an hour. Six years later the processing capacity of the dairy was doubled by the installation of new plant and when, in 1943, the Society took over the largest private retail milk business in Sleaford, the Society's sales of milk in that area rose by more than 100%. In the closing months of the war, structural alterations took place at the Lincoln dairy and new plant, including new boilers and washing equipment for churns, bottles and crates, was installed. A year later a decision was taken to change over from the holding method of pasteurising to the newly developed high-temperature short time process. Tuberculin tested milk was made available from the Welbourn farm in the summer of 1948 and in a very short time the dairy herd at Welbourn was supplying 1,150 gallons a week. From 1934 the Lincoln dairy also produced large quantities of butter, which was sold in the Society's shops and also on the dairy rounds. This ceased shortly after the outbreak of war in 1939.

A large private processing dairy, Pinchbeck Dairies, in the village of Pinchbeck, just north of Spalding, was taken over on 1 May 1954 and this enabled an even wider area to be serviced. By the early 1960's weekly sales from the two dairies amounted to 86,000 gallons, of which 30,000 were sold from the Pinchbeck dairy.

At that time 90 rounds were operated, 60 of which were from the Lincoln dairy. Some of the rounds served scattered rural communities including Ancaster, Martin, Helpringham, Navenby, Welton, Coningsby, Ruskington, Skellingthorpe, Woodhall Spa, Heckington, Spilsby, Ingham, Nettleham, Wragby, Waddington, Billinghay, Tattershall, North Hykeham, Washingborough, Branston, Sleaford, Horncastle, Bardney, Saxilby, Metheringham and Welbourn. By the end of the 20th Century 120 dairy rounds were in operation.

In spite of the long distances which roundsmen had to travel, it was the department's proud boast that it never failed to deliver milk to customers, even when road conditions in the winter were at their worst. Even in flooding, milk was still delivered and in 1947, when the dairy was entirely cut off by flood water, the department still functioned and it was necessary for a large percentage of deliveries to be made by boat. Many letters were received from members complimenting the staff on getting the milk through in very trying weather.

In 1968, a rare example of co-operation was evident when Lincoln started processing milk on behalf of the Nottingham society for delivery to Boston and Skegness. From the beginning and for many years afterwards, milk was delivered seven days a week but by the end of 1975, with many more people having refrigerating capacity, all dairy rounds had moved to six day delivery, Monday to Saturday.

The dairy industry had been in decline for some years through falling sales and by 1980 was coming under attack from long life and imported milk. The doorstep delivery was also under threat from supermarkets which were starting to sell milk at deeply cut prices. Nevertheless, the board gave a commitment to continue to support the doorstep delivery, an important reassurance in a rural county such as Lincolnshire. In order to improve the viability of the milk rounds, the roundsmen started to carry a much larger range of merchandise, starting with other dairy products such as yogurt and cheese and ending with bottled water and grow bags. They were about to become the new generation of travelling shops. It was in those circumstances of decline that the board faced a difficult decision. The old dairy, which had served the Society well since 1929, was coming to the end of its useful life, but to build and equip a new dairy would be expensive.

The dairy continued to operate during the floods of 1947

Once again Lincoln Co-op adopted the positive approach and in June 1981 work started on building what became, on completion, one of the most modern dairies in Europe. It was the biggest capital project ever undertaken by the Society, aided by modest European and UK government grants. Milk production began in September 1982 and the dairy was fully operational by November. At the same time, production ceased at the Pinchbeck dairy. The following year was another important one for the dairy. On 28 August, the Society bought the businesses of Lincoln and Carlton Dairy, a major competitor, operating in Lincolnshire and South Humberside and D C Clarey of Market Rasen. The commitment to the dairy had not just been given in words, but demonstrated by these substantial investments. The business of Newark Dairies was bought in 1990 and later in that year, in an imaginative deal with Northern Dairies, further Newark milk business was exchanged for the Society's interests in South Humberside. Further emphasising its commitment to the dairy industry, the Society purchased, in 1994, Dairy Crest's milk business in Louth, Mablethorpe and Skegness. Also, on a smaller scale, the Society has bought many other dairy businesses over the years, often one-man dairy rounds previously supplied by the Society on a wholesale basis.

Above: inside the new dairy, opened in 1982

Below: Kool Kat promotes Milk in Schools

As the end of the 20th Century approached the shape and structure of the Dairy Department continued to change with a decline in doorstep deliveries. The loss of business was balanced by the acquisition of the CWS dairy trade in Boston and Skegness and part of the dairy business previously supplied by the Anglia Co-operative Society. Following the demise of the Milk Marketing Board in 1994 there was a period of instability in the industry. Much marketing activity had been in evidence in the Dairy Department, headed by the Society's mascot "Kool Kat" and a serious attempt was made to reintroduce milk into schools supported by a number of promotional activities.

As the 21st Century dawned, Lincoln was one of only five co-operatives still operating processing dairies. The continuing contraction of the industry presented several opportunities to acquire relatively new equipment from dairies forced to close and as a result Lincoln was able to update its own equipment at relatively modest cost which assisted the overall cost control. Vigorous efforts were being made to secure new business and in the early summer of the year 2000, after extensive development work, the manufacture of ice-cream was commenced under the "Clareys" label, the Market Rasen dairy

business acquired some years earlier. The initial success of the top of the range "Lap of Luxury" products encouraged the extension of the range to a more competitively priced Clareys Dairy Ice-Cream. The wheel had turned full circle, as the Society had produced ice-cream in the early 1930's and sold it from "Stop Me and Buy One" tricycles.

In April 2005 following a strategic review of the viability and prospects for the dairy and following the Co-operative Group's sale of their dairy business, Associated Co-operative Creameries (ACC) the previous year, which affected Lincoln's ability to participate in national contracts, the decision was taken to sell all of the dairy operations to a dairy farmers' co-operative, Dairy Farmers of Britain (DFoB). The sale marked the end of a very successful association between the Society and the dairy industry but the directors were pleased to pass on the dairy to a fellow co-operative business, run by farmers. The sale secured jobs for the staff and allowed a productive facility to continue in Lincoln. DFoB then supplied milk to all the Society's food stores and delivered doorstep milk around the county.

Sadly, DFoB collapsed on 3 June 2009. An enquiry by the House of Commons Environment, Food and Rural Affairs Committee concluded:-

"The way in which DFoB pursued its vertical integration strategy was over-ambitious, given its shortage of capital and the strength of its competitors in the processing industry. Farmers' optimism about taking control over their long-term future was a noble objective, but it was severely hampered by decisions that turned out poorly in practice.

No single factor caused the demise of DFoB, although the purchase of Associated Co-operative Creameries (ACC) for a total of £81 million in 2004 had lasting repercussions that made DFoB's future success unlikely. DFoB paid too much for ACC but, more significantly in the long term, it was not fully aware of the implications of what it was buying. The situation was exacerbated by poor communications and governance that was not always of the standard that members were entitled to expect.

We are satisfied that DFoB did not fail because it was a co-operative".

The Society had believed, as DFoB had believed, that the deal offered the best option all round, which it probably did, but success can never be guaranteed. The effort had been well motivated.

Duncan McInnes (centre, with baton)
and the Lincoln Co-operative Choir
in 1900

EDUCATION

*'... one of the greatest powers
for good in this City'.*

Although the provisional committee had declined, in 1861, to adopt the Rochdale Pioneers' rule 42 requiring the establishment of a fund for the intellectual improvement of the members and their families, the Lincoln Society's first rule book when it was printed, in Rochdale in 1863, did in fact contain a provision that 'a separate and distinct account shall be kept of the allowance (if any) for educational purposes' and fixed the number of education committee members at eleven. An education committee had been appointed on 27 November 1873 and George Hartley, president of the Society, was its president. Actually, there was no education grant until February 1877, when a quarterly meeting approved, by a narrow majority, a grant of 1¼% of the net profits for education. The first four quarters grants amounted to £32.19s.9d.

With the same spirit of self help that had characterised the Society's operation from the start, the committee set about raising funds by appealing to members, with the objective of opening a library and reading room, the first in the City to be available to the public. There were, of course, no public libraries around at this time. In their first report the committee declared: "Your committee feel assured that no arguments are necessary to show the immense importance and advantage of seeking, by the diffusion of knowledge, the intellectual, social and moral elevation of our fellow men. Towards the accomplishment of these objects we have great pleasure in announcing donations of five pounds each from Charles Seely MP and John Hinde Palmer MP." Seely was Member of Parliament for Lincoln from 1847 to 1848 and again from 1861 to 1885. Palmer was elected MP for the City at the general election of 1868 but lost his seat in 1874. He was re-elected in 1880 and held the seat until his death at the age of 75 in 1884. That five pounds might, on first impressions, seem a rather miserly amount for such worthy gentlemen to donate but, calculated by reference to the index of average earnings, it would now be worth in excess of £2,500, so it was, in fact, a very generous gesture. The committee also commented in the same report that 250 volumes of books had been presented by various members. They also appealed for further books and library requisites and for the loan of periodicals and newspapers for the newsroom.

In their report of 6 October 1875 the committee commented, "Your committee have much pleasure in informing the members that their first entertainment this season came off successfully on 11 October 1875, by which funds were increased. The Treasurer has now in hand the sum of £17.10s.1d and we have over 300 volumes of books".

John Hinde Palmer MP for Lincoln
as portrayed by Punch in 1883

Entertainments were organised in successive winters in order to raise funds and many members and other interested parties from the City volunteered their services for this exciting new development. More books and cash were donated and on 30 September 1876, a news and reading room was formally opened in the Silver Street premises by Dr. Benson, Chancellor of Lincoln Cathedral, later to be Archbishop of Canterbury. Hours were from 6.30 pm to 9.45 pm on weekdays, with a 3.00 pm opening on Saturdays.

Periodicals, a List of which will be seen hung up in the News Room; and would hereby solicit additional aid from anyone, either in Books, Papers, or Money, which will be thankfully received and duly acknowledged by any of the Committee or the Secretary.

The valuable services of the Rev. Canon HOLE have been secured to give us a Lecture in our Large Hall, on Thursday Evening, November 16th, on "VULGAR TONGUE." The Rev. Chancellor Benson and others have expressed their willingness to serve and help on this department.

On behalf of the Educational Committee,

JAMES CUNLIFFE, Secretary.

CASH ACCOUNT.

	£	s	d		£	s	d
To Cash in hand, July 4th	18	17	2	By Chairs and Stools purchased	4	13	7
„ Sale of Tickets and Programmes for Enter-				„ Table Covers...	1	6	7½
tainment	2	17	0½	„ Expenses of Entertainment	2	14	10
				„ Repairs	0	2	0
				„ Balance in Treasurers hands	12	17	2
	£21	14	2½		£21	14	2½

An interesting little cameo picture of the time can perhaps be captured from this cash account of October 1876

This venture was a great success from the start and three months after the opening the committee reported:"on Saturday evenings it is not unusual to see 40 persons reading at one time, this is all the more gratifying as at the commencement of the quarter it became necessary to adopt some means of preventing our readers from being annoyed by a number of boys and youths, many of whom, not having any connection with the Society, conducted themselves so badly that the committee determined to exclude boys altogether for a time". Later, boys were admitted by ticket only, 35 being issued, chiefly to the sons of members. At the same time regret was voiced at the facility not being available to women "whose domestic duties prevents them from visiting the news room". Another interesting reflection, perhaps, on how times and social attitudes have changed.

It was through the library that the Society first forged what were to become close links with the clergy and officials of the Cathedral. Dr. Benson had been present at the opening of the library and during the winter of 1876/77, Canon Hole gave a public lecture for the committee on "The Vulgar Tongue". The Lord Bishop and the Rev. Chancellor Benson, who was by then Bishop Designate of Truro, promised lectures and gave other support and through the Chancellor the library department received a grant of £5 worth of books from the S.P.C.K., the selection being left to the committee. The library was opened on 11 May 1878, when 11 books were taken out in the first hour. Between then and 5 October, a total of 675 volumes were borrowed, all on Saturday evenings between 7.00 pm and 8.00 pm. The committee explained that in buying new books: "Special attention is given to procure those which are most in demand among the members, ie standard works of fiction, popular histories and illustrated books of travel, but as the committee do not wish to shut out from the

library those who may wish to consult scientific works, books of reference and those which treat of specialities, it will be taken as a favour if a written request can be forwarded to the secretary", who was by this time Duncan McInnes. Old papers from the news room were sold: the daily papers at 9.45 pm on the day of publication, local weeklies when four days old and the comic and high-class weeklies at the end of the week.

In addition to maintaining the library and news room the committee organised lectures and discussions not only in the City but in the country areas. At one of these, held at Welbourn in the autumn of 1880, the church school room was crowded and the meeting terminated with an exhibition and singing by members of the education committee. The new Chancellor of the Cathedral, Canon Leeke, who presided at one of the lectures, said that his predecessor had pointed out the store to him on his arrival in Lincoln and had said, "that is one of the greatest powers for good in this City". Another clerical visitor, Canon MacDonald of Manchester, told the same audience that the first thing he would do when he returned home would be to summon a meeting of his parishioners and give them a lecture on co-operation, which he had learned that night. An indication of the educational methods which the committee used at this time was given by McInnes in a paper to a Midland Sectional conference. If they got an obstructive member, he said, they put him in the chair at their discussion meetings and tried to convert him.

But the committee had much higher aspirations than that. The Rev. J. Fowler, MA, who had been Master of Lincoln Grammar School, presiding at a gathering to celebrate the 5th anniversary of the opening of the reading room, said that in future they would, by bursaries and exhibitions, pass on the apt sons of members from the elementary schools to the grammar schools and then to the universities. Canon Worledge, who was vice principal of Lincoln Theological College, told the gathering that as long as Canon Leeke and himself had the direction of students for holy orders, they might rely upon it that the great co-operative system should be placed before the students in its proper light as a great, if not the greatest, force for good now at work.

In 1882 the library was opened from 1.30 pm to 2.30 pm on Fridays for the benefit of country members who came in to market. One of the greatest drawbacks to the work of the committee at this time, according to McInnes, was the fact that hundreds of working men put in so much overtime that "their lives were little, if anything, better than the life of a beast of burden. They could not be said to live, they existed, they vegetated on the face of the earth which God had given man to enjoy".

In the summer of 1883 the library had to be closed for three months for repairs. So badly had the books been used, or rather misused, by some of the borrowers that more than 250 volumes needed thoroughly repairing, whilst many others deemed to be beyond repair had to be destroyed. In order to avoid a repetition a librarian was appointed and anyone returning damaged books was called on to pay for them.

A 19th century public reading room

Another facility introduced in 1889 was the provision of a refreshment room, with tea and coffee bar, on market days and Saturday evenings. The opening hours were, however, extended soon afterwards. The menu looks very tempting.

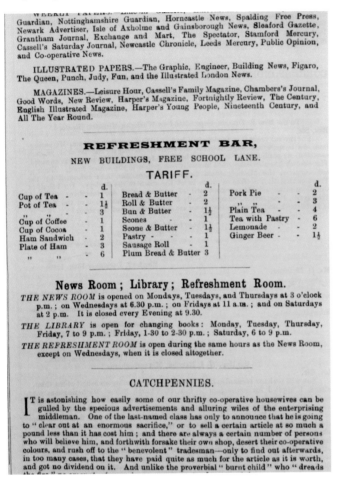

News Room; Library; Refreshment Room.

This refreshment bar was part of the new and improved facilities which were made available to the education department by the extensions to the Silver Street premises and which, like their predecessors, were opened by Dr. Benson, who was now Archbishop of Canterbury. The new library, nearly 30 feet long, had a patent indicator to show which books were available and which had been lent out. The reading room was a lofty apartment nearly 40 feet long and was described at the time as "one of the lightest rooms ever built for the purpose". The refreshment service took place in, what was described as, "a conversation room", which was more than 30 feet long and the committee are said to have had particularly in mind the needs of the country members when it was planned. The opening of the new department was marked by a festival on Saturday 2 November 1889, during which tea was served in the Corn Exchange to 2,800 people.

There was a wide choice of reading matter available in the news room, including *The Standard, Daily News, Daily Chronicle, Daily Telegraph, Pall Mall Gazette, Manchester Guardian, Manchester Examiner, Leeds Mercury* and the *Sheffield Independent*. Local newspapers regularly on display were the *Lincoln Gazette, Lincolnshire Chronicle, Horncastle News and the Spalding Free Press*. Magazines included *Leisure Hour, Cassells Family Magazine, Good Words, New Review, Harpers Magazine, The Queen, Building News, Fortnightly Review* and *All the Year Round*. McInnes resigned from the secretaryship of the committee in 1890 after 14 years in that office. Totally unconnected with this event was a resurgence of noise in the library, but this time it was decided to deal with the problem by displaying a "Silence" notice, rather than exclusion.

Sick nursing classes had now been organised for women, with an average attendance of 43, whilst a singing class for children had 250 members. The library had a stock of 2,335 books, 1,165 having been added in one year, with total issues of nearly 30,000. Saturday evening was the busiest time with a turnover of nearly 9,000 books during the year.

Gymnastic classes for girls and boys were added and children's festivals and entertainment were organised. Messrs. Hutchins and Liversedge, "Irish and Negro comedians", were engaged for one of these events, which, when advertised, boasted: "two hours continuous fun may be anticipated, plantation songs, clog dances, and sketches". The Drill Hall was engaged for a flower show on 27 August 1898 and this was the forerunner of many similar and highly successful events.

A branch library was opened at Welbourn in October 1898, with 300 volumes and 9 boxes of books were also sent for circulation in the neighbouring villages. The Welbourn venture lasted 6 years, when a lack of readers caused it to be withdrawn. Lantern lectures were, however, rather more popular in the villages. A senior choir had now begun to make a name for itself and in February 1899 sang a cantata "Magna Charta" and for the first time the choir provided the entertainment at the Society's annual festival on 27 January 1900. Later, the choir took part in a big co-operative festival at Crystal Palace. Interestingly, the singers paid their own expenses, 5s each. The junior choir was founded in 1901 and made its first appearance at one of the flower shows and at a children's festival, when they sang an operetta, 'Bo-Peep's Picnic', with Polly Kirkby as Bo-Peep and Thomas Sharpe as 'Bob Batter'.

This was also an era of picnics, by wagonette. Typical of them was one held in mid summer 1904 when the education committee organised a propaganda meeting at Clifton on Trent. Friends and members of the choir went in brakes and wagonettes, through Doddington and Thorney Woods. After a tea, which was said to have been 'splendidly served' to 120 people, a concert was held in a field with glees and choruses by the choir. A "racy and powerful speech" on co-operation was delivered by the committee's secretary. Even more idyllic was a similar event held at Hackthorn Park in August 1904. This time the wagonettes drove through Sudbrook, Scothern, Dunholme and Welton. Tea was served under the great trees in the park and a concert was given on a terrace overlooking the lake.

For many years the senior choir, conducted by Mr. D. E. Hirst, who was a chorister at Lincoln Cathedral, not only provided a useful source of musical activity for members of the choir, who numbered nearly 100, but also provided pleasure to thousands of the Society's members and friends. In addition they backed up the Society's propaganda efforts in the country districts. No winter programme was complete without three or four village concerts and a great many outlying areas were visited in this way.

Many good causes in the City also benefitted from their efforts. One notable event was a Sunday evening concert in aid of a fund set up by the Mayor of Lincoln for the victims of the typhoid epidemic which swept the district in 1905. In 1912 the **Record** reports that concerts had been given to raise funds for a local church activity. When private traders had been asked for help by these churches, the churchgoers had been told to go to the Co-operative Society for help, as they did for their

The senior choir was conducted for many years by Mr D.E. Hirst, chorister at Lincoln Cathedral

goods. The education committee saw this as an opportunity to help the churches concerned and to do useful propaganda work for the Society. Many new members were brought into membership as a result. The junior choir, which was seldom less than 120 strong in this period, was constantly recruiting new members from around the area and was extremely popular at local concerts.

The instructor of the gymnastics classes for many years was Sergeant Roberts, who was a drill sergeant at the local military depot. He was followed by Sergeant-Instructor Bentley who, in 1910, had a class of 43 girls and 55 boys. Each season's instruction was followed by a public display of gymnastics. When the First World War began the then instructor, Sergeant Davison, was recalled to his regiment, the Scots Greys and for the remainder of the war Mr H Clarke took over, whilst the ambulance class instructor, Mr T Trafford, who was associated with the St. John Ambulance Brigade, was called up and served in a military hospital. He was succeeded by Mr Jeffory.

For most of the war the military authorities were in occupation of the large hall, where choir rehearsals and classes normally took place and there were periods when activity was almost at a standstill, but the junior choir continued to be active and gave a series of monthly concerts at local military hospitals. One former junior choir member, Leonard James Keyworth, was one of the first servicemen to be awarded the Victoria Cross during the war. During a senior choir concert at Bassingham, a Belgian refugee joined in the proceedings with a Belgian version of 'Tipperary' in Flemish.

The library, which had experienced some decline in the early years of the war, became extremely popular later on and in 1918 issued 64,353 books and this increased to 72,798 the following year. When activities were resumed in the autumn of 1919 the gymnastics class had the largest membership in its history. A dancing class, which was started for members and their sons and daughters over the age of 16 at the same time as gymnastics resumed, had twice as many applicants as could be accommodated. A valuable wartime innovation which was continued for many years was the award of two or three scholarships for the sons of members, tenable at Lincoln Technical School.

A decline in the use of the news room led to it being closed at the end of 1931, but the library remained open and reported an increase in users. The space vacated by the reading room was converted to a recreation room equipped with billiard tables. Subscriptions were 6d a quarter, payable in advance. This continued to be a

(illustrations courtesy Mr Eric Croft)

Cartoon drawn by Lincoln artist A.E. White in 1905 blames members of Lincoln Corporation for the typhoid epidemic- caption reads: "why not boil them for ten minutes in their own water"

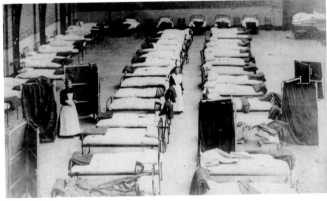

Dixon Ward at Lincoln County Hospital prepares for victims of the epidemic

A few months before the start of the Second World War, the decision was taken to appoint a full time education secretary, but before it could be implemented the war had started and it was not until the end of 1946 that an appointment was made. The first holder of the post was Mr H G Clode, who had held a similar position with Doncaster Society and under his direction the department took on a new lease of life. He was succeeded in September 1949 by Harold Thompson, who came from Manchester and Salford Society. When Thompson died suddenly in 1957, Ron McCartney took over the post. McCartney left in 1963 to be replaced by Arthur Shearsby and in 1966, George Elsey, a former Mayor of Lincoln, was appointed to the position.

The war years had been difficult ones for the education department. The choirs continued to operate but with a marked shortage of men in the senior choir. A valuable service was the provision of a soldiers rest and recreation room which was run by the department. Youth clubs and other youth activity were organised by a full time officer and the library was re-organised.

After a chequered history following the war, the senior choir was disbanded in 1959, but a year earlier a new choir, the Swanpool Co-operative Girls Choir had been formed. By the early 1960's this had a membership of 35 to 40 each year and was conducted by Maurice Lancaster. The choir won a number of prizes at musical festivals in the area. Various attempts were made to form other choirs in the years following, notably at Ermine, Bracebridge and St. Swithins, but they gradually faded away and the Swanpool choir itself folded in 1975 when most of the choristers failed to re-join after the summer break of 1974.

An amateur drama group, the Co-operative Players, was revived in 1958 under the direction of the producer Tom Pickering. This group enjoyed some success for a while and also won trophies at a number of local drama festivals, but was disbanded in February 1962. In 1964 the Lincoln Folk Song Club was formed and in March 1965 it was reported to have 430 members and this rose to nearly 700 by September of the same year. The club proved very popular and was supported by professional singers for a number of years. Like other groups, it had its ups and downs and eventually closed in June 1968.

The Gainsborough and Lincoln Society education committees had been working closely together since the mid 1960's, then, when Gainsborough Society formally merged with Lincoln in 1968, it brought with it a choir and a Music, Speech and Drama Festival. The Gainsborough and Lincoln festivals merged in 1970, the event being held in each location in alternate years, but

popular activity right into the Second World War, when it was thrown open to members of the forces. After the premises had been requisitioned by the Ministry of Works, the Institute, as it was known, did not re-open. A 16mm sound film projector came into use in 1936 and this gave first class service for many years, being in particular demand at country propaganda meetings. An innovation in 1937 was the holding of a children's camp on the Society's farm at Welbourn, with the Welbourn branch manager being responsible for the catering. This was the first of many, including two harvest camps which were held after the war, in collaboration with the War Agricultural Committee, one of them being attended by 120 children.

the festivals finally ended shortly afterwards. The Gainsborough choir ceased to operate in 1972. Gainsborough also brought a Darby and Joan Club to the merged society, which still operates to this day.

The library finally ceased to function in May 1960, after a very useful life of 84 years, and the remaining books were sold to the Lincoln Friends of the Hospital Association.

A change in the operation and control of the Society's educational work took place in the autumn of 1959. The education committee was then reduced from 12 to 6 in number and its functions were prescribed as those of member education, youth and cultural work. Weekend and summer schools etc were run, together with courses on consumer affairs. Staff training became the responsibility of the board of directors and the education secretary took on responsibility for the Society's publicity and public relations, in addition to his

educational duties. What they had done was to create a position where the post holder was responsible to the board of directors, through the managing secretary, for part of his duties and directly to the education committee for another part. Not ideal in terms of governance.

In 1968 the education committee changed its name to the Member Relations Committee and at the same time changed its constitution so that four members were appointed by the board of directors and three were elected from the membership, supported by a part-time secretary. A grant of £1,000 per annum was allocated, but activity had declined to such an extent that in some years they did not even spend that amount. There was the occasional fashion show or product demonstration and the odd social event, but the department reached its lowest point by the late 1970's and must have been on the point of collapse. But that was all about to change.

Silver tipped conductor's baton engraved with the inscription -
1928
Co-operative
Choir, Lincoln

Membership and Community Stand
at a county show

MEMBERSHIP AND COMMUNITY

15

'...the dividend card...firmly restored the link between membership and dividend. The pattern of events had gone full circle'.

In the early days, the members were very closely involved in almost every aspect of the Society's activities and there were many member events, exhibitions, festivals as well as educational, social and cultural experiences. Members outings were, for about twenty years, a major happening in the co-operative calendar. This level of activity tailed off over the years as a result of lifestyle changes. Two major internal events added to the decline: the introduction of professional management in the 1940's put too much distance between the Board and the members and the change to dividend stamps in 1970, which meant that non-members could obtain virtually the same benefits as members without having to join. This trend was, however, reversed in the 1990's as the Board sought to re-engage with the membership and introduced the dividend card in 1998, which firmly restored the link between membership and dividend. The pattern of events had gone full circle.

The changing levels of activity is clearly demonstrated by the fact that the grant for Member Services activity has gone from £1,000 in 1980 to nearly £300,000 in 2011 and membership has risen from around 50,000 to over 200,000 in the same period.

From the very lowest point in the late 1970's the level of activity gradually started to increase during the 1980's. A part time Member Relations Assistant was appointed and a number of new events were introduced. Many of these were in support of the trading divisions: travel promotions, photographic, gardening and freezer evenings and hair and beauty demonstrations. The co-op fashion show became quite an event in Lincoln in the 1980's.

There were also events aimed at children including Breakfast with Santa, a Teddy Bears Picnic and a number of competitions. More serious subjects were occasionally tackled as with the Bereavement Conference and Environmental evenings, but the profile was still fairly low.

All this changed in 1993 with the launch of Area Member Groups, based on a single shop or a group of shops in a small, geographically tight locality.

Unlike systems operated by co-operatives in other part of the UK, these groups were informal, unelected bodies.

The objectives were simple: to manage the Community Action Fund (a pot of money to be distributed to local good causes), to arrange social, cultural and educational events locally, and to facilitate two way communication between the membership and the management.

Recruiting new members in 1994

Horncastle was chosen for the first group and this was launched in September 1993, and later rolled out to the rest of the Society's area. Groups now operate in Lincoln North and South, Horncastle, Newark, Gainsborough, South Lincolnshire, Long Sutton, Market Rasen, Sleaford and Grimsby.

A number of minor changes have been made over the years, but the groups largely operate in accordance with the original concept and feed into the democratic structure of the Society.

Another significant change in 1993 was the decision to enhance the profile and concept of the Society's Annual General Meetings (AGMs). Up until this point, there had been the main meeting in Lincoln, plus branch meetings in Newark and Gainsborough, resulting from the mergers. All were rather low key and fairly poorly attended. The geographical spread of the AGMs now

Santa at Spalding in 1996

includes Horncastle, Spalding and Grimsby. From a low base, attendance has steadily increased to 741 in 2010.

1994 was 150 years since the formation of the Rochdale Pioneers Society and a number of events were organised to mark the occasion. Concerts were held all over the county, but the two highlights were both held towards the end of the year and both in Lincoln Cathedral.

The first was an exhibition of co-operative banners from all over the country, mainly historical, but including a brand new one made specially for the occasion by Horncastle Area Members Group. The exhibition attracted thousands of visitors from around the world.

The second event was a carol concert involving the Foss Dyke Band and the Orpheus Male Voice Choir, with an attendance of over 700. This concert was intended to be a one-off event, but such was its success that it has been held every year since and now attracts well over 1,000 people.

1996 saw a return to the Lincolnshire Show for the first time in many years. In the 1960's and 70's the

Society's pedigree Ayrshire Cattle had been regular prize winners but with the sale of the farms, attendance at the show ceased. The Society's presence is now a considerable one, showcasing, amongst other things, our range of locally sourced products.

In 1997, the Society launched Kool Kidz Klub for children aged 5-11 years and Club 12-16, started some time later, was subsequently re-named Activate. The clubs organise a range of activities and involve the young people in the running of them, introducing a new generation to the concept of co-operation. There are currently over 3,000 members of the two clubs.

Also in 1997 the Member Relations Committee was re-named Member Services Council and expanded to include Directors, senior managers, all Member Groups, Co-operative Ladies and employees.

One of the most important events in the Society's recent history, was the introduction of the dividend card in 1998. Dividend stamps had served the Society well for nearly thirty years, but it was now time to embrace new technology. The smart card system exactly mirrored the "old" stamp system. The initial allocation of points onto the dividend card had a pre-determined value in line with the value of dividend stamps. At the end of the financial year, an additional bonus, or Final

Display of co-operative banners in Lincoln Cathedral to celebrate 150 years since the formation of the Rochdale Pioneers Society

Kool Kat and friends celebrate the launch of Kool Kidz Klub on 2nd November 1997

Dividend, which is dependent on the profitability of the Society, is recommended to the AGM and if approved is paid to members. Initially, this bonus was paid into share accounts but is now paid directly onto dividend cards. Final dividend started at 20p for every £1 of dividend points earned in 1998, and by 2010 had reached 75p. Dividend card is very flexible, enabling much promotional activity. Currently 5 times points are awarded on local produce, fresh fruit and vegetables, fair-trade goods, pharmacy lines and funerals. Dividend card represented a return to a "genuine" co-operative dividend and has been a huge success and the major factor in the surge in membership since 1998.

End of an era - the last dividend stamp is issued in November 1998

A mobile exhibition trailer was created in 2000, visiting local shows throughout the summer to talk to members about the benefits of membership. Since then hundreds of shows have been visited and many thousands of members and non-members have heard the co-operative message.

Impressive results for the first Charity of the Year

In 2001/02 the idea of charity of the year came to fruition. The first was LIVES and the amount raised was £18,000. In 2010 the charity of the year, chosen by members, was Macmillan Cancer Support and £90,000 was raised.

The Society sponsors many local organisations both large and small. In 2002 the Society started its sponsorship of Lincoln City Football Club and the Lincolnshire Co-op Community Stand. Also in 2002, the members magazine "Esprit" was launched which is now published three times a year.

Member groups support many local good causes with grants of up to £500. In 2003, a Community Dividend Scheme was introduced, to award grants of up to £2,000 determined by the Member Services Council. In 2010 grants amounted to £121,000. At the same time a community dividend card was launched to enable community groups to collect points and receive a bonus.

In 2005, a "Healthy Habits" programme was started to teach children the benefits of a healthy lifestyle. This ran for five years and engaged hundreds of young people. In 2010 an alcohol awareness programme was introduced in schools.

Members are encouraged to play an active part in all aspects of the Society's life and perform a vital role in our democracy through Member Groups, Kool Kidz and Activate, the AGMs, elections, social, cultural and educational activities.

Chef Jamie Oliver lends a hand with the Healthy Habits programme

CO-OPERATIVE WOMEN'S GUILDS

The Co-operative Women's Guild started in England in 1883 and played a very active part in the co-operative movement for many years. It provided cultural and social opportunities for female members and led a number of campaigns for women's rights. It still exists, but times have changed, numbers have reduced and it is less active now than previously.

The first steps towards the formation of a guild branch in Lincoln were taken in October 1888 when a public meeting was held in the City. That meeting was addressed by Margaret Llewellyn Davies, a towering figure in the women's guild movement for many years who was president of the co-operative congress in Brighton in 1922. The meeting was also attended by Mrs Lawrenson from the National Guild and Mrs Cracroft of Hackthorn Hall who was a close friend of the Society.

Women's Guild, Bracebridge Branch 1911

Four years went by before anything else happened and there was another meeting, held in November 1892. Again, Miss Llewellyn Davies was the speaker and 'all women connected with the Society, either as employees, members or wives or daughters of members', were invited. The guild was formed, a provisional committee elected and members were recruited very quickly. An early item of expenditure by the new guild was £7.7s.5d for gymnasium fittings, not for guild members, but for a class of young girls. Mrs Hodgett was the first president of the Lincoln branch. One of the first events for the new guild was a 'public tea' at which a new committee was elected. Mrs Hodgett was president of the national Guild Congress at Blackpool, in 1901

and the **Record** reported that **"Her business ability in the chair is said to have excelled each of her predecessors".** Two years later Mrs Hodgett again presided over the national Guild Congress and on this occasion it was held in Lincoln. The national Guild Congress was held in Lincoln in 1942 and again in 1992 when on this occasion it was said to have been one of the most successful they had ever held.

Lincoln started with one women's guild branch at the centre but by 1961 there were eight and in 1974 nine branches including Gainsborough, Washingborough and Birchwood and membership exceeded 400.

Members changed the name of the organisation to the Lincoln Co-operative Ladies in 1999 and at that point ceased to affiliate to the national guild organisation. There is now just one branch previously known as Central and average membership is around 50. The ladies meet weekly and take part in outings and other activities.

The Womens Guild (Lincoln Co-operative Ladies) has done excellent work for well over 100 years and indeed has provided many Lincoln Society directors over the years from its membership.

Women's Guild, Conference at the Lawn 1992

Gainborough Adventure Playground

The first National Co-operative Development Agency (CDA) was established by Jim Callaghan's government in 1978, mainly to promote worker co-operatives. It was wound up in 1989. After this, a number of local CDAs were set up around the country, usually by Labour controlled local authorities and with all the attendant bureaucracy.

Nothing happened at local government level in Lincolnshire and Lincoln Co-op simply watched developments.

By 2002 Lincoln Co-op decided that an attempt should be made to set up a CDA in Lincolnshire but wanted a less formal, more action-focused structure.

A dinner was arranged to which were invited many parties whom the Society thought might have an interest in starting a CDA: the County Council, a number of District Councils, Business Link, Lincoln University, Prince's Trust, Lincolnshire Development, the Credit Union network, various quasi public bodies and charities. Presentations were made and questions answered. The bodies attending were invited to make a contribution towards the establishment of a CDA and a sufficient number responded positively to enable a start to be made. A business adviser was appointed with minimal administrative support.

The Lincolnshire CDA started as a department of Lincolnshire Co-operative and began to help prospective social/co-operative enterprises throughout the county. A steering group was established, drawn from those contributing to the start-up costs.

The organisation continued in this way until 2007, by which time the entity had grown to such an extent that the informal structure was no longer considered appropriate.

Lincolnshire Co-operative Development Agency (CDA) was incorporated in August 2007. Members were recruited and a Board of Directors elected from the membership. The Secretary of Lincolnshire Co-operative became the Secretary of the CDA. The lead adviser became Chief Executive.

The CDA has helped many small groups become established as social enterprises. Its funding now comes from Lincolnshire Co-operative, bids against public funds, project income and the Co-operative Enterprise Hub (part of the Co-operative Group). The CDA currently has in excess of 200 members and has supported over 300 organisations to date. A very wide variety of organisations have been assisted with small grants ranging from community groups, projects for children and the elderly, arts and crafts and transport-related enterprises.

Lincoln Castle was one
of the two main venues
for the 1998
Co-operative Congress

CO-OPERATIVE CONGRESS

16

*'...one of the most enjoyable...
and brought enormous credit to the
Society and the City of Lincoln'.*

113

The Co-operative Congress is the annual gathering of co-operative activists. Its purpose is threefold: it is the annual meeting of the Co-operative Union (now Co-operatives UK), it is an opportunity for society delegates to discuss current issues and it is a chance to meet fellow co-operators in a relaxed atmosphere.

It has often been described as the Parliament of the co-operative movement, but it is hardly that, as decisions are not binding on societies, except in respect of Co-operatives UK itself.

The first Congress was held in London in 1869 and the event was generally held in urban towns and cities until the Second World War, then mainly at seaside resorts, now a mixture of each.

Attendance at the 1869 Congress was 107 and remained in the hundreds until the 20th Century, then between 1,000 and 2,000 until 1950. From 1951 until 1964 delegate numbers generally exceeded 2,000, after which attendances started to decline. In recent years delegate numbers have been around 500, due to mergers between societies.

Beginning with the first Congress in 1869, a Congress President was elected to preside over the event; to begin with, a President was elected for each day, but from 1896 a single President was elected for the whole Congress. Being President was considered the highest honour in the UK Co-operative Movement, with societies nominating individuals for the position in recognition of their contribution to the movement. A ballot was then held, in various forms over the years, to determine who should be elected. The President chaired the Congress and gave a keynote address. The position of president was abolished in 2007. The style and content of congress has also changed significantly, being more like a trade fair, with less formal debates. The length of the event has reduced also, to just two days, having run for five or six at its peak. Congress has been held in Lincoln twice – in 1891 and 1998.

1891

Just 30 years after Parker and his fellow workers had opened their first small store in Napoleon Place, Lincoln Society was host to the Co-operative Congress, a remarkable tribute to the strength and importance of the Society in the co-operative landscape at that time.

It was said at the Glasgow Congress of 1890: "If the Lincoln Society succeed in receiving Congress as well as they have succeeded in all their other co-operative efforts, the delegates at the Congress of 1891 will have ample grounds for being well satisfied." What a wonderful tribute.

580 delegates attended from all over Britain.
The Congress was held on 18, 19 and 20 May at the Drill Hall in Broadgate, but most delegates arrived on Saturday 16th and many stayed over until Thursday 21st.

Delegates at Lincoln's first Co-operative Congress in 1891

Delegates were provided with a list of hotels and inns with tariff rates for bed and breakfast and 'attendance', ranging from 2s.6d at the Sloop Inn or the Horse and Groom, to 4s at the Durham Ox, or 6s.6d at the Saracen's Head, the most expensive. It was also said that accommodation at private lodgings could be obtained from 2s.

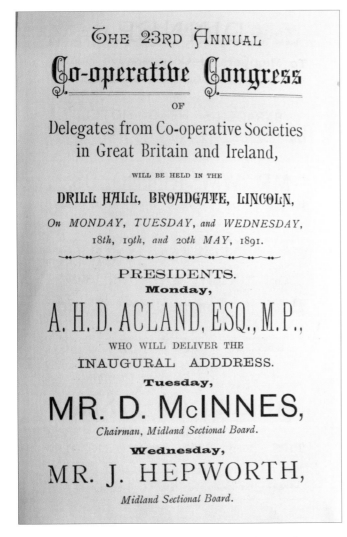

The President on the first day was Sir Arthur Dyke Acland, a liberal politician and writer, who was a strong supporter of co-operation. The honour of the presidency on the second day was given to Duncan McInnes in his capacity as Chairman of the Midlands Sectional Board.

There was what was described as a dinner at 2.00 pm on Saturday 16 May at the Saracen's Head hotel, chaired by William Reynolds, President of Lincoln Co-operative Society and in the evening a public meeting and concert was held in the Drill Hall with solo vocalists and a selection of Glees and Part Songs sung by the Lay Vicars of Lincoln Cathedral.

Church services were held at 10.30 am on Sunday 17 May, at Newland Congregational Church where the preacher was Rev. J D Jones and in Lincoln Cathedral where the preacher was the Lord Bishop of Lincoln at 3.00 pm.

An exhibition by Co-operative Productive Societies was held in the Corn Exchange from Saturday 16 May to the end of the Congress. The exhibition was opened by the Mayor of Lincoln, E Pratt Esq. The list of exhibiting societies paints an interesting picture of the nature and extent of co-operative productive activity at this time and the following list gives a flavour:-

Bromsgrove Nail Forgers
Hebden Bridge Fustian
Kettering Boot and Shoe
Leek Silk Twist Manufacturing
London Bass Dressers
London Stick Manufacturing

In all nearly 50 productive societies participated in the exhibition.

Four Prize Papers were presented during the course of the Congress.

1. *The best method of bringing co-operation within the reach of the poorest of the population.*

2. *How best to consolidate and improve the position of productive societies.*

3. *How best to utilise the increasing surplus capital of the movement.*

4. *The best means of bringing co-operation and trade unions into closer union.*

On Monday 18 May the 8th annual meeting of the Women's Co-operative Guild was held in the Co-operative Hall on Silver Street and a further concert, this time described as a Conversazione, was held in the Drill Hall on Tuesday 19 May.

What was described as "a ramble through the city", which was included in the Congress handbook, will be of great interest to Lincoln residents and visitors alike. It starts at the Midland Railway Station and the principal venues visited are listed below.

• St Mark's Church in St Mark's Street
• Portland Place Chapel in St Mary's Street, close to the central station
• St Mary-le-Wigford Church
• St Mary's Conduit
• The Corn Exchange (now owned by Lincolnshire Co-operative)
• St Benedict's Church

- Thomas Cooper Memorial Chapel
  (also in St Benedict's Square)
- Brayford Pool • High Bridge • Stonebow • Guildhall
- Newland • Newland Congregational Church
- The Masonic Hall
  (also on Newland close to Lucy Tower Street)
- The Racecourse
- Mint Street Congregational Baptist Chapel
- St Peter at Arches Church (on the north side of
  Silver Street, close to the Stonebow, now removed and
  re-erected as St Giles Church on Lamb Gardens)
- The Butter Market (just round the corner from
  St Peter at Arches, on the High Street)
- City Assembly Rooms (above the Butter Market and
  occupied by the Mechanics Institute)
- Theatre Royal
- St Martin's Church (now the offices of Jobcentre Plus,
  top of Orchard Street)
- The Jews House
- The Bishop's Hostel (Diocesan Theological College)
- Blue Coat School
- St Michael on the Mount
- House of Aaron the Jew • The Castle
- Exchequergate • The Bishop's Palace
- Grecian Stairs • Chancery • St Mary Magdalene
- Church of St Paul in the Bail
- County Assembly Rooms
- Bailgate Wesleyan Chapel • Newport Arch
- Rasen Lane Chapel
- Saxon Street Free Methodist Chapel
- The Old Barracks (Burton Road)
- The Work House (Union Road)
- Lunatic Asylum (Union Road, now
  The Lawn complex)
- Penitent Female's Home (Carline Road)
- St Nicholas Church • The Foss Dyke Canal
- St Peter in Eastgate Church • HM Prison
- The County Hospital • The Arboretum
- Monk's Abbey
- Schools of Science and Art (Monks Road)
- The Sessions House (bottom of Lindum Hill)
- Wesley Chapel (known locally as Big Wesley)
- Methodist Free Church (Silver Street)
- Lincoln Equitable Co-operative Industrial Society –
  central stores and offices
- Drill Hall • St Swithin's Church
- The Liberal Club
- Stamp End Works (Clayton & Shuttleworth)
- The Sheaf Iron Works (Ruston, Proctor & Co)
- The Globe Works (Robey & Co)
- Stamp End Locks • St Andrew's Church
- Canwick Road Cemetery
- South Park

- County Pauper Lunatic Asylum (close to South
  Park and the South Common)
- St Botolph's Church
- St Peter at Gowts Church
- The Hall of the Great Guild of St Mary (top of
  Sibthorp Street)
- Hannah Memorial Chapel (on the site of the present
  Thomas Cooper Memorial Church)

Quite how long it would take to do this particular
'ramble' is anyone's guess. There are also many pages
devoted to descriptions of the Cathedral.

Congress sittings were held from 10.00 am to 1.00 pm
each day and from 2.00 pm to 5.00 pm. Luncheon was
provided for delegates in the Agricultural Hall on
Monks Road.

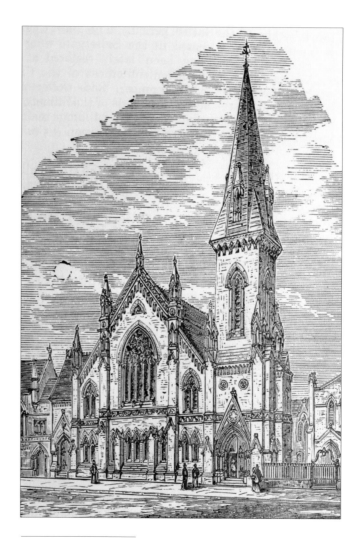

Newland Congregational Church, venue for Congress
church sevices and one of the many sites visited on the
"ramble through the city"

116

1998

The Co-operative Congress came back to Lincoln in 1998 after a gap of 107 years. Nearly 1,000 delegates and guests enjoyed three wonderful days in the City. For the first time the CWS Annual General Meeting was held on the same weekend.

Delegates arrived on either Friday 22 May or Saturday 23 May and were accommodated at various hotels and other venues in and around the City, including the Inland Revenue Residential College, Lawress Hall at Riseholme, and the Petwood Hotel at Woodhall Spa. A fleet of buses transported delegates around. In order to accommodate all the Congress events, the whole of The Lawn complex was taken over and a huge marquee was erected in the grounds of The Lawn, where the main Congress sessions were held. A further marquee was erected in the grounds of the Castle and many other rooms in the area were used for various one-off events.

Main Congress sessions were held in a huge Marquee in the Lawn complex

Marquee in the grounds of Lincoln Castle

The Congress President was Alan Middleton who had, by that time, been a Director of the Lincoln Society for more than 30 years and was also a member of the Board of the Co-operative Union.

The events got under way with a pre Congress dinner at the Judges' Lodgings on Friday 22 May at which the great and the good of the Co-operative Movement were present.

The CWS AGM was held in the Congress marquee on Saturday 23 May. This was followed by a 'welcome reception' for all delegates in the same location on Saturday evening.

The main Congress began on Sunday 24 May with the opening ceremonies followed by the presidential address. Lunch was provided at a series of fringe meetings in The Lawn buildings or the various marquees. After a full business session in the afternoon, there was a reception and banquet in the Castle marquee, at which the Lincoln Symphony Orchestra entertained and the evening ended with fireworks and a piped band finale.

The Annual General Meeting of the Co-operative Union was held on Monday morning and a luncheon for all delegates was held in the Castle marquee, sponsored by the Co-operative Insurance Society. After another full business session in the afternoon, delegates attended a pre-concert buffet reception in the Castle marquee, sponsored by the Co-operative Bank. The whole weekend was rounded off by a magnificent concert by the East of England orchestra in the Cathedral.

The Congress was widely regarded as being one of the most enjoyable and well organised in living memory and brought enormous credit to the Society and the City of Lincoln. Co-operators throughout the UK still talk about 'the Lincoln Congress'.

Alan Middleton makes the presidential address

Nettleham Foodstore - opened in 1962

INTO THE SECOND CENTURY

17

'Superstore shopping became available to everyone, in the centre of the City, with a municipal bus station alongside and a 400 space car park on top'.

So many things had changed for working people in the first century of the Society's existence that Parker and his colleagues would be amazed and proud. Disposable incomes were far higher, there was much greater mobility and even car ownership was a fast growing feature in the lives of ordinary people. Rooms in squalid houses and riverside warehouses had been replaced by quality supermarkets and superstores. The Society started its second Century 16 years after the end of the second world war as an established organisation, accepted by the community, highly regarded and valued by its members, providing good services and a cash dividend. By the 1960's, consumers were becoming more aware of their power, retailing had changed dramatically in the 100 years since 1861, but there were few hints of the revolution that lay ahead. As early as 1948 the Society had experimented with self-service at the sub-central branch and it was judged to be such a success that other conversions quickly followed. Throughout its history the Society has constantly upgraded to keep pace with modern developments and to meet the needs of its members and customers. It has also been necessary to close units where they have become uneconomic and move branches as the population has moved. Stand alone butchery and non-food shops had been largely eliminated by 1961, for the most part incorporated into larger composite units.

During the 1950's the Board determined to gain a more substantial presence in Lincoln City Centre. A number of shops were purchased just south of the High Street level crossing. One of them was a wet fish shop, a well known family business "Smalley's", and another was the medieval 'Whitefriars', which was eventually to become home to the jewellery department.

Society store located in the former Great Northern Hotel stable block - south of the High Street level crossing

By this time, the Society was experiencing real problems in maintaining a high cash dividend, credit, delivery and death benefit, in the face of increasing competition. In response, the first instant dividend store opened in one of these properties on 18 August 1961. The experiment dispensed with the traditional dividend and cut prices deeply. It proved popular with the members and was to be repeated at other branches later.

Directors were now offering two alternative types of trading: traditional dividend and instant dividend. The directors declared that they felt there was still a place for the traditional dividend, but it was a dilemma. In their 1962 report the directors announced: "Prices, especially in the grocery trade, are becoming very keen but we are doing everything possible to meet all competition. The two services which we gladly give to our members, of delivery and credit, are very expensive". It was becoming clear that the traditional dividend on food just had to go.

An important purchase in 1960 was that of the Town Hall Cinema in Market Rasen. A new store was opened on the site in March 1962. In the 1980's another site was assembled in Market Rasen by purchasing Marshalls garage and a piece of land from the National Westminster Bank. This enabled the Society to erect a large new supermarket, which opened in May 1987. Further pieces of land have since been acquired which has enabled extensions to both store and car park, now one of the Society's finest and an asset to the town of Market Rasen. In 1961, the Society bid £100,000 for the former Regal cinema in Lincoln High Street, but was unsuccessful; the building was later sold to Littlewoods. The growing Birchwood estate in Lincoln saw its first co-op shop open in September 1962, whilst new food stores opened in North Hykeham, Pinchbeck, Bracebridge Heath and Nettleham. A chemist shop had been purchased in Sincil Street in the 1950's with two other shops adjoining. The first Sincil Street supermarket opened on this site in 1964 alongside a revamped chemist's shop.

The Society had had an interesting history in regard to liquor licensing with many opponents claiming it was against co-operative principles, but by 1962 the Society were actively promoting off licences for Christmas drinks.

In 1961 the decision was taken to change to annual financial reports and half yearly meetings, dispensing with the quarterly meetings.

The Society's Managing Secretary, Duncan McNab, who had been Lincoln City Sheriff in 1962/63, left in 1964, to join the London Society, the largest in the country. Stanley Bett, his assistant, who had worked for the Society since the age of 17, was appointed to succeed him.

By 1967, trade in all traditional grocery branches was falling with only the instant dividend shops showing increases. The message was clear and a rapid conversion programme was embarked upon. A method of trading known as 'Krazy Kuts' had been tried very successfully at other societies, in particular at our neighbours in Gainsborough and Newark. This form of trading was very basic. All fixtures were removed from the shop and goods were offered for sale in cardboard boxes stacked on wooden pallets. It presented an image of cheapness and the first trial in Lincoln was at Winn Street branch in August 1967. As with the first instant dividend shops Krazy Kuts branches paid no dividend, offered no credit or delivery service and as purchases were not recorded they did not count for death benefit. The experiment proved to be such a success that over the next few years all branches were changed to this method of trading. It was a vital move, the Society's image did suffer, but the change had been necessary. A base line had been established from which the Society could build. Krazy Kuts formed a very important bridge from a form of trading which had served the Society well for over one hundred years, to the start of a new beginning and the fine range of modern stores we have today and which started to emerge in the 1970's.

The Society opened its first modern supermarket on 20 April 1967 next to Whitefriars in Lincoln High Street. Although small by today's standards, it was yet another demonstration of the Society's determination to keep pace with modern retailing developments. The building itself met with some opposition from the local history society and the public, as it obscured the view of the recently restored Whitefriars building with only a narrow passage between the two.

By 1969, technology was starting to play a greater part in the business. The check office had been mechanised and members' share accounts transferred to computer, via the CWS computer bureau.

The major event of 1970 and another very significant one, was the introduction, on 12 November, of dividend stamps. This was a national scheme run by the CWS and was facilitated by the Trading Stamps Act of 1964. Under the scheme, members and customers received stamps every time they made a purchase, which they affixed in a special book provided for the purpose. Completed books could be exchanged for goods, or for a smaller amount of cash, or could be deposited in a member's share account. Now, non-members could benefit from co-operative trading, although members received an additional bonus for every book presented. Unfortunately, this did weaken the link between membership and dividend. Many people did not join the Society, judging that the additional members' bonus

The Society's first modern supermarket, on Lincoln High Street

Dividend Stamps introduced in 1970

was insufficient to make it worth bothering. The system did, however, prove very popular and was used for nearly 30 years with great success to return profits to members and customers and as a promotional tool. The scheme finally ended in 1998 with the launch of the dividend card. The withdrawal of Lincoln Society from the National Dividend Stamp Scheme saw the closure of the scheme nationally.

For over 60 years the Society's grocery warehouse had occupied a three storey Victorian building in Firth Road, rented from British Rail. This facility, which serviced the Society's largest trading department, was both inefficient and costly to operate, clearly quite unsuitable for the adoption of modern trading techniques. Early in 1973 a modern warehouse on Doddington Road in Lincoln, vacated by S.P.D. (Speedy Prompt Deliveries), the distribution arm of Unilever, was acquired and extended. This significant investment in a modern distribution centre was made at a time when many societies, faced with similar problems, were opting in to the developing CWS-owned Regional Distribution Centre System. The Lincoln move was accompanied by a change in the historic management structure and the appointment of a Food Trades Officer to achieve integration in the food departments. In 1975, changes in legal requirements forced the end of slaughtering at the abattoir, first opened in 1919, and the former cold storage facility on the Doddington Road site was converted into a Meat Distribution Centre, thus bringing together total food distribution onto the one site. This did not, however, last for long because, as the food division grew in size and importance, it was necessary to move into additional warehousing at the corner of Doddington Road and Whisby Road, a unit first acquired for the non food departments.

On 1 April 1973 Value Added Tax (VAT) replaced Purchase Tax and Selective Employment Tax. Also in that year, the branch committee conference, which had been a feature of the Society's democratic structure for nearly 100 years, was discontinued through lack of interest. Later in the year the Board decided to honour its long serving employees. Gold watches were presented to all employees with 25 years service. 105 men and 8 women, with a total of 4,210 years service between them received the award. Over 100 attended the actual ceremony on 29 November and there has been a reunion every year since, at which new members of the '25 Year Club' are presented with their watches. Later, the scheme was extended to recognise those employees who had completed 40 years service.

The giving of credit, which had been a problem for Lincoln and other co-operative societies since the very early days, was gradually starting to change. Krazy Kuts had removed it from the grocery shops and the plastic card was to take over in other departments. Barclaycard was first accepted in Co-operative House in 1971 and the Society introduced its own 'Co-op Card' in 1975, at the same time winding down the old Trading Club system which had operated since the 1930's. The Society now welcomed credit customers, interest was charged on the Co-op Card outstanding balances and records were kept on computer.

The Society was extremely disappointed that an application to build a superstore on the dairy field at the corner of Dixon Street and Boultham Park Road was rejected by the planning authorities in 1973. However, the Society determined to continue the upgrading of its branches and shortly afterwards new units were opened at Welton, Branston, Metheringham, Waddington, Washingborough, Woodhall Spa, and Spalding. Welton, Branston, Metheringham and Woodhall Spa were all very successful and have been extended, refitted or rebuilt several times since. Spalding was incorporated into a larger development later on but Washingborough had to be closed because, as new housing developments took place, the Society's shop was on the very edge of the village. It was necessary to withdraw the food offering from Waddington due to competitor activity, but a pharmacy branch and post office continues in the same unit. A new store was acquired in the Market Place at Wragby in 1976. The Society went into Cherry Willingham for the first time when two units were bought on The Parade and opened on 3 April 1979. Two major openings took place in 1980 on the fast growing estates of Brant Road and Birchwood. Both units incorporated the latest retailing developments and both were situated in prime positions in new, modern shopping centres, providing a wide range of goods and services for the shopper. Birchwood opened on 11 September and Brant Road on 9 December. Each of these developments illustrated the Society's determination to follow the population, as new estates and dormitory villages grew and the older areas of the City saw their population decline.

On 12 November 1977, Stanley Bett, whose job title had been changed the previous year to Chief Executive Officer, retired after 47 years service, 13 of them as Chief Officer. He had steered the Society through some difficult years which had seen dramatic changes and left it in good shape and with a promising future. Tom Agar, his number two for 13 years, was appointed to succeed him. 1980 ended with two further honours. Alan Middleton, a Director of the Society for 14 years, was elected to the Central Executive of the Co-operative Union, the first time anyone from Lincoln has achieved such a position and Tom Agar was elected to the CWS Board, also a first.

After long and protracted discussions involving Lincoln City Council and others, and following a planning inquiry, the City Council eventually accepted the Society's tender for the redevelopment of Thorngate car park and planning approval was received on 1 July 1976 for a 35,000 square foot superstore at the rear of Sincil Street. Now at last the Society could compete with the biggest and the best on equal terms. Superstore shopping became available to everyone, in the centre of the City, with a municipal bus station alongside and a 400 space car park on top. It was the biggest development ever undertaken by the Society. The store was opened in a carnival atmosphere by the President, Alan Middleton, on 15 August 1978 and contained food, furniture, electrical, audio, floor coverings and kitchens. It was a very proud moment for the Society. It quickly proved to be a huge success and facilitated the re-organisation of the remaining city centre departments. The Society's board room and main offices were moved to a new location on the top floor of Co-operative House in 1979.

The premises of the well known Lincolnshire family business of Achurch & Sons in Ruskington were acquired and a fine new store was erected and opened on the site in November 1985, together with a pharmacy and post office. The unit has been extended and refurbished on a number of occasions since.

In 1982 a 14,000 square foot supermarket with petrol station was opened at Galley Hill in Sleaford. In 1989 the store was revamped and a national 'DIY' retailer was brought onto the site which was re-launched as

President Alan Middleton (right) opens the new Sincil Street store with Dr Who (Jon Pertwee) in 1978

the 'Northgate Centre'. Unfortunately this mix did not seem to work very well and in the face of competitor activity, the Society withdrew from the site and relocated to a new position on Lincoln Road in the town, together with the post office. It was completely rebuilt in 2008.

Unfortunately some very small uneconomic branches had to be closed and there was a touch of sadness when, in the 1980's, Welbourn, the Society's first country branch was closed having served the community for over 100 years and also Newport in the historic part of Lincoln. The handcart, used at Newport in the days of order delivery, had some years earlier been placed on permanent loan with the Museum of Lincolnshire Life, where a small replica co-operative shop was also created.

This handcart from the Newport branch is now in the Museum of Lincolnshire Life

Also in the Museum of Lincolnshire Life is this replica of a co-operative shop

An application was made to East Lindsey District Council for a 10,000 square foot store in Horncastle, but the planners considered that to be too large. Approval was given for a 7,500 square foot store in January 1984 and the Watermill Centre opened in November of that year. The store was so successful that it was extended twice, eventually to a size of 14,500 square feet, almost double the original store. The range in the Watermill Centre included food, electrical merchandise and housewares, together with a coffee shop. There was some nervousness about this unit which was the best in Horncastle by a very long way. A number of national multiple food operators had been attempting to secure a site in the town for a number of years. Fearing that if and when one of them was successful, the effect on the Watermill Centre would be disastrous, the Board agreed to sell to a competitor.

Horncastle was not however abandoned and other units have since been acquired in the town, including a convenience food store in High Street, a pharmacy, the main post office, a funeral home and a travel outlet.

In 1983, a piece of land was purchased from Barclays Bank in Long Sutton. More land was accumulated over the next three and a half years and a modern store opened in the town in November 1986, after winning planning permission on appeal. A petrol filling station was developed on the site shortly afterwards. This store, which is undoubtedly one of the Society's finest, has been extended and refurbished many times since and remains a great asset to the Society and to the town of Long Sutton.

One of the early co-operative principles had been political and religious neutrality, but the Co-operative Party was founded in 1917 'to promote its values and principles'. The Lincoln Society did not join at that time. The Co-operative Party is an independent registered political party with strong links to the Labour Party. However, a Lincoln Society Co-operative Party branch was formed in 1943. This functioned for nearly 40 years but in a very low-key fashion and meetings were generally poorly attended. In 1981 the Society's members agreed that it should be wound up and shortly afterwards the Board of Directors determined to return to political neutrality. That position has enabled it to work with all political parties for the benefit of the membership and the community.

Legislation introduced by Harold Wilson (above) and Edward Heath in the 1960s had lasting consequences for the co-operative movement.

18

THREE SIGNIFICANT FINANCIAL EVENTS

'The very survival of the Society was at stake; drastic action was called for and taken'.

Shortly after the Society entered its second century, three significant financial events took place which affected not only Lincoln but every other co-operative in the country. Life would never be quite the same again.

Resale Price Maintenance (RPM)

The first, in 1964 and one of the most significant events of that year, which had a rather dramatic and long lasting effect on the finances of the Co-operative Movement, was the abolition by Ted Heath, President of the Board of Trade, of resale price maintenance. This was a device by which manufacturers controlled the selling price of their products. Therefore, with all retailers selling at the same price, the co-operative dividend was the only discount available. Following its abolition competitors started to make significant cuts in prices, which customers found very attractive. Co-operatives had no option but to follow them. Gross margins, which had contributed to the provision of high dividends for so many years, declined rapidly. This was a double blow for co-operatives. Trade was lost but the dividend, which had been the traditional method of fighting competition, was also under pressure. In their report of 4 September 1965 the directors commented, "we are keeping under close scrutiny the effects of the abolition of Resale Price Maintenance and we are pledged to pursue a competitive price policy". The abolition of RPM was the beginning of the end for many co-operative societies, but Lincoln fought back with alternative strategies.

Edward Heath, President of the Board of Trade in Sir Alec Douglas Home's Conservative government abolished Resale Price Maintenance in 1964

Selective Employment Tax (SET)

What was probably the most severe blow of all to strike the Co-operative Movement was the imposition in the budget of 1966, by Jim Callaghan as Chancellor of the Exchequer in Harold Wilson's Government, of Selective Employment Tax. This tax, which was presented as an attempt to transfer labour from the service sector into manufacturing, cost the Lincoln Society £72,500 in the first year and was increased by 50% in 1968 and by a further 28% in 1969; all this at a time when the net profit of the Society was only £400,000.

The very survival of the Society was at stake; drastic action was called for and taken. It was accepted, however reluctantly, that the Society could no longer sustain delivery, credit and death benefits, as well as a dividend at 1s.3d in the pound. The first step was to reduce the dividend on bread and milk checks to 9d as an alternative to charging for deliveries. Later, a delivery charge of 6d was introduced, but this proved so unpopular that it was discontinued very quickly.

Substantial turnover was lost so the move was counter productive. Nevertheless further economies were necessary. The move towards instant dividend food shops, with no credit, delivery or death benefit was accelerated. It was also considered essential to reduce the heavy transport costs and over the next few years a total of 132 vehicles were taken off the road. This is how the **Co-operative News,** reacted to selective employment tax.

"Nothing that has happened since Mr Callaghan introduced his so-called selective employment tax proposals has modified our view that this is a thoroughly bad and dishonest measure. It taxes the people's food, it will provide free gifts, without any sort of selection, to all types of manufacturing industry, and it will not result in a single distributive employee being transferred to manufacturing. Indeed Mr Callaghan has himself admitted, in spite of his talk about the growth of employment in distribution, that such transfers are not the real basis for his proposals. His aim has been to raise additional revenue and it cannot be denied that if the Government is to go ahead with its desirable social benefit schemes it must tap additional sources, or increase existing ones. He has fallen for the obvious charms of a simple measure which does not obviously hit the ordinary citizen by raising the standard rate of income tax, or adding to purchase tax.

But its very simplicity is also its weakness. All manufacturing industry qualifies for a free gift of 7s.6d. per man, whether it is engaged in producing machine tools for export, or fruit machines or horror comics for use at home. All distribution – except the one-man shopkeeper – must pay."

To those who had survived the removal of RPM it was another devastating setback, it felt like a punishment for providing the services which the members wanted. Yet again the number of societies fell.

Chancellor James Callaghan introduced Selective Employment Tax in the 1966 budget

IN THINGS ESSENTIAL, UNITY; IN THINGS DOUBTFUL, LIBERTY; IN ALL THINGS, CHARITY

CO-OPERATIVE NEWS

Telephone: TRAfford Park 2991

NOT SO SIMPLE TAX

NOTHING that has happened since Mr. Callaghan introduced his so-called selective employment tax proposals has modified our view that this is a thoroughly bad and dishonest measure. It taxes the people's food, it will provide free gifts, without any sort of selection, to all types of manufacturing industry, and it will not result in a single distributive employee being transferred to manufacturing. Indeed Mr. Callaghan has himself admitted, in spite of his talk about the growth of employment in distribution, that such transfers are not the real basis for his proposals. His aim has been to raise additional revenue and it cannot be denied that if the Government is to go ahead with its desirable social benefit schemes it must tap additional sources, or increase existing ones. He has fallen for the obvious charms of a simple measure which does

Millom

Then, in 1969, a small society in Cumberland, Millom, went into liquidation. The event received national coverage in the press, radio and television. A senior official of the Co-operative Union went on a popular early evening TV programme, NATIONWIDE, to be interviewed about the affair. It was suggested (yet again) that the financial structure of co-operative societies was weak and there was even an attempt to question the stability of the Co-operative Permanent Building Society.

There was a run on co-operative share capital. In Lincoln this amounted to more than £100,000, but in some parts of the country it was much worse. Once again Lincoln's financial strength saved it from serious trouble.

The incident made the movement very nervous about further liquidations and this resulted, over the next few decades, in many mergers, some of which were not necessarily in the best interests of the wider co-operative movement. Strong larger societies started to bail out their smaller and weaker neighbours. This led the small and weak to believe that they could take risks with their society's finances, safe in the knowledge that a 'lifeboat' would always be there to rescue them. It led to some very reckless acts. The Millom affair also caused co-operative societies to review their financial structures and move away from their dependence on members share capital. In Lincoln this amounted to no more than a policy of financing capital programmes from retained profits; in many other cases it meant a recourse to bank borrowing which led to serious troubles of a different kind. There are two final ironies to 'Millom'. The first is that the Millom members received more than one pound for every pound of share capital, therefore nobody lost a penny. The second is that the Co-operative Permanent Building Society changed its name to Nationwide and, as a result of that, Lincoln Society in common with many others, severed its connection with them because they had removed the name Co-operative from their title, although they remained a mutual and still are.

The Society's first travel destination was the Great Paris Exhibition of 1900

19 TRAVEL

'The coach, a 33 seater, will be the last word in luxury and particular attention has been paid to ensuring the maximum comfort of passengers'.

The first reference to the Society having been involved in the travel trade appears in the Society's **Record** of 1899, announcing that the Society had started an agency for Cook's Excursion Club to take members on personally conducted excursions to the Great Paris Exhibition, of 1900. Subscriptions of one shilling per week were required from members and a total of 61 subscriptions, to take part in the excursion, which presumably meant that the total cost was £3.1s. For this, members would leave Lincoln on Saturday afternoon, spend Sunday, Monday and Tuesday in Paris, where reserved accommodation was secured. Breakfast and dinner was provided each day and two admittances to the exhibition. All fees to servants and porters were paid, luggage was conveyed on arrival and departure, and an excursion to the palace and grounds of Versailles was included.

The next reference to travel describes a rail trip to London in 1924 as a "great success", but unfortunately no other record of the outing exists. However, we can take it that it was a great success as it was repeated the following year, 1925. On this occasion the maximum number permitted was 550 and all of the places were taken up. The format of these outings was that the Society hired a whole train which departed from Lincoln very early in the morning. Passengers were served breakfast on the train. On arrival at the destination, coaches were hired to take the members to various places of interest. Luncheon and high tea were provided as part of the tour. At the end of the day passengers re-boarded the train, were served supper and returned to Lincoln arriving in the middle of the night. On this occasion the London train stopped at Harmston and Leadenham on both journeys. A Manchester trip in the same year gave members the opportunity of visiting CWS factories. The cost of the outing was 27s for London and 18s.9d for Manchester; a savings club was arranged for members.

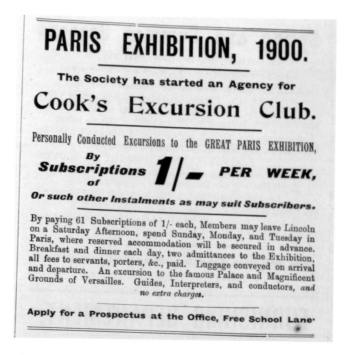

PARIS EXHIBITION, 1900.

The Society has started an Agency for

Cook's Excursion Club.

Personally Conducted Excursions to the GREAT PARIS EXHIBITION,

By Subscriptions of 1/- PER WEEK,

Or such other Instalments as may suit Subscribers.

By paying 61 Subscriptions of 1/- each, Members may leave Lincoln on a Saturday Afternoon, spend Sunday, Monday, and Tuesday in Paris, where reserved accommodation will be secured in advance. Breakfast and dinner each day, two admittances to the Exhibition, all fees to servants, porters, &c., paid. Luggage conveyed on arrival and departure. An excursion to the famous Palace and Magnificent Grounds of Versailles. Guides, Interpreters, and conductors, and no extra charges.

Apply for a Prospectus at the Office, Free School Lane.

The next members' outing was to Edinburgh in 1929 in conjunction with Messrs Cook & Sons and the London, Midland and Scottish Railway Co. The format appears to have been the same, a long train journey in each direction with breakfast and supper served on board, coach tours around Edinburgh, including luncheon and high tea. On this occasion the cost was 32s.6d. The 1930 outing was to Torquay, 356 members taking part this time.

From this point on, the outings were a regular feature in the Society's calendar and proved particularly popular with members, who saved up throughout the year in order to participate. The format had been clearly established and was not significantly changed.

In 1931 the "Day Trip", was to Glasgow, Kyles of Bute and Inveraray and included a 180 miles steamer trip in

Members about to embark on an outing to Edinburgh in 1929

"calm water". The cost was 35s which equates to around £90 today. This was described as a fine opportunity for members who would like to see some of the beauty spots on the south-west coast of Scotland.

The 1932 outing to the Isle of Wight sounds a very interesting one. The train departed from Lincoln Central Station at 3.00 am and travelled to Portsmouth. Members were served breakfast on the train. On arrival at Portsmouth they transferred to the Isle of Wight ferry and were transported to the island. On arrival they boarded a number of coaches for a full day tour, including luncheon and high tea. After tea they once again boarded the ferry and returned to Portsmouth where they spent the evening or at nearby Southsea.

At 10.00 pm they once again boarded the train and were served supper before arriving back at Lincoln the next morning. The cost was again 35s. The 1933 outing was to Rhyl and North Wales, 1934 Penzance and Cornwall and 1935 Loch Tay and Taymouth Castle.

In 1936 the destination was Margate which included a tour of the Kent and Sussex coasts and concluded with an evening in London; theatre tickets were available. Northern Ireland was the destination in 1937 and the journey involved a short sea trip from Stranraer to Larne. In 1938 the outing returned to Glasgow and on this occasion included a visit to the Empire Exhibition and a motor coach tour of Loch Lomond and the Trossachs. In 1939 the outing returned to Devon, 329 members participating this time.

Members outings were suspended for the duration of the war but in 1947 the committee announced that they had entered into an arrangement with WTA (Workers Travel Association) for holidays and outings, the Society acting as agents. The first outing after the war was in 1949 to Llandudno.

The format appears to have been exactly the same as the pre-war outings but on this occasion it was arranged via the CWS Travel Service. The 1950 outing was scheduled to go to the Wye Valley but had to be cancelled due to a poor response as the numbers did not reach the minimum required to justify the expense. The outing would have cost £1.12s.6d.

The directors' report of 24 June 1950 contained this statement: "We have pleasure in announcing that we have purchased a motor coach which will be delivered and available for hire as from August bank holiday. The coach, a 33 seater, will be the last word in luxury and particular attention has been paid to ensuring the maximum comfort of passengers. When any of our members are contemplating an outing they should apply to the general office for a quotation".

A very special members outing in 1951 visited the Festival of Britain in London. After the stresses and strains of war and rationing this was a big event and was said to be one of the finest ever held in this country up to that time. The Society reserved a special train for the first Saturday in June, which left Lincoln early in the morning and returned from London late at night. As ever, meals were provided throughout the day. The outing on this occasion was arranged on a non-profit basis. Several hundred members, many of whom had paid in advance by instalments, travelled to London and many others who had failed to book early enough were disappointed. In addition the newly purchased motor coach was used to convey other parties.

From that point on, the Society's focus on the travel business appears to have changed. The Society's motor coach and others hired in for the purpose were mainly used for outings. In 1952 a coach tour was to the Lake District, with an early start, breakfast, dinner and tea provided. On 6 June 1953 there was an outing to London to view the Coronation decorations.

The Society continued to arrange members' outings, sometimes a day trip, sometimes a full week's holiday and to act as agent for other tour operators including the CWS Travel Service, the WTA and the WEA (Workers Education Association), but this was still very much a part time adjunct to the duties of a clerk in the general office.

In 1979 the decision was taken to establish travel as a separate department, a manager was appointed and a unit created for the purpose in Co-operative House. This was an immediate success: the business grew very rapidly, far exceeding even the most optimistic expectations. Over a period of time, branches have been established throughout the Society's trading area and later on some of those in edge of town locations, with car parking, have proved very popular with members. In 2002 the Society entered into a closer working relationship with the Co-operative Group, giving access to a national brand, improved marketing and better buying terms, but the Society still retained its own identity.

The Society currently operates ten travel branches at Tritton Road and Carlton Centre in Lincoln, Sleaford, Balderton, Gainsborough, Spalding, Long Sutton, Grimsby, Louth and Horncastle.

Horncastle travel branch

Holland Brothers
Jaguar showroom on
Outer Circle Road, Lincoln.

PETROL STATIONS
& MOTORS

20

'...the Society was selling the Mini, Metro and Maestro - thousands of them...'.

There had been talk about the Society's possible entry into the motor trade for some time: many co-operative families were now car owners and motoring was no longer the preserve of the wealthy. The first reference in print appears in the directors' report of September 1965, when it was announced "that work would start, during the next half year, on the petrol station and motor showroom at Newland". The motor showroom did not happen, but a petrol station did open on Newland on 14 January 1967, next to the transport depot. Also in the 1965 report, members were warned that work would commence "some time next year" on the Inner Ring Road (Tritton Road) and that this would cut through the Society's sports field, "which had afforded healthy recreation and pleasure to staff and members since 1934". The sports field was, in fact, compulsorily purchased and the only compensation which the Society received for its loss was £9,000 and the retention of a strip of land for a petrol station which opened on 11 April 1968. Tritton Road was intended to be a dual carriageway road and the Society's petrol station was to be on the northbound carriageway. The dualling did not actually come about, which is why the petrol station was set so far back from the road. The land to the east of Tritton Road now forms part of the sports field of the Usher School on Skellingthorpe Road.

Top - the Society's sports field in 1967

Below - Tritton Road under constructi[on] later the same ye[ar]

(photos courtesy Lincolnshire Library Service)

Gainsborough petrol station opened in 1973, in North Street, opposite the Northolme football ground, home of Gainsborough Trinity Football Club. Newark petrol station opened in Albert Street in 1986, next to the Society's food and durables store in Victoria Street. Following this, there was a period of rather rapid growth in the number of filling stations, triggered in part by a change of supplier from Mobil to Fina. As part of the deal, the Society acquired three new stations, at Otter's Bridge near Saxilby, Riseholme Road and Outer Circle Road in Lincoln. Sleaford petrol station opened on Lincoln Road in 1987 and over the next few years further stations were added at Spalding, Whaplode, which incorporated a food store and post office, and at Carholme Road in Lincoln, the latter known as "Winning Post" because of its proximity to the old racecourse. At all of the petrol stations, great efforts were being made to improve the quality and range of the merchandise carried in the forecourt shops. In no case is this more true than at "Winning Post", where a 2,900 square foot convenience store was later developed on the site. A small petrol station was opened at Long Sutton alongside the Society's new food store in 1987.

In 1992 the Society assumed operational control of three filling stations owned by Fina, at Holdingham Roundabout, Thorpe Lane End and Newark Road in

Lincoln, but control was later relinquished when the deal came to an end. Gibbet Nook, near Coningsby, joined the Society's portfolio of filling stations in 1997, the novelty here being a coin operated maggot dispensing machine for the benefit of visiting fishermen. New petrol stations were acquired on Roman Bank, Skegness and Bracebridge Heath in 1999 and a brand new development was completed in 1998 on the Springfields Roundabout in Spalding, incorporating a McDonald's drive-through restaurant. A new petrol filling outlet supplied by JET was acquired along with a new convenience food store at Eastwood Road, Boston in 2000.

The petrol retailing market has changed significantly since the Society first entered it in 1967: margins have become tighter, the superstores have become dominant players and volumes of traffic have made some units virtually inaccessible. For these reasons, it has been necessary to close some stations, including the first two, Newland because access became so difficult on a busy road and Tritton Road because of competitor activity from the superstores. The Society currently operates ten petrol filling stations at:-

Winning Post, Lincoln
Gibbet Nook, Coningsby } Supplied by Total

Riseholme Road, Lincoln
Outer Circle Road, Lincoln } Supplied by Texaco
Springfields, Spalding

Eastwood Road, Boston
Long Sutton
Whaplode } Supplied by BP
Otter's Bridge, Saxilby
Albert Street, Newark

Winning Post petrol station and convenience store

MOTORS

The Society entered the motor retailing business in its 125th year, 1986; substantial cash balances had been accumulated and it seemed a logical move. When the long established family business of R. M. Wright Ltd. became available, the Society moved quickly and a deal was completed on 28 February. A substantial site on Outer Circle Road was acquired, together with the Austin Rover main dealership for the Lincoln area. The business was well respected but had lacked investment. With no background in the motor trade, the Society's officials had a great deal to learn. The Lincoln operation traded as Wrights Lincoln Ltd. and this same format was to be followed as other dealerships came into the group. The business of T. C. Harrison of Newark was acquired later in 1986 and in 1987 the Sleaford and Spalding branches of Holland Bros. of Boston. In 1987 the Fenton and Townsend business in Sleaford was bought and Wrights, Sleaford moved into a much improved location with a petrol station alongside. In December 1986 the Society acquired the main Austin

Rover dealership in Newark. By this time, the society was selling the Mini, Metro and Maestro - thousands of them - and it was a very profitable business. This all changed when Rover group was acquired by BMW in 1994 and all three of these models disappeared over the next few years. In addition the franchise for the sale of Yugo cars had been obtained and a dealership was established on Outer Circle Road in Lincoln. The Yugo experiment did not last very long. Austin Rover changed to Rover in 1989, moving further up-market and introducing a fine range of top quality cars.

The motor group entered Gainsborough in 1993 with the acquisition of the main Rover dealership. In the same year a Nissan franchise was obtained in Spalding, incorporated alongside the existing Rover dealership, which was upgraded in a newly-constructed show room in 1994 and this presented as a very good site. A similar

Wrights showroom on Outer Circle Road

133

development was completed the following year on the former dairy site at Farndon Road, Newark, with a joint Rover/Nissan showroom albeit, in accordance with motor trade practice, split into two separate units.

1 May 1995 was a very significant date for the motor group, as it was on that date that four new dealerships were added to the group: C S Scotney's Citroen operation in Boston, Holland Bros. Rover dealerships in Boston and Skegness and the Holland Bros. Jaguar operation in Boston. Holland Bros. was now a wholly owned subsidiary of Lincoln Co-operative but continued to trade under the Holland Bros. name, which was a well respected brand in Boston and Skegness. The Society was awarded the Jaguar franchise for the whole of the county of Lincolnshire in 1997 and now had two sites, one on Outer Circle Road in Lincoln and one in Boston, both trading as Holland Bros.

In 2000, BMW, having first removed the Mini from the deal, sold what was left of the Rover business to the Phoenix Consortium and the future of the group depended on the new models which were to be developed. The MG marque was re-introduced in an effort to boost image and sales. By this time, losses were being incurred in the motor group and it became necessary to start to close some of the smaller Rover dealerships. Also, both of the Nissan operations were closed together with Citroen in Boston. The MG Rover part of the motor group continued to incur losses into the early part of the 21st Century until the whole thing was brought to a head when MG Rover collapsed in 2005.

The Society had been in the motor trade slightly less than twenty years and it had certainly had its highs and lows. It went into the business for all the right reasons: co-op members were buying cars, Austin Rover was a British company and Lincoln Co-op was protecting British jobs. In the early years it was very successful, selling lots of cars; the quality may not have been of the highest order but the members liked them and bought them. Rover Group tried to go up-market, with the associated rise in prices, but the customers did not go with them. The sale of Rover to BMW was a disaster and the attempted rescue by the Phoenix Consortium in the end also failed. It was, in many ways, a classic business case study: the cost base was too high. This was evidenced by the fact that when MG Rover collapsed and the Society had to sell its remaining stock of cars at one-third off the list price, they sold the entire stock and could have sold more had they had them.

The Holland Brothers dealership continues selling and servicing Jaguar cars at Lincoln.

Holland Bros. circa 1912

Nissan dealership opened in Spalding in 1993

Wrights Rover Gainsborough

Spalding society's store in 1909

CO-OPERATIVE MERGERS IN LINCOLNSHIRE

21

'Where there has been no co-operative activity in an area for many years...it is always difficult to re-establish the ethos'

Over the years there have been a number of mergers between co-operative societies in Lincolnshire. Horncastle joined Lincoln in 1887 and whilst it was not technically a merger, when the Market Rasen Society went into liquidation in 1892, its members joined Lincoln and Lincoln Society moved into its main shop. The tiny Hackthorn and Cold Hanworth Society transferred to Lincoln in 1900.

In 1904 the Louth Co-operative joined the Great Grimsby Society and in 1927 Skegness transferred to Nottingham. In 1954 Boston Society also joined up with Nottingham and in the same year, Spalding transferred to Lincoln, bringing with it a central store in Winsover Road and four branches. Lincoln soon extended its trading area even further by opening an emporium in Long Sutton, more than 50 miles from the centre of the city. Various improvements were made to the Winsover Road store and in 1995, after an eleven year battle to acquire sites and planning permission, a brand new store was opened, the Winsover Centre. This was a mix of food, non-food, travel and a cafe. The main post office came into the centre at a later date. For a variety of reasons, including almost immediate new competitor activity, it did not really work and the Society finally withdrew from the site in 2011. The Society currently has six branches in the Spalding area at Wygate Park, Whaplode, Gosberton, Sutton Bridge, Crowland and Long Sutton, the biggest and the best.

In the mid 1960's there was a plan to form a Lincolnshire Co-operative Society. This was to be achieved in two stages; Grimsby (no longer Great

No. 19 Branch: HACKTHORN.

Hackthorn and Cold Hanworth Society transferred to Lincoln in 1900

apparently) joined Scunthorpe in 1966 and the following year, Lincoln and Gainsborough merged. The final piece of the jigsaw was to be put in place by all four combining, after the earlier mergers had settled down. Lincoln and Gainsborough came together very well, all back-office and support functions were transferred to Lincoln and the integrated society was soon functioning as an efficient and effective unit. Unfortunately that was not so in the case of Grimsby and Scunthorpe: the two operations carried on pretty much unchanged, few economies were made and little benefit materialised from the merger. So when Lincoln came to look at the situation some time later, the financial position of the enlarged Scunthorpe Society was so weak that the Lincoln Board declined to go through with the ultimate merger. Scunthorpe was virtually forced to join CRS in 1973 because of deteriorating trade results.

But the Lincoln/Gainsborough merger was judged to have been a success. Gainsborough had not been badly managed, but it did lack the resources to further develop the business in the way that was needed. Gainsborough had a departmental store on the Market Place, which housed its headquarters and it also brought a number of small branches to the new business. Various improvements were made to the Market Place store until in 1986 the Society proposed to West Lindsey District Council a major re-development of Gainsborough town centre and received a favourable response. The scheme, the biggest ever undertaken in the town, involved the closure of Heaton Street and took five years to complete. The "Lindsey Centre" opened on 23 July 1991, incorporating a food hall, re-modelled departmental store, a ten unit shopping mall and a 500 space municipal car park. The former Crown Post Office was brought into the department store, which also featured an imposing glass lift. A high quality restaurant was added a year later. Sadly, some time later, the grocery operation was forced to close due to competitor activity, but the rest of the development continues to operate. Lincolnshire Co-operative currently has four branches in the Gainsborough area at Misterton, Kirton Lindsey, Queensway in Gainsborough and a fine convenience food store at Morton, fractionally to the north of the town.

In 1971, Grantham and Retford societies transferred engagements to Nottingham, despite quite an effort to tempt them to Lincoln. Why did so many societies go to Nottingham when Lincoln would have seemed a more logical move? We don't know. Nationally, it was often a question of which society offered the retiring

Chief Officer the best departure package, but there is no evidence that this is what happened in the case of Nottingham. By 1992, however, Nottingham itself had run into financial difficulties and merged with CWS.

The Gainsborough Society's branch at Misterton

On 29 January 1983 the Newark Society transferred its engagements to Lincoln. Nottingham could undoubtedly have tempted them in their direction, but supported a move to Lincoln. The financial situation at Newark was weak and the shops were of a poor standard. The co-operative reputation in Newark was very low and Lincoln had much work to do to improve the image. Newark central premises and offices were in Kirkgate and they brought five branches into the merged society. Major refurbishments were undertaken at Kirkgate and when the District Council invited tenders for a major town centre re-development, involving some of the Society's property, a scheme was submitted in conjunction with local developers. After many delays, which the Society did not understand, the contract was awarded to a rival bid from House of Orange. It was a bitter disappointment and the Society felt a deep sense of disillusionment at the way the whole process had been handled. The compulsory purchase order could have been fought and the scheme delayed for, perhaps, years but in the end a deal was struck.

The site of Easons Motor Traders on Victoria Street was acquired and a new modern food store opened on 5 August 1986, also including furniture and electrical, with a petrol station alongside. The premises at Kirkgate and Paxtons Court were constantly upgraded and a travel branch added, together with the main post office, but it was never a great success, possibly due to the buildings' labarynth configuration and the Society finally withdrew from Newark town centre in 2008, save for the post office.

A property, bought initially as an investment, at Lakeside, Balderton was eventually opened as a quality food store and the travel branch moved in during 2008. The Society currently has eight branches in the Newark area at Sutton-on-Trent, Collingham, Churchill Drive, Lincoln Road, Victoria Street and Barnbygate in Newark, Balderton and Witham St Hughs; the latter opened in 2010 in response to requests from residents in the village.

By 1998, CRS had gradually withdrawn all its services from Grimsby and Cleethorpes and there were no co-operative shops left, where once there had been many. Less than forty miles from Lincoln and with a combined population of 150,000, almost twice that of Lincoln, it was a terrible indictment. Grimsby/ Cleethorpes had become a co-operative desert. Lincoln Society decided that something should be done about it and that an attempt should be made to re-introduce co-operation to the area. It was, and still remains, a difficult challenge. Where there has been no co-operative activity in an area for many years and all the shops have been closed and sold off, it is always difficult to re-establish the ethos.

The glass lift at Gainsborough's
Lindsey Centre

Something that has taken 25 years to run down is likely to take at least that long to build up again.

The first move came in 1999 in the form of a pharmacy business on Grimsby Road, Cleethorpes, which was so large that it was down-sized and a convenience food store range was introduced alongside. The pharmacy was later relocated to a better position. The following year businesses were acquired at Holton-le-Clay and on the Willows estate in Grimsby and from then on, new stores were added to the portfolio on a regular basis in the Grimsby/Cleethorpes area.

Pharmacy at Wybers Wood, Grimsby

Witham St Hughs foodstore & pharmacy opened in 2010 in response to requests from residents.

Shortly after the Humberside adventure had commenced, it was decided that Lincoln Society's services could be extended to the whole of Lincolnshire, including Boston, Skegness and Scunthorpe which had all been poorly served by national co-operative operations. Opportunities would be taken in these areas, as and when they presented themselves. As a result of these policies, Lincolnshire Co-operative currently has the following operations in these areas, where previously independent societies had once operated. Some outlets have been bought, some have been built from scratch.

Grimsby/Cleethorpes

Food	Holton-le-Clay The Willows Coniston Avenue, Grimsby Waltham Cambridge Road, Grimsby Wybers Wood, Grimsby Convamore Road, Grimsby Nunsthorpe, Grimsby
Pharmacies	Cleethorpes Wybers Wood
Funeral Home	Mark Tyack

Scunthorpe

Food	Westcliffe, Scunthorpe Willoughby Road, Scunthorpe Messingham
Pharmacy	Westcliffe, Scunthorpe

Boston

Food	Argyle Street, Boston Eastwood Road, Boston Woodville Road, Boston Old Leake
Pharmacy	Liquorpond Street Tawney Street Kirton

Skegness

Food	Roman Bank, Skegness Chapel St Leonards

The first phase of
Co-operative House was
completed in
November 1963

CO-OPERATIVE HOUSE

22

'...another disaster, in the form of a
second but, on this occasion,
massive fire which completely gutted
the building'.

(photo courtesy Mrs J.E. Fields)

The Silver Street frontage of the original 1873 building - boarded up prior to demolition

(photo courtesy Lincolnshire Library Service)

Top -
the junction of
Bank Street and
Silver Street in
December 1963

Below -
the same
view in
October 1964

Following the opening of Silvergate House in 1960, the Society moved to develop the departmental store on Silver Street and Free School Lane. Initially it was intended that this should be achieved in three phases, but it was actually done in two. Departments were temporarily relocated in other premises, including an old chapel on Silver Street which the Society had acquired some time earlier. The "Old Chapel", which was described in the 1891 Congress handbook as the Free Methodist Chapel, stood to the east of Free School Lane, next to the Conservative Club. The Silver Street store had served the Society well since 1874, but was now quite inadequate to serve the needs of members in a new era. Demolition started in March 1961 and the building programme commenced in May of that year. The first phase was completed and the store opened in the name of "Co-operative House" in November 1963. To enable the second phase to proceed, the Chemist's and Optician's were moved into Silvergate House and work commenced in January 1964. This part of the development was nearing completion when it met with something of a setback.

On Sunday 9 May 1965 the building was struck by fire. Fire appliances attended from four brigades, including a turntable ladder from Mansfield. A ten year old Lincoln boy, appearing before Lincoln Juvenile Court, later admitted responsibility for starting the fire, together with his younger brother and younger sister. Fortunately, the fire damage was restricted to the top floor, but considerable damage was caused to the rest of the store by smoke and water. At this time all of the reserve stock of beers, wines and spirits for the whole Society was stored in this building. Most of the labels were washed off the bottles by the water. As was the case with many co-operative societies and some other businesses, in an emergency the Works Department was sent in. Unfortunately the brief was not very clear. It is apparent that Works Department operatives undertook some tasting and testing. By lunchtime they were no longer capable of any type of work and their services had to be withdrawn. The bottles were then returned to the CWS where a more scientific method of testing was organised. The rest of the stock in the store had to be examined and decisions taken urgently as to whether it was suitable for sale or not. That which was considered unsuitable was taken by lorry and deposited on a rubbish tip close to the dairy. Shortly afterwards several hundred people descended upon the rubbish tip on foot or by car, van or even taxi and availed themselves of some real bargains. One man appeared before Lincoln Magistrates and was fined £15 for looting. When the official sale commenced a few days later, huge crowds attended and the damaged stock was cleared very quickly. Co-operative House was opened in full on 14 October 1965, incorporating, among other things, ladies and mens fashion, footwear, haberdashery, hardware, wallpaper and decorating materials plus a food hall. It was a development of which the Society was justly proud.

This store traded successfully until 11 February 1969 when it was struck by another disaster, this time in the form of a second but, on this occasion massive, fire which completely gutted the building. The fire brigade arrived quickly, but could do nothing to save the building, as black smoke filled the skies over Lincoln. Departments were temporarily re-housed in other property and a decision had to be taken whether to reinstate or demolish and rebuild. The Society preferred to reinstate but the Local Authority were uneasy. They appointed consultants to work alongside the Society's own experts and the whole structure was examined inch by inch. Nine months elapsed before approval was given to reinstate, by which time three quarters of the loss of profits insurance had been eroded. The original building had been very open plan and free flowing. However, such was the understandable nervousness on the part of the fire authorities and planners, that the replacement building was much more compartmentalised, although probably more fire safe. Co-operative House was re-opened on 2 October 1970. The store was completely refurbished in 1994 and re-launched as "Silvergate". The ladies fashion floor was refitted to a very high standard and incorporated some very popular labels. At this time, Silvergate was a major player on the Lincoln ladies fashion scene.

Silvergate traded well until 1999 when, with Lincoln's commercial centre having moved south, a painful decision had to be taken. The Lincoln departmental store was relocated from Silver Street, where it had traded for 125 years. Some of the departments, including men's and women's fashion, footwear and gifts were accommodated in premises owned by the Society since 1975, the former Corn Exchange building. Others, including photographic and toys, were relocated to a re-vamped Moorland Centre on Tritton Road. The Silver Street building was re-developed as an entertainment and leisure complex, together with accommodation for the University and it was renamed

"Thomas Parker House" in honour of the Society's founder.

The Society's principal non-food operations are now at the Home stores on Tritton Road in Lincoln and Market Place, Gainsborough, but some small electrical items are carried in food stores.

(photo courtesy Lincolnshire Echo)

Firefighters tackle the blaze at Co-operative House on 9th May 1965

4 Brigades Fight Flames: Boy (10) On Arson Charge

FIRE SWEPT THE SECOND FLOOR OF LINCOLN CO-OPERATIVE SOCIETY'S NEWEST STORE LAST NIGHT, CAUSING DAMAGE PUT BY ONE ESTIMATE AT NEAR THE £250,000 MARK.

And today, as the work of clearing up the mess, and fully assessing the damage began, a 10-years-old boy was due to face Lincoln Juvenile Court on a charge of arson.

The fire was in the first phase of Co-operative House, the building at the corner of Silver-street and Freeschool-lane. The second phase, which continues along Silver-street and down Bank-street is in the course of construction and was due to be opened in the summer.

added to the difficulties of the firemen.

Among those who watched was Mr. Duncan McNab. He is a former managing secretary of Lincoln Co-op who left recently to take up a similar position with London Co-operative Society.

of the society and some of his staff.

Mr. Bett, who said he could not attempt to assess the damage yet, said the second floor was used as a store for the whole of the chemist's stock; the wines and spirits stock, drapery, furnishing, lino, carpets, etc.

Refreshment for the firemen was provided by Lincoln Sportsmen's Club. The chairman, Mr. Les Buckthorp, and Mrs. Buckthorp, Mr. and

JTW Mitchell
Chairman of
the CWS
from 1874 to 1895

CO-OPERATIVE COMMISSIONS

23

'In 1958 there were 967 retail societies, of which 166 operated only one shop and 650 had fewer than 10'.

There have been three commissions which either referred to or directly related to co-operatives or co-operation.

The Royal Commission on Labour
This commission, established by Parliament, to examine the conditions of the working man, was held towards the end of the 19th Century. The Chairman was the Duke of Devonshire.

Giving evidence before the Commission, on 25 October 1892, J T W Mitchell, a director of the CWS, was asked to describe the methods of a Society located in an agricultural district. He said:-

"Lincoln Society will furnish the best example of this type of Society. Propaganda work by the Lincoln Co-operative Society was begun in 1877 out of sympathy for the conditions of the agricultural labourer classes, rather than from a desire on the part of the Society to invest capital. As capital accumulated, however, and these branches were found to be remunerative as investments, renewed propaganda efforts were put forth by the Society.

At each place the first members to join are invariably labourers engaged in agricultural work; afterwards platelayers and other railway employees, cottagers, village artisans and farmers become members and in some instances clergymen and large tenant farmers and land proprietors also.

At any of these branches whenever a desire is expressed by members for the appointment of a local supervisory committee, one is allowed to be elected but this committee is entirely subordinate to the general committee or directors of the Society. At some branches business meetings are held periodically, quarterly or half yearly when the accounts of the Society are submitted and the members present record their votes for the directors and other officers of the Society. At branches where no desire is expressed for such meetings none are held.

A large portion of the trade at these branches is done by vans and part of this business is simply the exchange of one class of commodity for another, groceries, bread, flour, drapery, boots and clothing being given at market rates for dairy and farm produce.

The Society occupies to some extent the position of a bank for the working classes who, from time to time, withdraw from their share capital (accumulated dividends) to buy seed for allotments, pigs for fattening and outfits of clothing for sons and daughters emigrating or leaving home for farm or domestic service.

Small growers obtain a market at their doors for what they produce, as the Society purchases farm and dairy produce and sells it to its town members direct. Through their membership in the Society, the agricultural labouring class receive some degree of training in local Government".

Mitchell also explained how advances on mortgage, without deposit, were made by the Society. He also referred to the possible establishment of large district farms with labour-saving machinery, on which the shareholders could be employed for the greater part of their time, while continuing to cultivate allotments or small-holdings during their spare hours. With the help of their families they could thus assist in the system of small farming which Mitchell reported was already rapidly spreading in south Lincolnshire.

He went on, "The Society can buy land at so many years purchase and continue to hold it, its members tilling such land for wages. The establishment of a creamery on co-operative principles has already been mooted at one branch where the system of agriculture pursued is clearly suitable for such a venture and local opinion is unanimous that it should be a department of the Society rather than an independent concern".

The Independent Co-operative Commission
This Commission was set up by resolution of the Edinburgh Co-operative Congress of 1955.
The principal concern seems to have been the failure significantly to expand the co-operative share of trade since the war. It reported in 1958.

Hugh Gaitskell was the Chairman of the 1958 Commission

The members of the Commission were:-

The Rt. Hon. Hugh Gaitskell, Leader of the Labour
Party, in opposition - Chairman
Miss Margaret Digby OBE
Prof. D. T. Jack CBE, JP
Dr. J. B. Jefferys
Col. S. J. L. Hardie DSO, LL.D
J. T. Murray
Alderman F. Pette JP
Lady Hall

The Secretary of the Commission was Tony Crosland
who had been Member of Parliament for South
Gloucestershire from 1950 to 1955 and was to be
Member of Parliament for Great Grimsby from 1959 to
1977. Crosland also became a Minister in the
Governments of Harold Wilson and Jim Callaghan.

All members of the Commission were described as
"suitable persons not engaged in co-operative
management or administration". The co-operative share
of total retail trade at this time was approximately 11%.
It was noted that this was, "scarcely higher than it was
before the war". In 1958 there were 30,000
co-operative shops and 250 factories. There were two
separate Wholesale Societies, one for England and

Co-operative
Independent
Commission
Report

Wales and one for Scotland and there were 967 retail
societies, of which 166 operated only one shop and
650 had fewer than 10. Those societies were together
paying dividends to customer members in excess of £40
million per year, but this was often at the expense of
retained profits and there were major concerns about the
ability of the Movement to fund its future development.

Following 35 meetings, spread over almost three years,
a range of visits, and formal and informal consultations,
the Commission produced its report which,
unfortunately, also contained a minority report from
Col. Hardie, dissenting from the main findings by
recommending the establishment of a single national
society for England and Wales, plus one for Scotland,
combining retail, wholesale and manufacturing
interests.

The majority report comprised 51 recommendations,
many of which refer to issues and debates long
forgotten. Recommendation 13, for example, proposed
the clearly radical idea that "the Movement should be
more willing than it has been in the past to recruit from
Grammar Schools and Universities". Similarly the idea
that "the ideal number of societies is in the region of
200 – 300" has long been overtaken by events.

However, there is much in the report that was ahead of
its time and is still in many ways relevant. The
Commission was clear about the respective roles of
Boards and of management. "Boards should
concentrate on major policy and ultimate supervision,
leaving the detailed management to the paid officials
and all societies should, if necessary with the help of
outside business consultants or the Co-operative Union,
create a clear management structure, with unambiguous
job specification and an explicit chain of command".

This theme was further expanded on with regard to
the CWS, where the key recommendation was that the
then full-time elected Board should become part-time
and confine itself to supervising and sanctioning major
policy and altogether eschew interference in detailed
management.

The Commission had much to say on the subject of
dividend and price policy, arguing that the Movement
should "sell at market prices and treat dividend as a
residual", that is, it should aim to match local
competition, and not expect the dividend to
compensate for higher prices. Concerning the dividend,
the Commission assumed, without spelling it out, that
the dividend was an essential element of a co-operative.
However, recognising that societies were increasingly
paying out dividend which they should have retained, it
recommended that societies should stabilise dividend at

a level, high enough to act as an effective inducement to trade, but not so high that it could not be maintained for a period of years ahead, and that they should allocate the remaining surplus and any increases in surplus, to reserve.

In looking at the financial performance of the Movement, the Commission was again ahead of its time in terms of introducing "return on capital employed" as the crucial measure and recommending that investment decisions should be taken on the basis of a comparison of relevant rates of return on capital. Even more significantly, it recommended that the greater proportion of co-operative capital expenditure in the next few years should take place, not in the production but in the retail field. In part, flowing from this, the Commission recommended that a "co-operative retail development society" should be set up to plan and operate national chains of specialist shops, involving the surrender of the notion that a local society can claim a permanent monopoly of co-operative trade in its own area.

Finally, recognising that the Movement was likely to be faced with ongoing change, the report recommended that it should formally examine both major constitutional issues and its basic trading policies, at least once a decade.

What happened next? Regrettably, not much. The idea of a retail development society led to the establishment of Shoefayre, but little else happened immediately. In 1964 though, the Board of CWS grasped the nettle and set up a Joint Re-organisation Committee, under the chairmanship of Sir Leonard Cooke, which reported in August 1965. This report led rapidly to the replacement of the then full-time CWS Board with an elected part-time Board and brought in professional management, in a structure which has broadly lasted until today.

This led in turn in the late 1960's to a programme of tackling declining market share, the old fashioned image and inadequate shops, with the launch of a co-op logo, the first national TV advertising campaign and Operation Facelift, a national refurbishment programme.

At the same time the Co-operative Union published, in November 1967, a regional plan, aimed at reducing the number of societies from 467 (there having been a large number of failures and forced mergers in the meantime) to a more realistic 50. Its report, almost ten years after the Independent Commission, said: "If the serious warnings of the Independent Commission had been heeded, the Movement would be in far better shape

Shoefayre was established as a result of the Independent Co-operative Commission

to withstand the impact of new problems which have developed".

The activities of the late 1960's and early 1970's led to a halt in the decline; in the mid 70's there was even, briefly, a period when the Movement was showing growth again. But the Independent Commission's call for a formal re-examination of the constitution and trading policies at least once a decade went unheeded thereafter and with some notable exceptions, the Commission recommendations were ignored, or brought about by force of circumstances rather than being freely and willingly adopted.

The Co-operative Commission 2000
Towards the end of the 20th Century there was real concern that the Co-operative Movement had lost its way, sales and profitability were falling and its impact on the lives of the people had been significantly reduced. So late in 1999 the establishment of a Co-operative Commission under the patronage of the then Prime Minister, Tony Blair, was announced. The Commission's brief was to examine the performance of the Movement in the second half of the 20th Century, its current activities and structure, with a view to proposing a realistic course of action to improve the effectiveness, performance and contribution of the UK Co-operative Movement to the economic and social life of the country. The situation was rather more desperate than at the time of the previous Commission; market share had fallen from 11.7% to 3.4%, net surplus had fallen from 6.3% of sales to just 1.1%.

Members of the Commission were:

John Monks, General Secretary of the Trades Union Congress – Chairman

Alan Donnelly, Former Member of the European Parliament – Secretary
Hazel Blears, MP for Salford
Lord Simon of Highbury – Former Group Chief Executive and then Chairman of BP
Lord Fyfe of Fairfield – Former Chairman of the CWS
Gerard Hill – Vice President of Scottish Midland Co-operative Society
Mervyn Pedelty – Chief Executive of the Co-operative Bank
David Pitt-Watson – Commercial Director of Hermes Lens Asset Management
Bill Connor – General Secretary of the Union of Shop, Distributive and Allied Workers
Bob Burlton – Chief Executive of Oxford, Swindon & Gloucester Co-operative Society
Pauline Green – Chief Executive and General Secretary of the Co-operative Union, former Member of the European Parliament and Leader of the Group of European Socialists
Alan Middleton – Director of Lincoln Co-operative Society and of the Co-operative Union

the co-operative advantage

Creating a successful family of Co-operative businesses

social goals

commercial success

competitive advantage

The Report of the Co-operative Commission January 2001

The Commission started its work early in 2000 and produced its report in January 2001. The main recommendations affecting Lincoln Co-operative Society are briefly summarised below:-

Boards of Co-operative Societies must establish challenging targets for the commercial performance of their society.

The commercial performance targets should include Return on Capital Employed, which should achieve a minimum of 10% as a first step.

In order to implement and monitor the commercial and social performance of societies, the Co-operative Union should be given responsibility for establishing a Commercial and Social Performance Panel.

Co-operative societies should conform to the co-operative accounting standards and adopt a standard system of financial reporting.

The Co-operative Union should establish challenging Key Social Performance Indicators for performance in relation to co-operative and social goals and should monitor the performance of individual societies.

Boards of societies should ensure that the key performance indicators for commercial and co-operative & social performance indicators are presented to the society's members annually.

Re-investment in the business must always be the first claim on profits, but where a society is trading profitably, the Commission recommends that the minimum commitment to the members and the community dividend should be 10% of the profit and that the distribution ratio between individual and community dividend, should be 70% to 30%.

The Board of every co-operative society should aim to ensure that an increasing proportion of the society's customers become members and that an increasing proportion of the society's business is conducted with members.

All societies should update and refine their membership records urgently to delete the names of obviously dormant members and establish a membership file that accurately reflects current membership. Societies should thereafter maintain regular contact with their members so that the membership becomes a valuable asset to the movement.

All societies should adopt best practice in increasing participation and strengthening democracy via a range of tried and tested balloting procedures.

Societies which have not yet adopted the seven rule amendments designed to set high turnout thresholds as a defence against hostile takeovers or attempts at demutualisation and/or to secure the transfer of assets to another co-operative organisation, should do so at the earliest opportunity.

The maximum size of boards should be 15, except in the case of CWS, where the maximum ideally should be 20 members.

The Chief Executive and Financial Controller, as a minimum, should serve on the board of a co-operative **(recommendation 31.1).**

Boards should introduce a skills audit and should be empowered to fill any skills gaps identified by the appointment of two external independent directors.

Ongoing training for all directors should be addressed regularly by all society boards. The Co-operative Union and the Co-operative College should develop a new qualification that meets the minimum requirement for elected directors to execute their duties and responsibilities adequately.

Societies should review their remuneration policies in order to reward appropriate senior managers so as to attract talented people from outside the movement. The remuneration package should be based upon the profitability and social achievements of the successful co-operative business and not on turnover alone.

There were also recommendations affecting the Co-operative Retail Trading Group (CRTG), Co-operative Financial Services (Co-operative Bank and Co-operative Insurance Society), CWS, Co-operative brand issues, Co-op logo, distribution, e-commerce and the new technology, new ventures and a national membership card.

The Co-operative Union were to be given responsibility for the implementation of the Commission's recommendations.

The Commission's work took almost a year and at times it was a difficult process. One of the problems was that most of the non-co-operative members of the Commission knew very little about co-operatives.

Some of the co-operative members, particularly those associated with the Co-operative Union, Dame Pauline (as she was to become), Burlton and Middleton had difficulty with some of the recommendations. There were many side meetings and consideration was even given to a minority report, but in the end it was considered that that would have been too destructive. Whilst there were many good points in the report, and

Tony Blair was the patron of the Co-operative Commission 2000

many unhelpful ones had been removed, it was recognised that some of the recommendations would have been unacceptable (particularly 31.1 above) to many, if not most of the retail societies. However, as the Co-operative Union had been given responsibility for implementation, it was eventually concluded that the principles enshrined in the recommendations could be achieved in a different way, within the Movement itself.

Following publication of the Commission's report, entitled "the co-operative advantage", the recommendations underwent scrutiny and debate. Presentations were made around the country, including one at Lincoln and many members contributed to consideration of the findings. A Special Congress was held in Manchester in November 2001, when the Co-operative Union made a series of proposals to achieve implementation of the Commission's recommendations. In some cases member societies were given a choice of a number of methods of implementation. The Co-operative Union proposals were endorsed by the Special Congress almost unanimously.

The Lincoln Society had played a major part in the work of the Commission and following its publication and the Special Congress, detailed consideration was given to the recommendations and the proposals. The principles behind the report were fully endorsed by Lincoln Society, which made a number of rule changes as a result - in fact, being the first retail society to appoint external independent directors, following a skills audit.

Standing : F. STEPHENSON (*Cashier*), G. BACON, W. H. GOLDSTEIN, H. BELL, W. HEWSON, G. HARLEY, G. WARD.
Sitting : W. B. HOWARD, W. COULSON (*Treasurer*), C. OSTICK (*President*), G. HARRIS (*Secretary*), M. SMALLER.

The Committee of Management
in 1910

DEMOCRATIC CONTROL AND MANAGEMENT

24

'The word 'Governance' was now starting to be used more often... the first code was published in the early 1990's'

The way in which the Committee, or Board, exercises its control has changed many times over the Society's 150 year history. The relationship between the various players is important in any business but in a co-operative an appropriate relationship between the members, who own the business, the Board, who direct the business and the management, who manage the business, is absolutely vital.

The one constant throughout all of the Society's long history has been the post of Secretary, from Thomas Parker (1861) to Duncan McInnes (1882-1902) and now to Jane Powell, the current Secretary.

The duties of the Secretary are many and varied and include: advice and support for the Board, ensuring compliance with rules and regulations, legal issues and making returns to regulatory bodies. The Secretary is the glue that holds it all together and working closely with the Senior Officer, the Secretary makes it all happen in a proper manner.

In the early days the committee did virtually everything, including the delivery of groceries to members' homes, although there was an employee, the storekeeper Thomas McTurk, himself a former member of the Committee. However, it is clear that the committee were very hands on and were effectively managing the business; they were in fact, sometimes referred to as "the Committee of Management".

Following the move to Silver Street in 1874, there were a number of General Managers responsible for buying stock. They were sometimes referred to as buyers. In the late 1870's something of a power struggle developed between the managers and the committee, but the membership eventually decided that the power should properly reside with the committee.

In 1875 James Cunliffe was appointed Cashier. In some annual reports in the years following, he was described as "Manager", but whatever his title, he was now the head of the paid workforce. Cunliffe was replaced by Fred Stephenson in 1881 and Charles Mackinder succeeded Stephenson in 1921.

In the late 1870's and early 1880's there had been some reckless buying by the managers and the committee acknowledged control weaknesses. Eventually however, the committee showed their frustration by abolishing the general manager posts and establishing, in 1886, a number of departmental committees with a departmental manager reporting to each one. There were committees for: Boots, Butchery, Buildings, Coals, Drapery, Tailoring, Mill and Bakery, Finance, Grocery, Livestock and Rolling Stock. This move was

judged to have been a success as the Society's results generally improved and the improvement was maintained.

The Society's minutes throughout the years of the late 19th and early 20th Century indicate how closely members of the committee attended to the Society's business. There was no general manager and the cashier was the senior official. As a result the main committee and the sub-committees dealt with a mass of detail. They inspected property, bought horses, accompanied buyers and generally "managed" the Society. In 1910 they received £5 a quarter in fees, the President and Treasurer received £6 each and the Secretary £10.

Branch managers in 1910

Once a year, they were allowed to go on a picnic by brake. In 1910 it was to Welbourn via Stapleford Woods and a limit of 3s.6d was placed on the catering budget. Another privilege was the right to shoot on the Society's land at Lower Bracebridge. And what detail they attended to. They granted the Welbourn employees the use of a horse and van to attend the annual meeting of the Sick Club; they authorised the Secretary to "cycle over to Riseholme" to enquire about land to let, a journey for which he received 2s.6d in expenses, and they ordered an investigation into a report that a horse had worked on Easter Monday for a private party without permission. They interviewed managers and staff and issued formal warnings about what might happen if trade did not improve or if leakages were not reduced.

Occasionally the minutes give rise to speculation, as when the committee decided to meet the growing trade at the sub-central branch by providing the manager with a new dray, a man and a set of harnesses. No mention of a horse. They moved managers and staff around according to performance, determined opening and closing times and took charge of the stocktaking arrangements. This structure survived more or less unchanged until the end of the Second World War in 1945, when Mackinder retired as cashier and John E Harrison as Secretary. Their replacement was A. R. Chance, who came from Chipping Norton Society and was given the title of Chief Executive Officer and Secretary. Very little else is known about Chance, except that he stayed only two years, leaving in 1947 to go to the Oxford Society. His replacement, with the job title of Managing Secretary, was Duncan McNab.

Although there was a new job title, there was no job description and the relationship between the Board and the "Managing Secretary" does not seem to have been very well defined. There was no scheme of delegation and no list of matters which were reserved for Board decision. It was not clear who could appoint or dismiss whom (both the Managing Secretary and Directors interviewed candidates for appointment and conducted disciplinary interviews), or what levels of expenditure required Board approval, if any. There were no budgets and no management accounts.

What is clear though, is that there had been a shift, almost by default, of power from Board to management, but without the controls or the checks and balances which are so essential to make such a system work. The Board had effectively ceded control of the Society to the Managing Secretary without actually making a positive decision to do such a thing. Departmental committees were abolished in 1948.

Stanley Bett was appointed Managing Secretary in 1964 when McNab left for London and the same arrangement continued into the 1980's, when the words "Corporate Governance" entered the co-operative vocabulary for the first time. This made people think "who was responsible to whom?" and "what were the proper reporting lines?" On closer examination, what had been happening was that department managers were reporting directly to the Board with the Chief Executive present as an observer. Tom Agar replaced Stanley Bett as Chief Executive in 1977 and department managers ceased visiting Board soon after.

The word 'Governance' was now starting to be used more and more often. Very slowly things started to change and in the light of corporate governance disasters inside and outside the Co-operative Movement, the Co-operative Union started to develop a Corporate Governance Code of Practice. The first code was published and approved in the early 1990's and this has been reviewed and revised on a regular basis ever since. Lincoln Co-op has been deeply involved in this process through its Director, Alan Middleton, who was also a Director of the Co-operative Union (Co-operatives UK).

Keith Darwin was appointed Chief Executive in 1992 and he and the Board determined that Lincoln Co-op should work towards being at the forefront of good governance. A schedule of matters reserved for the Board was developed so that everyone knew where the authority to make decisions rested and many more controls were put in place. The Board had again taken effective control of the Society, whilst allowing the Chief Executive sufficient flexibility to manage the business on a day to day basis. The current Chief Executive has also worked with the Board to further enhance the quality of the governance arrangements.

The Board are proud to proclaim today, that Lincolnshire Co-operative now has the best corporate governance system of any co-operative in the UK.

Alan Middleton has been deeply involved in the Corporate Governance Code of Practice as a Director of the Society and also as a Director of the Co-operative Union (Co-operatives UK).

President Eileen Bangay presents medical equipment provided by the Healthcare Fund

The Society has a policy that approximately 25% of its net surplus should be distributed to members in the form of dividend or to the community in the form of grants. These are some of the funds.

Healthcare Fund

Conscious that the Society was prevented by law from giving a dividend on NHS dispensing, the Board determined in 1993 to establish a Community Healthcare Fund. This fund gives benefits to patients of medical practices within the Society's trading area and also assists schools, community groups and other NHS-based organisations with community health-related projects. Donations have been made in response to a very diverse range of applications from medical equipment, fittings for doctors' waiting rooms, keep-fit appliances, diagnostic, convalescent and recuperative tools.

Since 1994 grants totalling over £700,000 have been made to many hundreds of different organisations.

Co-operative Development Fund

The Society chose to mark the new millennium with the establishment of a fund to help new and emerging co-operatives and social enterprises. A very wide variety of organisations have been assisted with small grants ranging from community groups, projects for children and the elderly, arts and crafts and transport-related enterprises.

Since 2000 over £400,000 has been donated through this fund.

Education Fund

Lincolnshire Co-operative has had an objective of supporting education since the very beginning and a fund was established as early as 1877, but this was to support work within the Society itself. The Education Fund was set up in 1998 to support educational projects out in the community.

Quite often schools and colleges have to provide matched funding in order to access public funds. Many schools in Lincolnshire have achieved specialist school status in this way with help from the Education Fund. Since 1998 grants amounting to over £400,000 have been made from the fund.

In 2005 Branston Community College (now Branston Community Academy) achieved Business and Enterprise Specialist School status and shortly afterwards entered into an innovative partnership with Lincolnshire Co-operative. This provides valued links and joint working projects bringing specialist expertise and real life experience to the school and contact with a new generation to the Society and the chance to demonstrate co-operative values in a practical way.

The partnership has been a huge success for each party and in 2010 the National Council for Educational Excellence produced a summary report of the way the partnership was managed as a model of best practice.

The members' meeting held on 15 November 1995 authorised the Board to make contributions up to £1 million to the proposed new University of Lincolnshire, at their discretion, over a ten year period.

In 1997 the Lincoln University Campus was created on Brayford, initially as part of the University of Lincolnshire and Humberside. The complex now includes a Lincoln Co-operative Lecture Theatre, a Chair of Health Studies and a Lincolnshire Co-operative Medical Centre.

The University Students Union was set up first as a co-operative, aided by the Society, but was converted to a company limited by guarantee when the co-operative structure proved slightly impracticable, but the Society continues to support them.

Right from the beginning the Society has worked very closely with the University and continues to do so.

It is fair to say that the University has transformed Lincoln. The University has been a driver for greatly increased economic activity and a job creator. It has produced a pipeline of talented young graduates, some of whom have worked for the Society while studying or joined as graduate trainees. Many more young people have been brought into the City.

President for 1997 David Fall (right) presents the first instalment of the Society's £1 million grant support for the University to Vice-Chancellor Professor Roger King.

152

The Society started its own "provident club", a savings and loan facility, as early as 1898 and in 1931 started a "Trading Club", which was loan only. Admitting that the decision had been taken "more or less reluctantly", the committee said it was because so much non-food business was being lost to competitors "which should be ours". It was an immediate success, with 2,529 members being recruited in the first year. This is hardly surprising as, like today, there were plenty of unscrupulous "loan sharks" out there in those days. Money was scarce, but members knew that they could trust the Co-op to give them a fair deal.

The system worked by way of credit coupons or vouchers, which came in denominations ranging from 2s.6d to £5. The minimum loan was £1 and the maximum £5. The coupons could only be spent in the Society's shops. Members paid an entrance fee of one shilling in the pound, which was the Society's credit charge, and then repaid at the rate of one shilling per week for every pound borrowed, over a period of 20 weeks. Once the final repayment had been made the member was issued with a dividend check.

The scheme was operated by a number of "Trading Club collectors" supported by a small office staff. The collectors, all men, issued the coupons and went round the county collecting the repayments each week, mainly on bicycles. At one time there were as many as twelve collectors employed, travelling all over the Society's trading area and two or three people involved in the office as back up. Twice a week, on

Tuesdays and Fridays, all the collectors went into the main office to pay in their collections, obtain more coupons and have a staff meeting.

In some more remote areas the collector would issue the coupons and members were allowed to make repayment at a local branch, the collector calling to pick up the money once a week.

The "Trading Club" scheme was very popular with members for over 40 years. It is not known whether anyone ever calculated if the amount paid by members in entrance fees exceeded the amount paid to the collectors in wages and travel costs.

The scheme started to slow down in the 1960's and 70's as credit cards, including the Society's Co-op Card, and other forms of credit became more popular and the scheme was finally closed down in 1975.

Since then, the Society has supported the establishment of a number of credit unions in Lincolnshire as that network has grown.

Sincil Sreet in 1970
(photo courtesy Lincolnshire Echo)

PROPERTY

25

'...the need to secure future services for members, whilst at the same time supporting the general commercial and economic well-being of the area'.

(photo courtesy Lincolnshire Echo)

The Sincil Street Inquiry

In 1971 a potentially very serious problem developed for Lincoln Co-op in the City of Lincoln. The Corporation announced plans for a central area redevelopment, which would have had a devastating effect on the Society's presence in the Sincil Street area. A compulsory purchase order was served for the grocery and pharmacy in Sincil Street, but the Society was not to be offered any priority in securing premises on lease in the new development, or any preferential terms.

A public inquiry was ordered and the Board determined to fight, as official objectors, although it was recognised that their chances of winning were slim. Unable to enlist the services of any of the top planning lawyers, who were all engaged in major London inquiries, the Society was fortunate to obtain the services of a young criminal barrister, but one who had never before dealt with a planning matter. He was Edwin Jowitt, who went on to become The Honourable Sir Edwin Frank Jowitt, a High Court Judge of the Queen's Bench Division. From that point everything changed. Jowitt worked with tremendous energy, often through the night, examining the case in minute detail. When the inquiry was eventually held, the Society's principal witness was Stanley Bett and due to his skill and knowledge and the

brilliant advocacy and cross examination of Jowitt, they won against all the odds. The whole process had taken two years. It was the longest running inquiry of its kind in the City's history, lasting 123 hours over 25 working days. Jowitt featured prominently in two marathon cross-examinations. He questioned the City's Director of Planning for a total of ten and a half hours, and followed this up by questioning the Planning Consultant, Hadley James Buck for eight and a half hours.

In May 1975, following the 1974 local Government re-organisation, the new Lincoln City Council invited tenders for the re-development of the Thorngate Car Park at the rear of Sincil Street, which formed part of the now defunct development. Assisted by the CWS, the Society submitted a scheme which, after several visits to Manchester and Nottingham by the City Council, was successful and accepted in September 1975. This was the start of what was to become the Sincil Street Superstore, now the City Square Centre.

Lincoln Corn Exchange and Market Company Ltd.

In 1974 the Society identified another opportunity to strengthen its presence in the City of Lincoln which

The former Newmarket Hotel was converted into shops.

McDonalds became tenants of the Corn Exchange building.

would have provided an alternative fall-back plan in the event that, despite their success in defeating the earlier Corporation proposals, their tender for the new Thorngate Scheme should fail. Together with Simons, a local building contractor, a new company was formed, Cosim of Lincoln Ltd, and a substantial shareholding was acquired in the Lincoln Corn Exchange and Market Company Ltd (LCE). This company had extensive property holdings in that part of the city centre covered by the now defeated development proposal. The following year the partners made a bid for the remaining shares in LCE. Over 92% of shareholders accepted the offer and the bid therefore became unconditional under the Companies Act. The Society owned 75% of the company and Simons 25%. Plans were immediately announced to upgrade and renovate the LCE property portfolio, retaining the historic buildings and essential character of the area that the earlier proposed development would have swept away. LCE was to become a very important part of the Society's business over the next 35 years.

The Exchange Arcade was completely refurbished in the following year as the company declared a determination to clear up the whole area and make it more attractive to the public. Additional land and buildings were acquired including land to the rear of a row of small shops in the Newmarket area.

The Queen Hotel in High Street was bought, mainly for the land at the back, which was to unlock the way to further successful developments. The hotel was sold on, but the back land, together with the Newmarket properties, now demolished, enabled a large retail store to be built for W H Smiths on Cornhill. There was much discussion at Executive as well as Board level, as to how the further development of LCE should be financed, by selling the W H Smiths building or by borrowing. Eventually it was decided to sell and the remainder of the old Newmarket site in Cornhill was developed. The Society's former supermarket in Sincil Street was brought into the scheme as well as other Sincil Street properties and large units were built for a number of national retailers, including Evans and Mothercare. The markets area was completely revamped with a new canopy and the Newmarket Hotel was converted to shops. Industrial units were developed on out of town estates, in part to help stimulate the economy and provide employment.

As Co-operative House was redeveloped, Silvergate House was no longer needed for trading, so part was let to Mecca as a nightclub. A new market hall was created at the rear of the Corn Exchange building, linked to the Local Authority market. This incorporated a number of small shops, one of which was let to McDonalds, the American fast food outlet. The Silvergate Restaurant was let to Whitbread as a nightclub.

Lincoln Corn Exchange and Markets (1991) Ltd

On 1 January 1991 LCE was re-organised, with Simons and Lincoln Co-op parting company. The Society became 100% owners of a new company, Lincoln Corn Exchange and Markets (1991) Ltd., taking 75% of the assets of the former LCE, mainly the retailing elements. A number of the properties retained by Simons were subsequently bought back into the company. In 1994 the Abbey National bank (now Santander) moved into prestigious new accommodation at the front of Exchange Arcade and some years later Waterstones moved into the other end. Also in 1994 the company acquired the Stonebow Centre in Lincoln. In 1995 a new restaurant was built on the Moorland Centre site which was leased to the award winning Elite Fish and Chip Company. The Riverside Centre at Sleaford and the Lakeside development in Balderton, Newark were also acquired in 1998 and 1999 respectively. Once vacated in 1999, Co-operative House was extensively re-modelled and the ground floor and basement let as an entertainment complex with the upper floors being leased to the University. In 2001 the company acquired the Lloyds/TSB premises in Bank Street, the General Accident building on Brayford and the former Royal Insurance offices on Silver Street.

A shopping parade in the Riddings area of Scunthorpe was acquired from North Lincolnshire Council in 2003. Much needed investment was made into this project where a new food store was created for the Society joining the post office which was already on site.

In 2004, responding to an urgent appeal, the Society bought the Dynex property on Doddington Road, saving the business and many jobs. Becor House in Lincoln was also acquired around the same time and investment was made in a number of small industrial estates, mainly in rural areas with the objective of supporting the local economy. The tenants are nearly all local businesses and the uses range from storage to technical and skilled trades.

The Society's property holdings provide an income stream which underpins the economic performance of the business, provides a return on capital not immediately required for trading operations and offers opportunities for the further development of services to members. There is also the potential for capital growth which strengthens the Society for the longer term. In considering property investment decisions the Society is always conscious of the need to

Lakeside Balderton

secure future services for members, whilst at the same time supporting the general commercial and economic well-being of the area. All investments are local and many have made a real contribution to improving the fabric of Lincolnshire towns and villages. When undertaking development projects the Society always tries to use contractors from the area, further contributing to the health of the local economy.

Birchwood

On 22 January 1991, a 50% interest was purchased in a newly formed company, Newcoop Properties Ltd. This company acquired the Birchwood Shopping Centre in Lincoln and over the next two years the centre was refurbished and extended. The remaining 50% of the shares were subsequently obtained by the Society and the company was transferred into LCE. In 2007 the Society announced plans for a comprehensive redevelopment of the centre, significantly upgrading the existing units and introducing some new ones. Apartments and offices were also introduced. The scheme was completed in 2010.

Birchwood Centre was extensively redeveloped in 2010 to create a modern community hub

Lindongate

A plan for the possible redevelopment of a large section of the Sincil Street area, from the railway to the river, was first discussed in 1988. The development had to be put on hold however, when planning consent was granted, on appeal, for a massive expansion of retail outlets on the former St Mark's Station site to the south west of the city centre. But the idea did not go away, has been resurrected several times since and is still very much alive today.

Two development partners have been appointed. The first, Wates, did buy some properties in the area, but as the scheme dragged on with little progress being made, they eventually lost interest and those properties were acquired by the Society. One of those acquisitions was a car park bordering Pelham Bridge and St Mary's Street, which includes the site of No. 1 Napoleon Place the Society's first shop, opened in 1861. The second partner was Modus who ran into financial difficulties and had to withdraw.

The Society has itself bought properties in the Sincil Street area, including the Grand Hotel which is intended to facilitate a redesign of the transport network and a new transport interchange for bus and train passengers. Prince Charles took a keen interest in the plans for the bus station and surrounding area when he visited Lincoln. His Prince's Foundation for the Built Environment has helped to ensure that the area is developed in sympathy with the ancient fabric of the city. It is hoped that outline planning approval will be achieved in 2011.

Lindongate

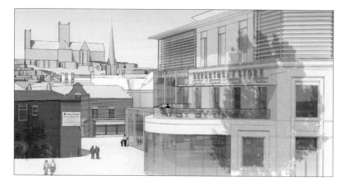

Carlton Centre

Carlton/Greetwell

In the 1980's the Society acquired some land on Outer Circle Road as a result of the purchase of the Lincoln and Carlton Dairy business and also bought the former Hillards supermarket on the corner of Bunkers Hill. The Hillards site was developed by the building of a 35,000 square foot store for a national DIY chain. In the years that followed other land was added, some purchased from the Church Commissioners, a somewhat painful and time-consuming process. Eventually a large site of some 90 acres was accumulated. It was decided that the front part of the site should be developed by LCE for retailing and other commercial purposes, whilst a new company was established with a local development partner, Universal Construction Services (UCS), to develop the back land for housing. The joint venture company was known as Greetwell Developments.

Both projects were successful and over the next 20 years many major retailers opened up on the Carlton Centre and some of the country's biggest names in the housing market bought tranches of land for residential development. From nothing, the Society had created a high quality mixed housing community with a district shopping centre and a wide variety of services and leisure facilities.

IN
MEMORY OF
THOMAS PARKER

ZILLAH PAULINA
DIED APRIL 1887 AGED 58 YEARS.

THEIR DAUGHTER
ROSAMOND EVA
JULY 1862 AGED 6 YEARS.

June 2011:
Stonemason Gary Daynes carves a new headstone in memory of our founder Thomas Parker.

FUNERAL SERVICES

26

'...a beautiful listed building...was painstakingly renovated to restore it to its former glory'.

FURNISHING DEPARTMENT.

We have pleasure in informing our members that this Department is now open, and that they can be supplied with all articles required in their households, at most moderate prices consistent with quality and workmanship. Appended is a rough price list representing Goods stocked, to which we are daily adding.

We have engaged a competent CABINET-MAKER and UNDERTAKER, and are now prepared to execute any orders in either branches at shortest notice. We earnestly solicit your inspection when purchasing.

FURNITURE.

	£ s. d.
Imitation Walnut Suite, in Brocaded Crimson Plush	8 15 0
Mahogany Couches, in Hair-seating .. from	2 14 0
Birch Couches, Stained Mahogany, in Hair-seating .... from	2 2 0
Stained Couch, in Leather-seating ....from	1 5 0
Gents' Easy Chairs, Mahogany, in Hair-seating .... from	1 9 0
Gents' Easy Chairs, Birch, Stained Mahogany, in Hair-seating .... from	1 0 0

French Bedsteads, 6ft. 6in. by 4ft. 6in., £ s. d. from 16s. upwards.

	£ s. d.
Flock Beds, complete, 6ft. 6in. by 4ft. 6ft. from	1 8 0
Feather Beds made to order, from samples of Feathers and Ticks.	
Wool Mattresses, 6ft. 6in. by 4ft. 6in. ..from	1 0 0
Straw ,, ,, ,, 8s., 9s. 6d., and	0 10 9
Wire-Woven Spring Mattresses, 6ft. 6in.....	0 17 0
Bassinette Perambulators, from £1 7s. 6d.	

CROCKERY.

Dinner Sets ....from 15s. upwards.
Tea ,, ... ,, 12s. ,,
Toilet ,, ... ,, 7s. ,,
Jugs (Sets of 3).. ....from 10d. to 4s. 3d.
Cups and Saucers, Tea .....from 2½d., 4d., 4½d., 5½d.
,, ,, Breakfast ,, 3½d., 6d., 9½d.
Basins, from 1½d. to 5d. Custard Dishes, from 4d. to 6d.
Tea Pots, from 3½d. to 2s. 9d. Cream Jugs, from 6d.
Cheese Stands, from 2s. 9d. to 4s. 9d. Egg Cups, 1d. each.

The first reference to a funeral service appeared along with the committee's report of 1 January 1890, in an advertisement for the furnishing department and read simply:-

"We have now engaged a competent cabinet-maker and undertaker and are now prepared to execute any orders in either branches at shortest notice. We earnestly solicit your inspection when purchasing".

This appeared in the next three quarterly reports in the same form, but no mention is made of this new service in the body of the committee's report, nor in any reports around this time.

By 31 December 1890 this notice had been reduced to:-

"Funerals furnished throughout by your own shop".

and shortly after it was reduced still further to a very simple block

• **FUNERALS FURNISHED THROUGHOUT** •

beneath references to watches, pianofortes, organs, harmoniums, washing machines and wringers.

It would appear that the service operated from the Works Department in Tanners Lane, where the coffins were made. In 1930 the Society purchased property in Portland Street for the Funeral Department where families could be seen, but the coffins were still made and polished at Tanners Lane. The Portland Street site, although extended and upgraded many times over the years, is still the Headquarters of the Funeral Division and houses the main Lincoln Funeral Home.

There is very little mention of this service at all in the committee's or directors' reports until well into the

second half of the 20th Century. It was then, and to some extent still is, a subject that is just too difficult to talk or write about. We do not know how much business was transacted or how successful it was but, based on what we know about the attitude of the early committees to under performing sectors of the business, we can assume that it was economically viable.

In 1976, nine years after Gainsborough Society merged with Lincoln, the Society took the opportunity to extend the service into the town by opening a new funeral parlour in North Street.

In the town of Sleaford the businesses of Smeeton's and Roy Slater were purchased in 1981 and a new Chapel of Rest was opened in Duke Street in 1985.

The Society had attempted to start its own funeral service in Newark, without success, so in 1990 the business of G E Rose in Beacon Hill Road was purchased.

In 1995 another business was acquired, that of M England in Horncastle and this was relocated to new premises in the Market Place.

The following year the service was extended to the south of the county with the purchase of Clubleys in Spalding and a new unit was opened in Holbeach.

In 2003 the business of Smith and Son in Hundleby was acquired and the search for better, more suitable premises, was started immediately. This was achieved in 2009, when the operation was relocated to the nearby town of Spilsby. Also in 2003 the Society bought Herrings of Boston Funeral Services, but by 2007 had outgrown the small premises on South Parade and acquired a beautiful listed building on South Square.

The property was painstakingly renovated to restore it to its former glory. This work was recognised by the Boston Preservation Trust and the Society received the Civic Pride Award for its re-housed funeral home.

Funeral home at South Square Boston

The service was extended still further in 2005, with the purchase of the businesses of V Walker in Louth and D W Bloomer which operates in Alford, Mablethorpe and Sutton on Sea. 2008 saw further growth with the acquisition of the Mark Tyack funeral service in Grimsby.

In 2010 the Society bought the former DVLA driving test centre in Proctors Road in Lincoln and this was converted to a funeral home to serve the northern part of the city and nearby villages.

The department has offered a monumental masonry service for many years and erected memorials on behalf of members locally. In 2006, however, this small team brought great credit to the Society by crafting a monument which was installed at Auchy-les-Mines in France as a war memorial to Lincolnshire soldiers who died in the assault on the Hohenzollern Redoubt in the Battle of Loos in 1915.

The monumental masonry team have since restored a number of war memorials in Lincolnshire, which have been greatly appreciated by the local communities.

The Funeral Services team have not restricted their activities to Europe however and following the Southern Asia Tsunami disaster in 2004, two of the embalmers spent time with the disaster response team in Thailand and one also spent time working in New Orleans following the hurricane there.

The Florists shop has operated for many years in Lincoln, mainly in support of the funeral service, but it also supplies floral arrangements for weddings and other events. The Society is also a member of Flowers Direct, which enables customers to send flowers anywhere in the world.

In 1904 a "Free Collective Life Assurance Scheme" was introduced and operated by the CWS and the Scottish CWS through their joint insurance department, the Co-operative Insurance Society (CIS).

The Society paid a small annual premium per member to CIS and both the member and their spouse were covered. Benefits were based on the members' purchases in the previous three years. The cover was entirely free to members.

In 1948 the scheme was brought in-house and operated by Lincoln Society. It was re-named the Death Benefit Fund but the benefit structure remained unchanged. When making this announcement in the quarterly report, the Directors reminded members of the funeral furnishing service, one of the few references to be found anywhere. The scheme was later re-named Funeral Benefit and in 2009 converted to Funeral Dividend, based on the cost of the funeral.

In 1990 the Society introduced a Funeral Pre-Payment Plan, whereby funeral arrangements could be made and paid for at today's prices with the funeral being conducted to an agreed standard without any further payment. In 2002 this was re-launched as the Funeral Bond and operated in conjunction with the Co-operative Insurance Society and now forms an important part of the division's portfolio.

War memorial to Lincolnshire soldiers at Auchy-les-Mines

PHARMACY

'...the Society started to offer ultra violet ray therapy, which was said to be achieving wonderful results...'

The earliest reference to anything pharmaceutical appears in the Committee's report of 5 October 1880, when it was announced that patent medicines were to go on sale. The list makes fascinating reading and seems to provide cures for almost every disease imaginable.

In the report of 31 December 1890 it was announced that arrangements had been made with Mr J F Harston,

Chemist, to provide for members' needs on a type of agency basis. Dividend was given on these purchases, where appropriate.

By 1912 the list of chemists participating in the scheme had grown considerably.

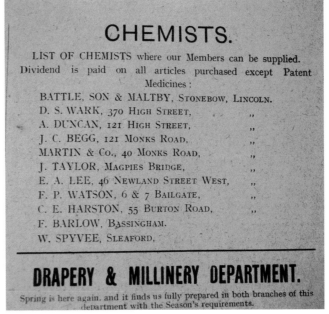

The first pharmacy opened by the Society itself came in 1928 at the top of Bank Street, in a building previously occupied by the Prudential Assurance Company.

This was followed a year later by another pharmacy on the fast growing Moorland Park estate in the city and in 1933 a branch was opened on Burton Road. A further branch was opened on Wragby Road in 1937.

The Society's first pharmacy opened in 1928 in Bank Street, Lincoln

Pharmacy branches in some locations have moved a number of times in the division's 80 plus year history. Some branches have been bought, sold, bought back and closed or sold again. Some have been relocated to better positions, perhaps closer to a doctors' surgery. In the 1970's branches were closed, the reason given at the time being an inability to recruit pharmacists; it seems more likely however, that it was an unwillingness to pay the 'going' rate of pay. At that time there was a national pay scale for pharmacists, which must have seemed very high by Lincolnshire standards. At one point there were just four branches left. It was because of a shortage of qualified pharmacists that the Society converted a pharmacy in Woodhall Spa to a food store very soon after buying it in 1947.

In the town of North Hykeham the branch in the old village was relocated to the Newark Road Crossroads, nearer to the doctors, but as the population of the town increased, a licence was obtained in 2003 to open a new branch at Hykeham Green, with a medical practice on site. What was known as the Central Pharmacy remained at the top of Bank Street until 1963, when it was moved to the ground floor of Silvergate House. It was moved on to the ground floor of Co-operative House in 1977 and finally relocated to Sincil Street, the store now called City Square Centre, in 1994.

In 1915 it was announced that arrangements had been made with several dentists 'of repute' to supply members' requirements in dentistry, on which full dividend would be paid.

In 1928 the Society started to offer ultra violet ray therapy, which was said to be achieving wonderful results and the following year a photographic service began. The Society had quite an extensive photography section in the 1980's, probably the best in the city, but with the departure of key staff and intense competitor activity on the part of national chains, the service was eventually discontinued.

The optical service had originally started as part of the jewellery department, but was transferred to pharmacy when that division was created. It continued until 1975 when it was sold to David Sims and Partners (the partners being CWS).

Having reached a low point in the 1970's, pharmacy started to expand in the 1980's. In 1988 four shops were bought which had previously operated in the name of 'Halliday'. These were on Monks Road, Brant Road and Newark Road in Lincoln and the Forum at North Hykeham. The small shop on the Forum was so successful that it was necessary to take a lease on two further units to increase the size of the facility and substantially improve the service.

In 1991 the Society entered into an agreement with two private chemists to develop a pharmacy adjacent to the new health centre on Cabourne Avenue on the Ermine Estate in Lincoln. The Society eventually obtained

Cabourne pharmacy opened in 1991

100% ownership of this business. Also in 1991 Tower Pharmacy, next to Newland Health Centre, was purchased, standing on the site of a well known local establishment of yesteryear, Sam's Cafe. Also in 1991 the Society bought back the St. Botolph's pharmacy in Lincoln. In 1992 pharmacies were acquired in Ruskington and Spilsby and in 1993 in Saxilby. Ruskington and Saxilby were later incorporated into more comprehensive developments alongside a food store.

In 1994, following some opposition from local doctors and a lengthy and rather acrimonious struggle, a new pharmacy was opened in Welton. A similar problem emerged in the village of Waddington, which was ultimately resolved.

1995 saw the opening of two new outlets, in Bracebridge Heath and on the Birchwood Estate. The mid 1990's was a very busy period for pharmacy with the division returning to Burton Road and also acquiring units in Boston, Metheringham and two in Gainsborough, one of which was relocated into the Lindsey Centre. Towards the end of the decade two businesses were acquired in Cleethorpes which were eventually combined.

The first pharmacy to be purchased in the new millennium was at Washingborough and this was followed by acquisitions at Skellingthorpe, West Parade in Lincoln, Swineshead and Kirton near Boston, on the Westcliffe Estate in Scunthorpe and Tawney Street in Boston.

Maltbys was purchased by the Society in 2009

In 2007 the Competition Commission forced Alliance Boots to dispose of some branches. These were to be sold off in tranches. The Society bid for and was successful in securing the units in Louth, Horncastle and Hull. A branch was also purchased from a local provider in the village of Nettleham in the same year.

The biggest single event in the pharmacy division's long history came in 2009, with the purchase of Maltby's, a pharmacy wholesaler with more than 150 customers and ten retail pharmacies at Cherry Willingham, Donington, Holbeach, Hunstanton, Wybers Wood in Grimsby, Molescroft near Beverley, Thornton le Dale, plus three in Scarborough.

The Society had worked with Maltby's for many years, in fact Lincoln Co-op was one of their very first customers when they started over 100 years ago. The wholesale business continues to run under the Maltby's name and the pharmacies have been re-branded Lincolnshire Co-op.

The development of the pharmacy service to date is completed by the purchase of a business in Branston adjacent to the Lincolnshire Co-operative convenience food store and the opening of a new branch at Witham St Hughs which is actually in the food store.

The pharmacy division is one of the largest and most successful in the Society. The financing of pharmacy operations is complicated and when the Government or the NHS takes the view that gross margins are too high, they make retrospective reclaims of prescription income, known in the business as 'clawback'. This can be very disruptive and makes life difficult when it comes to pitching bids to buy other businesses.

But the pharmacy division does more than dispense prescriptions. Most branches are now equipped with consulting rooms and provide a whole range of services including: free counselling and advice on health related matters, free health check days, Medicine Use Reviews, treatment of minor ailments, advice on smoking cessation and for those wishing to free themselves from drug addiction. A free prescription delivery service is provided where appropriate and work is under way to enable prescriptions to be electronically transferred from doctor to chemist.

A chiropody service is available in three locations, at Crossroads in North Hykeham, Sincil Street in Lincoln and at Gainsborough.

The department constantly seeks to develop new services for members and has been very successful in doing so. The Society currently operates 47 pharmacies.

Tritton Road Home store

THE LAST QUARTER CENTURY

28

'Some Lincolnshire Co-op branches are now open for up to 15 hours a day, reminiscent of the very earliest stores of 150 years ago'.

The last 25 years has been a period of unprecedented competitor activity. The Society has, as always, responded in a positive manner, by continuously refurbishing and upgrading its stores, including the introduction of the latest technology, new stock ranges, and competitive pricing policies. In addition, new stores have been opened, some in territory where the Society has not previously operated.

In 1986 the Society celebrated its 125th anniversary with many special events being held throughout the year. All members were issued with a 'Passport to Value' containing numerous special offers available to members only. As part of the celebrations the Society entered a float in the Mayor's Parade in Lincoln, which was awarded the prize for best float.

Towards the end of the 1980's the Society's transport depot vacated premises on the Brayford in Lincoln, which it had occupied from the dawn of the motor age, indeed some of the workshops had previously served as stabling in the era of the horse and cart. The department was relocated to new modern workshops to the rear of the motor group site on Outer Circle Road. The old premises, together with the redundant abattoir which had remained empty for some years, were sold to Holiday Inn for the construction of a new hotel.

A number of co-operatives successfully developed the 'late shop', or '8 till 8' concept during the 1980's. Lincoln Society's first experience with this idea was at the Queensway branch in Gainsborough in 1988. It was such a success that within five years most of the Society's food stores were operating on this basis. Long opening hours have, of course, now become very much the norm and 8.30am to 5.30pm, Monday to Saturday, with a closure for 1¼ hours at lunch-time, feels like something from a bygone age. Some Lincolnshire Co-op branches are now open for up to 15 hours a day, reminiscent of the very earliest stores 150 years ago.

A significant event in the Society's long history was the opening of the Moorland Centre in Lincoln on 29 March 1989. Its birth was preceded by a long and painful labour. In February 1985 a contract was entered into to purchase the former Dawsons Belting Works factory on Tritton Road, subject to planning approval for change of use for retailing. Consent was finally received in January 1988, after a three year struggle. Now renamed Lincolnshire Co-operative Home, it incorporates furniture, carpets, gifts, mens and womens clothing, footwear, travel, cafe, a small food section and a garden centre in a 70,000 square feet unit.

In the village of Bardney, the Board were faced with an interesting decision. The Society had traded in the same little shop for over 100 years, it was making a good net profit, but the building was deteriorating and the Society's image suffering. The problem was that if something in the order of £250,000 were to be invested in a new store it would still only produce about the same net profit as in the old shop. Once again, the Society decided to invest in the future. The new Bardney store opened on 20 March 1990.

In yet another new venture, a community store and filling station was opened in 1994 on the site of the old "Winning Post" petrol station, which was completely rebuilt and included a National Tyre Service depot.

The Moorland Centre opened in 1989

The new Bardney store - pictured in 1990

The development was so successful that the store was doubled in size in 2000 and provides a quality service for members in the West End of the City.

In 1992 the Society acquired a controlling interest in Lincoln Shop Equipment Ltd, a small company which sells and maintains point of sale equipment ranging from the very basic to the more sophisticated technology. The company derives approximately 50% of its turnover from the Society's own units with the balance generated from principally small businesses within the Society's trading area. Early in the 21st Century new premises were built for the company on the site of the Moorland Centre and in 2005 the balance of the shares were purchased so that it became a wholly owned subsidiary.

On 19 December 1992, Tom Agar retired from the post of Chief Executive. He had guided the Society through 15 years of rapid expansion and left it well equipped for the future. Keith Darwin, his deputy throughout that 15 year period, was appointed to succeed him.

In 1993, the Society purchased, initially as an investment, an office block in Tentercroft Street in Lincoln, Mountnessing House. Shortly afterwards, the tenants, Boeing, departed and in 1994 the Society decided to relocate its Board room and administrative offices from above the Silver Street department store. In honour of the former Chief Officer, the building was renamed Stanley Bett House.

The Society has been a member of the Co-operative Group Ltd (previously CWS) since 1875 and is still a corporate shareholder. Born in 1863 as the Co-operative Wholesale Society (CWS), it was owned and controlled exclusively by the retail societies, who at that time numbered around 50. One of the big problems with the CWS procurement function was that there was no discipline and therefore no loyalty. Societies could buy from them if they wanted to, or go it alone if they thought they could get a better deal elsewhere. It was against this background that the Co-operative Retail Trading Group (CRTG) was established in 1993. Discipline was mandatory; societies could only buy from the CRTG range. The Co-operative Group, now a significant retailer in its own right with individual members, accounts for approximately 80% of CRTG turnover. There is a CRTG Strategy Group and a Monitoring Group on which there are representatives of independent societies. CRTG has brought great benefits and continues to do so. In 2008, the current Chief Executive, Ursula Lidbetter, became a Director of the Co-operative Group following two of her predecessors, Tom Agar and Keith Darwin, in that role.

There had been discussions with Co-operative Retail Services (CRS) for some years regarding the co-operative presence in Alford. Eventually CRS agreed to sell their little shop to Lincoln Society who, shortly afterwards, transferred the business to a newly acquired former Spar shop and in September 1994 opened a new supermarket on the former cattle market site, acquired from East Lindsey District Council.

The last five years of the 20th Century saw no let up in development activity. Changes in population, shopping habits and retailing methods generally enabled the Society to return to three villages with fine new stores: Coningsby, Navenby and Spilsby, from which it had withdrawn some years earlier. New units replaced inadequate ones in Kirton in Lindsey and Collingham. The old store in Collingham was converted into a community police station. In extending its geographical boundaries still further, the Society reached the Lincolnshire coast with a new development at Chapel St Leonards within a few yards of the sea and arrived at the county's southern boundary with a new store at Sutton Bridge.

During the summer of 1999, Lincoln played host to over 12,000 caravanners participating in the 61st International Caravan Rally. A temporary supermarket was created on the Lincolnshire Showground providing a greatly valued service to visitors to the County, which proved to be an enormous success. The store, during its 10 day life, exceeded the turnover of the Society's largest permanent store.

Moving into the 21st Century the pace of events was no less hectic. In the year 2000, an independently owned convenience store was purchased in Crowland, in the south of the county and this was later refurbished and redeveloped. A replacement store was opened in Skellingthorpe in 2002 incorporating a post office and pharmacy. In 2003, the CWS bought a chain of small

Staff all set for the International Caravan Rally in 1999

convenience stores in the name of Alldays. They agreed to sell some of the shops to local independent societies. Lincolnshire was able to acquire the store in Caistor. The unit was not very satisfactory, operating as it did on several levels. The search for more suitable premises took some time, but eventually the Society bought the Talbot Inn, which was tastefully restored and opened as a 5,500 square feet convenience food store in 2010. Lincoln Co-operative had once had three stores in the Monks Road area of the City, but over time all had closed. It was felt that a return to the area was long overdue and again a long search ensued, resulting eventually in the purchase of a former Chapel on Monks Road itself. There was some discussion as to whether demolition or restoration was the best way forward, the planners preferring restoration. Although probably the more expensive option, the decision was taken to restore and a convenience food unit opened in 2004. At around the same time two local post offices were acquired and these were combined and moved into the store.

In 2003 a new neighbourhood shopping centre was created in the town of North Hykeham. This provided a focal point for the town, which had grown rapidly but in a rather disjointed way, with the commercial developments lagging some way behind the housing. The Hykeham Green Centre included a new doctors' surgery built by the Society, a Co-operative food store, pharmacy and post office, and several smaller shop units offering a good range of services.

Keith Darwin retired as Chief Executive in 2003. He had served the Society with distinction for 30 years, over 11 of them as Chief Executive. During his time with the Society, great progress had been made, both in terms of standards and Lincolnshire's position within the movement. After the brief tenure of Kevin Cooke, the present Chief Executive, Ursula Lidbetter, was appointed in 2004.

In Misterton the Society replaced the store from which it had traded for over 100 years, with a larger, more modern unit in 2005. This was so successful it had to be extended in 2007. The former store was converted for community use. A project which proved particularly challenging was to buy and re-open, in 2005, an old burnt out Quick Save on the Nunsthorpe Estate in Grimsby. A good deal of time, money and effort was invested in this unit, which was eventually rewarded and is appreciated by the local residents. Also in 2005 a convenience food store, post office and travel outlet were opened as part of the Society's Carlton Centre development in Lincoln.

Hykeham Green includes foodstore, doctor's surgery, pharmacy and post office

A major new village centre was completed in 2008 in Welton. Working closely with the local doctors' practice and the County Council, the development incorporated a new pharmacy, post office and food store for the Society, a public library and the doctor's surgery. The development had taken many years to bring to fruition, but the effort has been worthwhile.
Also in 2008 a new convenience food store was opened on Roman Bank in Skegness.

In 2009 the Society bought the food store and post office business of 'Bessies' at Old Leake, near Boston.

Lincolnshire Co-operative has always sought to respond to the wishes of its members. It has also, where possible, tried to source its supplies locally. In recent years, these two objectives have come together and have taken on a sharper focus. In customer surveys, members made it clear that local produce was important to them, so the Local Choice range was born.

Welton village centre opened in 2008

Like so many good things, the Local Choice scheme started in a small way but has grown steadily and is now an important part of the offer in foodstores and the Home Division.

Society members have consistently expressed a strong desire to have local products available to them and to be given the opportunity to support local producers through their purchasing decisions. Consequently, Lincolnshire Co-operative has worked closely with numerous local producers to provide a reliable network of retail outlets for their products.

Our foodstores stock products supplied by about 30 different local producers. Displayed on Local Choice stands are to be found free range eggs, flour, honey and jams, plum loaf, crisps and much more. Drinks include beers, cyder and fruit cordials. Gadsby's breads and confectionary items offer a local choice in the bakery section. There are also local meats, cheeses and pies in the range of chilled products and local ice creams take pride of place in freezer cabinets.

Non-food items such as Lincolnshire Charcoal and Walking Books from local authors are also available.

The Garden section at Lincolnshire Co-operative Home on Tritton Road, Lincoln has made the most of the

opportunities presented by the lively horticultural industry operating in the Society's trading area. Plants, bushes, shrubs, herbs and bulbs are available from a range of local nurseries and growers. Christmas trees grown in Louth have also proved a popular addition to Home's seasonal offerings.

Other locally-produced gardening products such as garden furniture, planters, stoneware, logs, bird feed and compost have helped establish the Garden section in an extremely competitive market.

Home's Bedding section offers duvets, pillows and mattresses from Fogarty of Boston and upholstery furniture from Lebus of Scunthorpe features prominently in Home's extensive Furniture range in Lincoln and Gainsborough.

Tony Ward
garden furniture

The meat is sourced from county farmers and prepared into the different cuts by the Society's skilled butchery team. Each piece of meat can be traced back to the individual producer and every animal is reared in Lincolnshire to the highest standards. With much public concern about meat quality and food miles, Lincolnshire Farm Assured was immediately attractive to Lincolnshire people and proved to be a great success. In 2008 the scheme was recognised with a prestigious national accolade. The Rural Action Award was presented to the Society's representatives at the glittering Business in the Community Awards for Excellence ceremony, at the Royal Albert Hall. This is a good example of what Lincolnshire Co-operative is all about and has been for 150 years: fair and ethical trading, supporting the local community, top quality products and paying a dividend to the members.

Lincoln Red cattle

Lincolnshire Quality Beef, Lamb and Pork was founded in the late 1990's in the wake of the BSE crisis. (BSE was a brain disease found in cattle, which made them stagger about, then fall over and die. It was also known as Mad Cow disease). At that time, consumers lacked confidence in meat products, so low prices for farmers became a big problem.

Overseas markets remained closed even after the BSE crisis ended. Global markets were extremely competitive in any case and particularly tough for small-scale producers to access.

In those dark days there was a real threat that livestock farming, so much a part of the life and economy of Lincolnshire, could be coming to an end, devastating for farmers, the end of the road for the local abattoir – a disaster for the county.

So Lincolnshire Co-operative got together with 20 local farmers to see what could be done. If we could create a local outlet for Lincolnshire meat, it would give the farmers a more dependable market and give customers reassurance, at a time when many were turning away from meat following one food scare after another.

The Society is presented with the Rural Action Award at the Royal Albert Hall

St Margaret's Gardens 1957

REFLECTIONS

'Lincolnshire Co-operative has changed significantly since 1861, but the focus remains on meeting the requirements of the membership'.

In 1861 conditions for working people were terrible, so it is no wonder that Thomas Parker and people like him all over the country wanted to do something about it.

Parker and his Lincoln Co-operative pioneers must have been more than a little nervous given the earlier failure of the Lincoln Flour Mill Co-operative.

But they went for it and trading started on 8 September for, what is today, Lincolnshire Co-operative Ltd. Would they be pleased if they could see today what became of their enterprise? We believe they would.

These were not business men or economists, they had no capital, they were building trade workers, simply trying to improve the lives of their fellow men, but the work they did was impressive, indeed it was inspirational. They showed determination, perseverance and a degree of probity which could stand as a model for those in business and public life today.

They moved fast, from shops in back street lodging houses and riverside warehouses - in 13 years they had brand spanking new premises on Silver Street. Two years later, the first branch store was opened in Bracebridge and others quickly followed. Lincolnshire was certainly at the forefront of efforts to take co-operation into the countryside and the first country branch at Welbourn opened just two years after the first city branch.

There was a great deal of public mistrust of private coal merchants in the 1860's, so an early entry into that business was no surprise and a move which met with immediate success.

In 1883 with the Society little more than 20 years old, they responded to the need for affordable homes and built houses for the members.

Society coal wagon in the Jubilee parade of 1937

Flour and bread were still staple commodities and despite the earlier failure, bread was baked and sold to members as early as 1867.

The move into farming did not quite achieve the success hoped for, but it did not fail and the spin off into dairying supplied millions of pints of milk to the members for over 80 years.

Long before there was any public provision, the Society started a library and reading room, which was soon followed by refreshment facilities in support. Nearly 40 years before the start of the NHS, the Society opened a Sick Appliance Room department to provide some comfort for its members. The first medicines were sold in 1880 and the pharmacy division still provides a first class service to members.

Billinghay store in the 1930s

From the refreshment room to the present coffee shops, the Society has always fed and entertained its members.

The members outings of the 1920's and 30's must have been magnificent occasions and were, of course, the forerunners to the present travel agencies.

The funeral service started in a very quiet way in the City of Lincoln, but a top quality service is now available throughout Lincolnshire and in Newark. As co-operative members moved from the bus and the bike to the car, the Society moved into petrol and motors.

The Society entered the property business almost by accident, buying the Lincoln Corn Exchange and Market Company as a back-up in case its bid for the Sincil Street re-development failed. However, having secured a property company, they made a success of it, and it has played a major part in the Society's development for nearly 40 years.

The decision to take up a position of political neutrality in the 1980's has been one of its most important decisions in recent years. This has enabled the Society to work with many more Councils and other organisations than would otherwise have been possible.

The introduction of the Dividend Card in 1998 has facilitated a reconnection with the members and membership and community activity is now key to all the Society's work.

Retail consumer co-operation enjoyed over a century of almost unbroken success and expansion, but that started to change in the 1960's and 70's. Many societies failed, but those failures were not exposed as they were usually merged with stronger neighbours or one of the, then two, national co-operative retailers. In the 1960's the ending of Resale Price Maintanance and the introduction of Selective Employment Tax presented real challenges and an actual co-operative failure, Millom, created many problems. The world of retailing was changing fast and it was the failure of so many co-operative societies to change themselves which led to their demise. By contrast, Lincolnshire responded to the need for change and changed itself very successfully.

The Society's financial performance places it at the top of most co-operative performance tables. Lincolnshire Co-operative now covers the whole of the geographical county of Lincolnshire and beyond, picking up along the way some former independent Lincolnshire societies and filling some co-operative deserts.

Society funeral vehicles in the early 1950s

The Board of any co-operative is key to its success or failure. With the introduction of professional management in the 1940's it became necessary to establish the correct balance of control between them and the Board. It would take many years to get this to the very best level. However, more than anything it is the willingness of the Lincolnshire Board to do its job and only its job, and to do it well, that sets it apart from so many boards of societies long gone. Beyond that, it has been the ability of the Lincolnshire Board to recruit and retain Executive Officers of the highest order that has been the secret of its undoubted success. Lincolnshire Co-operative has changed significantly since 1861, but the focus remains on meeting the requirements of the membership.

The Society also recognises a commitment to the wider community, with which it is fully integrated. Directors and officials serve on the Boards of many schools and colleges and numerous charitable and voluntary organisations. The Chief Executive works with many public, private and partnership bodies.

There are very few activities in Lincolnshire in which co-operators are not involved and frequently taking a leading role. The Society is actively involved in the social, cultural, educational and economic life of the area as befits one of the largest businesses in the county.

For the future, the Society will have a role to play wherever the consumer is disadvantaged and where private companies and plcs do not quite fit the bill, Lincolnshire Co-operative will be there.

The Dividend Card replaced stamps in 1998

PROGRESS OF THE SOCIETY

Year	Membership	Sales	Profit	Reserves	Dividend Paid
		£	£	£	£
1861	74	365	13	-	-
1870	850	15,842	1,157	32	994
1880	2,072	54,221	4,599	263	3,287
1890	6,123	147,557	15,496	3,158	18,272
1900	9,849	226,286	24,854	8,096	15,775
1910	12,871	344,764	38,001	11,855	24,879
1920	20,320	1,101,625	65,240	34,905	24,828
1930	25,659	942,446	65,944	27,665	15,429
1940	30,974	1,259,834	106,133	57,541	39,125
1950	38,651	2,815,113	193,136	96,000	149,387
1960	55,197	6,012,107	429,594	189,000	308,217
1970	75,130	10,204,467	259,426	582,060	163,871
1980	54,671	37,488,024	1,867,621	7,942,215	548,352
1990	57,400	127,137,000	7,362,000	28,836,000	1,169,000
2000	125,882	210,314,000	9,522,000	106,948,000	1,800,000
2010	187,124	277,830,000	20,572,000	247,980,000	4,001,000

Duncan McInnes

Duncan McNab

Duncan McInnes came to Lincoln from Fife where his father had been a coast-guard. He worked as a moulder at Robey's and had been on the committee since 1878. He was appointed as part-time Secretary in 1882, a position he held for 20 years.

To describe this man as a co-operative enthusiast would be a serious understatement. He played a dynamic part in the development of the country branches in Lincolnshire, was the driving force behind the house building programme and had a vision for co-operative manufacture and production, part of which was realised through the Lincoln Co-operative farms. Duncan McInnes was a highly respected writer and speaker on the principles of co-operation, both nationally and internationally. He drafted the first rules of the International Co-operative Alliance (ICA) in 1896 and served on the ICA Central Committee and Executive Committee, effectively the Board. He chaired the final day of the ICA Central Committee Meeting in Copenhagen in 1921. He was also Chairman of the organising committee for the ICA Congress held in Manchester in 1902.

Duncan McInnes made a remarkable contribution to co-operation in Lincoln. He was elected to the CWS Board and subsequently became Secretary of that Society, but continued as Secretary at Lincoln before resigning in 1902. He wrote the Society's 50 year history book.

Duncan McNab was born in Glasgow and his first co-operative appointment was at St. George Society in Glasgow as Cashier and Accountant. From there he became Assistant Secretary at Leicester Society and in 1947 was appointed Managing Secretary at Lincoln.

During his term of office, the Society carried out a vigorous policy of expansion: the number of grocery branches grew from 33 to 72, Silvergate House was opened and the complete re-building of the central premises was started. The Society's farming interests also extended significantly in this period.

He was Lincoln City Sheriff in 1962/63 and was a regular speaker on behalf of Lincoln Society at Co-operative Congress.

Duncan left to become General Manager of London Society in 1964, at that time the biggest co-operative society in the country. He is credited with co-writing the Society's 100 year history book.

Stanley Bett

Tom Agar

Stanley was born in Lincoln and served the Society from the age of 17, save for his service in the Royal Navy. After 16 years as Deputy, he succeeded Duncan McNab as Managing Secretary in 1964 and was subsequently re-designated Chief Executive Officer.

The radical re-shaping of the Society which became necessary in response to the rapidly changing retail scene and legislative initiatives, in particular the abolition of Resale Price Maintenance and the introduction of Selective Employment Tax, was undertaken during his period at the helm.

The Lincoln Corn Exchange and Market Company was acquired during this period. It was the firm foundation created at this time, when so many co-operative societies failed to respond adequately to the need for change, that enabled the Society to maintain and further improve its position.

He retired in 1977.

Tom originates from County Durham and joined Lincoln as Assistant Secretary in 1964, from Guildford Society, having served with several other co-operative societies. He was later appointed Deputy Chief Executive Officer and Chief Executive in 1977 when Stanley Bett retired.

The Society expanded significantly under his leadership with major acquisitions being made in the dairy, filling stations and pharmacy departments. The Society entered the motor trade in this period once again by acquisition and substantial investment was made both in the refurbishment and upgrading of the core business and continuance of property investment.

The solid financial base was strengthened to the point where the Society had few equals. A more active part in the affairs of the wider movement began with Tom's election to the CWS Board and subsequent appointment as Chairman of the Co-operative Bank.

He retired in 1992.

Keith Darwin

Ursula Lidbetter

Keith was born in Gainsborough and attended Queen Elizabeth's Grammar School and York University where he achieved an honours degree in history and politics.

On leaving York he obtained a place on the Co-op Graduate Training Scheme and his first appointment was with Plymouth Society.

When Lincoln advertised for a Food Trades Officer in 1973, Keith applied and was successful. He was appointed Deputy Chief Executive in 1977 and Chief Executive in 1992. In all these positions he drove the standards of shops and service forward. Sales grew from £12 million when he arrived to £224 million when he retired in 2003. Lincoln Society's performance was further strengthened during his tenure.

He was elected to the CWS Board and was appointed Chairman of that Society in 2000.

He was awarded the OBE in 2000.

Ursula was born in Lincoln and attended Lincoln Christ's Hospital School and Hull University, where she was awarded a first class honours degree in operational research and management.

On leaving Hull she won a place on the Co-op Graduate Management Development Programme run by the Co-operative College and in 1985 was recruited by Lincoln Society. Her first placement was at Co-operative House in Lincoln. She then managed the development of the Lindsey Centre in Gainsborough.

On returning to HQ she was appointed Research and Development Officer and later qualified as a Chartered Secretary. Ursula was appointed Assistant Secretary in 2000, Deputy Secretary in 2001, Secretary in 2002 and Chief Executive Officer in 2004.

Under her leadership the Society has moved even further ahead of the field in terms of performance as she has sought to improve links with the membership and the standards of service on offer to them.

Secretaries		Chief Officers
1861	Thomas Parker	
1861	Josiah Simpson	
1863	Thomas Jackson	
1865	William Walker	
1866	Charles Higgins	
1868	George Ufton	
1875		James Cunliffe – Cashier
1881	George Lewis	Fred Stephenson – Cashier
1882	Duncan McInnes	
1903	William Turner	
1909	George Harris	
1921		Charles Mackinder – Cashier
1930	John E Harrison	
1945	A R Chance	A R Chance – Chief Executive Officer
1947	Duncan McNab	Duncan McNab – Managing Secretary
1964	Stanley Bett	Stanley Bett – Managing Secretary
1976	Stanley Bett	Stanley Bett – Chief Executive Officer
1977	Tom Agar	Tom Agar – Chief Executive Officer
1992	Keith Darwin	Keith Darwin – Chief Executive Officer
2002	Ursula Lidbetter	Keith Darwin – Chief Executive Officer
2003	Ursula Lidbetter	Kevin Cooke – Chief Executive Officer
2004	Ursula Lidbetter	Ursula Lidbetter – Chief Executive Officer
2005	Jane Powell	Ursula Lidbetter – Chief Executive Officer

Lincolnshire Co-operative in 2010

- Achieved sales of £277 million

- Created a surplus of £20.5 million

- Distributed member benefits and dividends in excess of £5 million

- Has total reserves of £247 million

- Is one of less than 20 consumer co-operatives remaining in the UK

- Came top of the Co-operatives UK performance table for consumer societies in 2008 and 2009 for both trading profit and net profit

In 2011 Lincolnshire Co-operative has -

72 Food Stores
10 Filling Stations

47 Pharmacies

5 Coffee Shops

40 Post Offices

2 Home Stores

15 Funeral Homes
1 Memorial Masons
1 Florists Shop

10 Travel Agencies

1 Jaguar Dealership

The **co-operative** travel
at Lincolnshire Co-op

HOLLAND BROTHERS
EST. 1898

Over 200,000 Members

2,700 Staff

**and is
still serving the community.**

180